Third Edition

In OUR
Own Words

Student Writers at Work

REBECCA MLYNARCZYK
Kingsborough Community College
City University of New York

STEVEN B. HABER
New Jersey City University

CAMBRIDGE
UNIVERSITY PRESS

CAMBRIDGE UNIVERSITY PRESS
Cambridge, New York, Melbourne, Madrid, Cape Town, Singapore, São Paulo

Cambridge University Press
40 West 20th Street, New York, NY 10011-4211, USA

www.cambridge.org
Information on this title: www.cambridge.org/9780521540285

First published 2005

Printed in the United States of America

A catalog record for this publication is available from the British Library.

Library of Congress Cataloging in Publication Data

Mlynarczyk, Rebecca.
    In our own words : student writers at work / Rebecca Mlynarczyk ;
Steven B. Haber. – 3rd ed.
        p. cm.
    Includes index.
    ISBN-13: 978-0-521-54028-5 (pbk.)
    ISBN-10: 0-521-54028-3 (pbk.)
    1. College readers. 2. Report writing – Problems, exercises, etc. 3. English
language – Rhetoric – Problems, exercises, etc. 4. English language – Textbooks
for foreign speakers. 5. College students' writings, American. 6. College prose,
American. I. Haber, Steven B. II. Title.

PE1417.M537 2005
808'.0427–dc22

                                                            2004060839

ISBN-13 978-0-521-54028-5 (paperback)
ISBN-10 0-521-54028-3 (paperback)

In memory of my mother, Ruth Williams Adams, 1911–2003

R.M.

For Xiaolan, Jonathan, and Maya, whose love makes all things possible

S.H.

CONTENTS

PART III MORE FORMAL WRITING 125

Chapter 6 Families in Transition: Writing Based on Reading 167

Chapter 7 Issues of Identity: Writing Based on Research 207

INTRODUCTION

To the Instructor

In Our Own Words: Student Writers at Work is based on three beliefs:

1 Students learn to write by writing.

2 Students respond well when they are taken seriously as writers and are permitted to actively engage in writing as a communicative process.

3 Students are more highly motivated and successful when they are inspired by the writing of their peers and when they are encouraged to write about subjects that matter to them.

The distinguishing feature of this textbook is that approximately 85 percent of the readings are pieces composed by students in our own multicultural writing classes. These essays reflect the freshness of perception, knowledge, and originality of a rich cultural diversity. The essays are intended not as models but as sources of interest, discussion, and inspiration for further writing.

The positive response the book has received over the years has confirmed our belief in the importance of highlighting student writing. In 1992, the first edition of *In Our Own Words* received the Mary Finocchiaro Award for Excellence in the Development of Pedagogical Materials from the international TESOL organization. Teachers often tell us how much they enjoy using the book. And, most important, students who never before thought of themselves as writers have been motivated by reading the student essays in the book and have responded by producing engaging writing of their own.

Students in our classes are familiar with the experience of living or having lived in two cultures, the challenge of learning a new language or dialect, and the exhilaration and frustration of cultural surprise. Those who share the experience of cultural transition are naturally curious about the observations, sensitivities, tensions, and successes reflected in the writing of their peers.

Another shared experience is the recent arrival of our students at colleges and universities. Many are the first in their families to attend college. They may find being in a writing class where they are expected to master the requirements of academic discourse an unfamiliar and threatening experience. For such students, the presentation of student writing sends a clear message: You are welcome here; your writing is welcome here.

NEW IN THE THIRD EDITION

Benefiting from the suggestions of reviewers and instructors who have used the second edition of *In Our Own Words*, we have updated and revised the book in several ways:

- *Fifteen new reading selections by student writers*
  For teachers who have used the book before, the new readings offer variety. For students, these readings capture the concerns of a new generation of college students. For example, in "My Friend Nafiz," a student portrays "the bravest, toughest, and strongest boy in the school," who changed his life dramatically after his father died. In an essay entitled "Identity," another student describes her difficulties in reconciling the different aspects of her own identity as a Christian woman of color of Panamanian and Irish descent.

- *Five new reading selections by professional writers*
  Like the new student essays, these pieces provide variety and updated content. For example, "An Immigrant's First Day on the Job," published in *September 11: An Oral History* by Dean E. Murphy, gives a first-person account of an immigrant who began work at the World Trade Center on that historic day. Other new readings provide models of effective academic writing. For example, in "The Color of Love," psychologist Maria P. P. Root uses traditional research sources, such as public opinion polls and ethnographic interviews, in her analysis of changing attitudes toward interracial dating and marriage.

- *Updated writing topics*
  New topics, such as changing attitudes toward interracial marriage and the influence of race, ethnicity, and immigration status on personal identity, will engage students' interest as they begin to write more formal essays.

- *Internet activities to support the writing process*
  Each of the writing chapters now includes an Internet Search designed to help students use the resources available on the Internet to spark ideas for writing and gather information.

- *Contextualized revising and editing activities*
  Revising and editing activities are included at the end of every chapter to encourage students to see revising and editing not as afterthoughts, but as integral parts of the writing process. Chapters end with an Editing Checklist to encourage careful proofreading, with special attention to the grammar point highlighted in the chapter.

We hope that this third edition of our book will continue to inspire new writers and new writing.

GUIDING PRINCIPLES

In Our Own Words accomplishes its goals by:

- *Engaging student interest through reading selections written by other students on high-interest themes.* Students read essays by peers on such topics as changing family structures and interracial dating and marriage, subjects that are of immediate relevance to multicultural college students. The readings are intended as invitations for reflection and discussion rather than as models to imitate.

- *Increasing students' motivation to write.* We believe that good writing is contagious. One student's reminiscence about his childhood home evokes similar memories in other students. Another writer's description of her quest to establish a sense of personal identity inspires others to tell their stories.

- *Including classroom activities that encourage students to see writing as a social process.* These activities, all of which have been successful in our own classes, encourage discussion and social interaction among students as they work on their writing. Students learn to provide meaningful responses to the writing of their classmates through activities that teach the techniques of constructive criticism and through the Peer Response Forms included at the end of Chapters 3 through 7.

- *Encouraging students to reflect on their own writing.* The book includes three self-evaluation surveys, which students complete at the beginning, middle, and end of the course. These questionnaires encourage students to take an active role in assessing their progress in writing. In addition, Chapters 5 through 7 include a form entitled Writer's Plan for Revising. These forms encourage students to consider the feedback they have received from peers and perhaps from their teacher, to analyze how successfully they have achieved their aims for a particular essay, and to decide how to revise it.

STRUCTURE OF THE BOOK

Good writing does not just happen. *In Our Own Words* provides carefully designed activities, suggestions, and assignments to form the structure that enables developing writers to explore their own thoughts and find their own words. The book is divided into three parts and seven chapters. Information on the content of each part and chapter may be found on the next two pages.

Part I   STARTING OUT
          Chapter 1   Thinking of Yourself as a Writer

Part II   PERSONAL WRITING
          Chapter 2   Experiences
          Chapter 3   People
          Chapter 4   Places

Part III MORE FORMAL WRITING
          Chapter 5   Oral History: Writing Based on Interviews
          Chapter 6   Families in Transition: Writing Based on Reading
          Chapter 7   Issues of Identity: Writing Based on Research

Part I: Starting Out

Part I establishes the foundation for the rest of the book as students experience writing as a social process involving genuine communication.

In **Chapter 1**, students are encouraged to form a classroom community in which they can think and write about their attitudes toward and past experiences with writing. They can explore strategies for writing without worrying and consider ways of coping with common writing problems, such as choosing an appropriate topic or overcoming writer's block.

Part II: Personal Writing

In Part II, students write about topics of interest from their own experience.

In **Chapters 2**, **3**, and **4**, students write personal essays about experiences, people, and places that have influenced them deeply. These essays involve students in writing vivid descriptions but also in analyzing how their lives have been shaped by the experiences, people, and places they are writing about.

Part III: More Formal Writing

In Part III, students practice more formal writing as they begin to analyze their own experiences and attitudes in the light of larger societal forces.

Chapter 5 serves as a transitional chapter in which students use interviews they have conducted as the basis for an analytic essay. They may choose between interviewing someone and writing about a theme in that person's life, or interviewing one or more individuals for information on a topic of interest that will be the focus of their essay. In this chapter, students are introduced to the traditional academic practice of formulating a thesis statement.

In **Chapter 6**, students write a traditional reading-based essay using one or more print sources from the chapter. The topic is one familiar to every college student: how families are changing in the modern world. Not only do students comment on their print sources, they must also summarize and paraphrase ideas from these sources.

In **Chapter 7**, students write a brief research paper that includes identification of their sources according to APA or MLA style. As in the previous chapters, the topics are of high interest: (1) the influence of such factors as race, ethnicity, and immigration status on the formation of personal identity, and (2) an assessment of the possible advantages and disadvantages of interracial marriage. Students are required to use at least three research sources, one of which must be a reading in the chapter, another from the Internet, and a third that includes statistical information. They are encouraged to consider articles, books, and journals for their sources as well as personally conducted interviews.

Chapter Organization

In each chapter of Parts II and III, students do the following:

- Read and respond to some or all of the **Readings** at the beginning of the chapter
- Practice one or more of the **Techniques Writers Use**, which facilitate the type of writing called for in the chapter
- Do an **Internet Search** designed to generate ideas for writing or provide background information
- Draft an **Essay** based on one of the themes of the chapter
- Discuss the draft with a partner or group using the **Peer Response Form** at the end of the chapter
- Reflect on their own writing processes and on the feedback they have received (A **Writer's Plan for Revising** form is included at the end of each chapter in Part III.)
- **Revise** the essay in light of the feedback received
- Focus on correctness by doing the **Grammar in Context** tasks, which call attention to a typically troublesome grammatical structure
- **Edit** the essay, paying special attention to the grammar point highlighted in the chapter
- **Proofread** the essay and make needed corrections

In Our Own Words contains a wealth of activities. We hope that teachers will feel free to move back and forth among the different parts of the book, using those sections that suit the interests and needs of their students.

To the Student

This book is based on a very simple idea: People write better and learn more when they write about things that are important to them. Most of the reading selections in this book were written by students like you who were actively engaged in their own writing. But the essays didn't start out in the polished and correct versions that you will be reading. All of them have been revised by the student writers, often several times. Any remaining errors in grammar, spelling, and punctuation have been corrected, as is done for all published writing. However, the ideas, organization, and wording of these essays came entirely from their authors, the students.

We hope that you will enjoy the reading selections and that they, in turn, will make you feel like writing. We suggest some topics for writing, but we hope you will discover your own topics as well. As you move through the book, remember that different people learn in different ways. What helps the student sitting next to you may not help you at all. Try to figure out what works best for you.

Finally, a word about the book's arrangement. Textbooks have to be organized in a linear way, with a beginning, a middle, and an end. But the writing process does not usually work that way. As writers, we may begin by writing, then observing and taking notes, writing some more, then editing what we have written so far, going back and taking more notes, and so on. Sometimes we decide to throw out everything we have done and start over on a new subject. We hope that you will use this book in a way that suits your own writing process, returning to review the different sections as you need them.

But let's not spend any more time talking about writing. Let's simply start out.

AUTHORS' ACKNOWLEDGEMENTS

Rebecca wishes to thank her colleagues in the English Department of Kingsborough Community College, City University of New York, especially Professor Bonne August, the former department chair, with whom she co-edits the *Journal of Basic Writing*; Professor Marcia Babbitt, with whom she co-directs the ESL Program; and Professor Vanessa Santaga, with whom she coordinates the lower-level developmental courses. Professor Dulcie Repole, who died in 2004, was an inspired teacher and enthusiastic user of *In Our Own Words*. Three of the new essays in the third edition were written by Dulcie's students. Rebecca also wishes to thank the members of her writing group – Susan Babinski, Jane Isenberg, and Pat Juell – who regularly demonstrate the immense value of honest and supportive peer response.

Steve wishes to thank the faculty, staff, and students at New Jersey City University, specifically Dr. Joanne Bruno, Dr. Clyde Coreil, Dr. Lisa Fiol-Mata, David Trujillo, and Ruddys Andrade for their support.

We are grateful to our families for their constant love and support throughout the writing and revising of this book. Rebecca would like to thank Frank Mlynarczyk, Alex Mlynarczyk, Susanna Mlynarczyk-Evans, Bill Evans, Carol Williams, and Robert Asher. Steve would like to thank Xiaolan Gao, Jonathan Rui Haber, and Maya Lin Haber.

We are especially indebted to the professors who reviewed the second edition and suggested ways in which we could improve it. We would like to thank Linda Forrester, LaGuardia Community College, City University of New York; Patricia Goldstein, University of Wisconsin–Milwaukee; Emy Kamihara, Bloomfield College; Pamela L. Lee, Tidewater Community College; and Richard Morasci, Foothill College.

Many people at Cambridge University Press have helped to make the third edition of *In Our Own Words* a reality. We have been privileged to work with Bernard Seal, Commissioning Editor, whose keen editorial eye and strong sense of organization strengthened the book immensely. We are extremely grateful to Kathleen O'Reilly, Senior Development Editor, for her deep understanding of the philosophy of the book as well as her systematic work to help us improve it. We also wish to thank Heather McCarron, Senior Project Editor; Don Williams, Compositor; and Susan Ball, Copy Editor.

Finally, we extend our deepest thanks to the students whose writing appears in this book and to the many others who have been in our classes over the years. They have been our most important teachers.

Rebecca Mlynarczyk
Steven B. Haber

PART I
STARTING OUT

Thinking of Yourself as a Writer

Chapter 1

Thinking of Yourself as a Writer

Students often do not think of themselves as "real writers." Speaking as teachers with many years of experience, we strongly believe that you *are* real writers, with important things to say. We hope that the samples of student writing included in this book will help to convince you of the power of student writing. We also believe that the only way to improve as a writer is to write regularly and write a lot. Thus, even in this first chapter, we have included many writing activities to show you ways of exploring your attitudes toward and past experiences with writing, as well as strategies for getting words on paper and coping with common writing problems.

FORMING A CLASSROOM COMMUNITY

The activities in this book are designed to help you become a more effective reader and writer of English. In doing them, you will often be asked to work with a partner or small group of classmates. As any experienced writer knows, talking freely about ideas is a very important part of the writing process, and many of the group activities included in this book involve discussing the readings, developing plans for your own essays, or giving and receiving feedback on essay drafts. In classes where collaborative, or cooperative, learning is encouraged, students learn as much from other students as they do from their teachers. For this reason, it is important for you to start learning about one another and working together from the beginning of the course.

The three activities that follow give you a chance to get to know your classmates, to practice working with them in a collaborative way, and to begin to do some informal writing.

Getting Acquainted

This activity encourages you to get acquainted with your classmates by conducting an informal survey and then writing up your results.

1 Move around the room and try to find as many of the types of people listed below as possible. Write down their names in the blanks.

   a Find someone who is majoring in the same area that you are.

   ....

   b Find someone who is working at a job you would like to have. What kind of job is it?

   ....

c Find someone who speaks more than two languages.

....

d Find someone who has done a lot of writing in the past – either for school
   assignments or for personal reasons.

....

e Find someone who likes to draw or paint.

....

f Find someone who is an expert at using computers.

....

g Find someone who is a good cook.

....

h Find someone whose favorite kind of music is the same as yours.

....

i Find someone who likes to play a sport you like to play.

....

j Find someone you can call if you need to get homework assignments.
   Write down the person's name and phone number.

....

2 Now write up your results. Imagine your reader is a classmate who was absent
   on the day of the survey. Do not try to include everything, just the most
   important parts. Here are some questions you can use to focus your writing:
   • What did you learn about other members of the class that was <u>interesting</u>
     or surprising?
   • What did you learn that might be useful to you?
   • What did you learn that might be useful to others?

Looking at Similarities and Differences

As you work with your classmates, you will discover not only what you have
in common but also the ways in which you are different. In this activity, you
will interview a classmate using some questions about common situations in
everyday life. Based on your interview, you will write about how you are similar
and how you are different.

1 Working with a partner, interview each other using the questions below.
   Write your partner's answers in the blanks.
   a When you receive a bill, do you pay it right away, or do you put it off until
      the last minute?

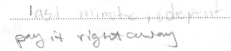

....

meyers - Briggs [handwritten notes at top]

b When you cook, do you follow the recipe exactly, or do you like to improvise?

sometimes improvise [handwritten]

c When you are eating, do you like to save the most delicious food for last, or do you eat it right away?

eat it right away [handwritten]

d When you go shopping, do you like to find things by yourself, or do you ask for help from the salesclerk?

find by yourself [handwritten]

e When eating at a restaurant or going to a movie, do you prefer to go alone, with one person, or with a group?

with group [handwritten]

f When you get a new piece of electronic equipment, such as a DVD or CD player, do you read the instructions before connecting it, or do you like to figure things out for yourself?

figure out [handwritten]

g When you draw or paint, do you prefer to copy a picture or make one up yourself?

prefer to copy a picture [handwritten]

h When you pack your suitcase, do you make a plan and fold everything neatly, or do you just throw everything in without any special order?

plan [handwritten]

i When you study, do you prefer to work alone or with someone else?

Both, make plan and fold everything [handwritten]

2 Look at the questions again and classify the type of information they ask for:

• Put an O next to any questions that have to do with whether someone is well organized.

• Put a C next to any questions that have to do with creativity.

• Put an I next to any questions that have to do with independence.

3 Based on the information you learned about your partner during your interview, write three guesses about your partner's personality compared with yours. *how we see things* [handwritten]

> **Examples**
> Chen seems more organized than I am.
> I may be more independent than Chen.
> Chen and I are both creative.

4 Try to form at least two generalizations about your partner that you can support with details from the questions you discussed. Now write a brief description comparing your partner to yourself. For example, "Although I may be more independent than Chen, she seems to be more organized than I am. . . ."

5 Discuss the results of the interview with another pair of students.

Silent Conversations

Writing and speaking are equally important forms of communication. In this activity, you will begin a spoken conversation with a classmate and then continue it in writing.

> **Example**
> Sophia and her partner, Zyary, had been talking about whether Sophia should hire a math tutor. Here is the way Zyary continued their conversation in writing:
>
> Sophia, as I told you before, the chemistry between people has to be positive in order to do something together. The first meeting you are going to have with your tutor should be like an interview. This is the moment when you analyze the person, see if there is anything in common between you, and also ask for her credentials. By doing this, you save time and maybe future misunderstandings.

1 Choose a partner to work with and agree on a topic of conversation that interests both of you, such as what you did over the weekend, what happened this morning, or something strange or unusual that you learned recently.

2 Talk with your partner for two or three minutes about this topic.

3 Now stop talking and, for the next five minutes, continue your conversation by writing.

4 Exchange papers and read each other's writing carefully.

5 Discuss with your partner what you noticed about the differences between communicating by speaking and communicating by writing. Use these questions to guide your discussion:

- Which was easier?
- Which took longer?
- Which form of communication do you prefer? Why?
- Would you feel the same way if you had been asked to do this activity in your first language or dialect? Why or why not?

6 Share the results of your discussion with another pair of students or with the class.

THINKING ABOUT WRITING

Attitudes Toward Writing

By the time students enter a college writing class, most of them have accumulated a variety of thoughts and feelings about writing in general and their own writing in particular. For some students, these thoughts and feelings are positive. But many students approach writing with feelings of uneasiness and fear. As you begin this course, it is important for you to take an honest look at your own thoughts and feelings about writing. Even if your feelings are not very positive, it is helpful to express them so that you understand how they might be affecting you as a writer. Once these thoughts and feelings are expressed directly, they can begin to change. The activities that follow will help you to examine your attitudes toward writing and your past experiences with writing.

1. Read the following excerpts, in which four students describe their attitudes toward writing in English. As you read, compare these students' feelings about writing with your own.

> **Student A**
>
> I like to write. I believe that writing is helpful to me both in school and for the rest of my life. Writing for me is fun. My habit is to write poems, and when I start writing, it's hard for me to stop. Writing makes me think, and it helps me to develop my ideas and put them into words.

> **Student B**
>
> I have mixed feelings about writing. Sometimes I like to write to my friends. It seems that I have a million things to write about. But sometimes I hate to write, and those times are usually when I'm writing an essay or something for work. When I want to write something, I have trouble getting my thoughts together and putting them down on paper. When I know I have to write something for school, I always get nervous and put it off until the last possible minute. Then I sit down and write very fast and try to get all my ideas out of my head before I lose them. After I hand it in, I try not to think about it. I think it's much easier to speak. I never seem to have any trouble thinking up ideas and organizing them when I'm speaking. But when I write, I have to think about so many things, it makes me feel like giving up halfway through.

Student C

I realize that English is important in school and in my later life. I want to learn good English so that I can be successful in my future. However, when people criticize my English writing, I get angry. Criticism makes me ugly. I know this is my shortcoming, and I intend to change it for good. If I don't change the way I feel about criticism, I will hurt myself in the long run.

Student D

My attitude toward writing in English? Well, the good thing is that attitudes can be changed as a person gets older; otherwise I wouldn't be here to write for you. I remember the way I used to feel about writing; I thought it was impossible for me to learn how to write. Now it is obvious to me that it takes patience, but I know I can be a good writer.

2 Now write freely for 10 to 15 minutes about your own attitude toward writing. Try to be as honest as possible even if you think your attitude is not very good. (If you have never done this type of writing before, refer to page 12 for a discussion of *freewriting*.)

3 Exchange your writing with a partner. Read each other's answers and then discuss them. Use these questions to guide your discussion:

- In what ways are your attitudes toward writing similar?
- In what ways are they different?
- Is there anything about your own attitude that you would like to change?

4 Share some of your answers with the class.

Past Experiences with Writing

1 Read these responses, in which students describe their past experiences with writing. As you read, think about how their experiences are similar to or different from your own.

Student A

Write about a pleasant experience you have had with writing.

Writing is one of my hobbies, and I enjoy it a lot. It started when I was about fifteen and was in love. (Ordinary, isn't it?) I wrote a couple of very bad poems for that girl, without any intention of sending them to her. For the first time I was writing for myself, without any rational reason. Just for fun, just to express my feelings. Later I forgot about the girl entirely, but I never stopped writing poems. There was always something to express, relations between people, usual events, even politics and caricaturing of other people's mistakes. I am still writing for myself, for fun and to document my opinions for the future. Someday I guess I will laugh at my present thoughts in the same way I now smile about my past.

Student B

Write about a bad experience you have had with writing.

My memories of writing for school assignments are of tension and frustration. I may have an hour to write on a particular topic – it doesn't matter whether it's an exam or a regular classroom essay – and my mind would just go completely blank. I would spend about half of the hour thinking about what topic to choose and what I am going to say about this topic.

Student C

How do you feel about writing in your first language compared to writing in English?

Thinking in one language and translating it into another one makes me feel like I am going to Haiti on foot because there is no bridge to walk on. I feel like more than an idiot who never went to school because I feel miserable when I cannot explain myself the way I would in my native language. My whole life has been difficult because my country has two languages, Creole and French. I have to think in Creole and translate it to French. Now it is even worse because I live in America. I have to speak, read, and write in English. I get a big headache every time the teacher gives me a writing test to do.

Student D

When you are writing a paper for a class, do you try to please yourself or the teacher?

I have done both kinds of writing – for myself and for the teacher. When I'm writing for myself, I find it easier and more carefree, maybe because I don't worry about the criticism and I'm not under pressure. Another thing is I don't have to worry about the grammar, punctuation, etc. I just write whatever I want without worrying. When I'm writing for the teacher, it is totally the inverse of writing for myself. I have to worry about the criticism and correction. I have to watch out for my grammar and be sure my information is correct. I'm under pressure when writing for the teacher, and that makes it worse.

2 Read the following questions and choose three of them that you think you can answer in detail. Then write about your past experiences with writing, using the three questions you chose as a guide.

- What are your earliest memories related to writing?
- Write about a pleasant experience you have had with writing. How did this experience affect your attitude toward writing?
- Write about a bad experience you have had with writing. How did this experience affect your attitude toward writing?
- How do you feel about writing in your first language compared to writing in English?
- Describe how writing was taught in your previous schooling by answering some or all of these questions: How often did you have to write? What kinds of topics did you write about? Give one or two examples. What kinds of comments did the teacher make on your papers? What was considered more important: the content of your papers (your ideas) or correct grammar and spelling (how you expressed them)?
- When you are writing a paper for a class, do you try to please yourself or the teacher? Explain.
- Have you ever done any writing for yourself only – letters to friends or relatives, journals, diaries, poems? If so, explain how this writing was different from the writing you did for school assignments.

3 Working in a small group, have each student read the answer to one question to the group. Go on to the next student without taking time for discussion. After everyone has read, discuss these questions:

- How were your experiences similar?
- How were they different?
- In your opinion, how have these past experiences influenced your attitudes and thoughts about writing?

WRITING WITHOUT WORRYING

One of the most difficult things for any writer to do is to get started on a piece of writing. Some students stare at the computer screen and think, "I have nothing to say. I have no ideas. My mind is totally blank." Others stop themselves from writing by thinking, "I have lots of ideas, but I'm such a bad writer that nobody will understand what I'm trying to say." The truth is, however, that there are always plenty of ideas floating around in your mind. And even if you are not an experienced writer, once you get some words written down, you will be able to refine and improve your writing through the drafting process. (You will learn more about the drafting process as you do essay assignments in Chapters 2–7.)

many ideas

In this section, we introduce some ways to write without worrying about being perfect. First, we suggest that you try the technique of freewriting. Next, we encourage you to start writing in a journal. Third, we offer some options for interactive writing. And finally, we ask you to try an experiment: writing with and without a dictionary.

Freewriting

write and writ
don't worry
about
grammer and
ideas

Freewriting is a technique that many people use when they have to write but are not sure exactly what they want to say or how to say it. The purpose of freewriting is not to turn out a finished piece of writing, but rather to discover a place to begin.

When you freewrite, you should not use a dictionary or worry about grammar or spelling. If you don't know how to spell a word, just do the best you can or write the word in your native language. In freewriting, ideas do not have to be connected or written out in complete sentences. The important thing is to keep writing. When you feel stuck, just keep writing, "I can't think of anything to say. I can't think of anything to say." Soon a new idea will come to you.

1 Read the following sample of freewriting, in which a student writes about her fear of donating blood at a hospital. As you read, think about how this writing is different from formal, academic English.

> Tomorrow, for the first time, I will give blood. Just the thought of it frightens me. I wonder how much the needle will hurt when it is put in my arm. Eck. Ooo. My heart is in my throat. My stomach is tight at the thought of it. Oh! Well, I know that it is a good action. Who knows? I know that I am a rare blood type and maybe someone will need it.

2 Now try this technique yourself. Freewrite for about 10 minutes without stopping. Write about anything that comes into your mind – for example, sounds you hear in the room, what you plan to do after class, or a problem that you are having at the moment. You will not have to show this writing to anyone; it is only for you.

3 Take a few minutes to read what you have written, and underline the part that seems most important. Did you discover any new ideas while you were writing?

4 Discuss your reaction to freewriting in a small group.

Keeping a Journal

Many professional and student writers keep journals in which they freewrite about any subject imaginable. The journal is the place to experiment with writing, to be as silly or as serious as you want. Some writing teachers require their students to keep a journal for class. Your teacher will tell you whether the journal is only for you or whether he or she will collect it from time to time or ask you to share some of your journal writing with other students. If your teacher does collect your class journal, he or she will respond only to the ideas and will not correct errors in grammar or spelling. If your previous instruction in English emphasized correctness above all else, loosening up to write in a journal may feel strange or even uncomfortable at first. But if you continue to write regularly in your journal, your writing will eventually become more fluent – and more correct.

Choose a notebook for your journal that reflects your taste; it can be a simple spiral notebook or something fancier. Alternatively, you can keep an electronic journal by storing all your entries in a folder on your computer. Try to write in your journal once a day for at least 10 to 15 minutes. You do not have to write a lot each day. Some days you may write only a few sentences. Other days you will write more. The important thing is to get into the habit of writing regularly.

1 Read the journal entry below, in which the writer is exploring an idea she had been exposed to in another course: how intellectual change takes place in cultures. As you read, notice how the writer "discovers" an important idea through the act of writing.

> I am studying the great philosophers (ancient and medieval). I learned that a movement of intellectual change started to happen around 600–500 B.C.E. A few people, the philosophers, started to move away from the mythological explanation of nature.
>
> The causes for this change may vary. There was a growth in freedom of thought, a beginning in literacy. But one reason strikes me especially. This was the contacts of people from different cultures.
>
> Now if we take a look around us, with the technology revolution, with the speed at which communication can travel from one part of the world to another, with the mix of cultures in the big cities – if we are not moving toward a big change, or refuse to believe in it, it is because we are blind.

2 In your journal, write for 10 to 15 minutes about one of the topics listed below. No one will look at this writing except you.

- a daily event in your life
- a memory
- a dream
- a secret

- a plan for the future
- a problem you are facing
- a reaction to something you have read
- an idea from another course

3 Rest for a minute or two and then reread what you have written. Then write your answers to the following questions: Did you discover any new insights? Would you like to continue writing about this subject the next time you write in your journal? How was the experience of writing in your journal different from the formal writing you have done for school assignments?

Interactive Writing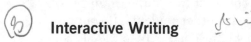

Most people find interactive writing, such as letters and e-mail, easier than more formal writing. Perhaps this is because we know exactly who the reader will be and we do not have to worry too much about writing "perfectly" with good organization and correct grammar. Another advantage of this type of writing is that we usually receive a response. Finally, as with freewriting or writing in a journal, interactive writing is another way to loosen up, get more comfortable with writing, and discover ideas about a topic.

1 Do one of the following activities:

- Choose a classmate you feel comfortable working with. Write a letter or e-mail to this person in which you discuss your feelings about living in the city or town where you currently live. You may want to write about how long you have been living there, whether you intend to stay or go somewhere else, and what you like or don't like about it. In your letter or e-mail, ask for a reply.

- Write a letter or e-mail to one of your classmates about something you have read recently. It could be a newspaper or magazine article, a book, an essay written by someone in your class, or an essay from this book. Tell your classmate the main idea of the reading and your personal reaction to it. Ask for a reply.

- Write a letter or e-mail to a younger friend or relative about what it is like to be a college student. You may want to address some of the following questions: How would you describe your academic course work? What are the professors like? How would you describe the social life of your institution? What advice would you give your friend or relative about the best way to prepare for attending college or university? Ask for a reply.

2 After you finish writing, read through what you wrote and discuss the following questions with a partner or small group:

- Did you enjoy writing this letter or e-mail?
- Was it easier than other writing that you have had to do?
- Did you write anything interesting that you could continue to explore in your journal?

Writing Without a Dictionary

In most of the writing activities in this book, we do not want you to use a dictionary – at least not in the beginning. The reason for this is that sometimes students spend more time looking up words than they do writing, and by the time they have found the word they were looking for, they have lost track of the larger idea they were trying to express.

As you do the following activity, you will be able to compare writing with a dictionary to writing without one. If possible, do this activity on the computer so that you can easily count how many words you write.

1 Write for five minutes about a person you know well. Use a dictionary (either English-English or bilingual) to look up any words that you do not know or that you are unsure of.

2 Pick another person you know well and write about that person for five minutes without the dictionary. If you do not know how to spell a word or you cannot think of an appropriate word, do one of the following:
  • Leave a blank space for the word and look it up or ask someone later.
  • Write the word, even if you are not sure it is correct. Put a question mark next to the word and check it later.
  • Write the word in your first language (if it is not English) and look it up or ask someone later.

3 Count the number of words in each piece of writing. Which is longer? Which do you think is better written? Why?

4 With a partner or small group, discuss the advantages and disadvantages of not using a dictionary until after you have finished writing. Base your discussion on the writing you just did as well as your past experiences in writing with or without a dictionary. Consider the following:
  • The amount you write
  • The quality of what you write
  • The enjoyment you get while writing

COPING WITH WRITING PROBLEMS

In the earlier parts of this chapter, the writing you did was informal. Much of what you wrote was read only by yourself or perhaps by a partner or a small group of classmates. You knew that you would not be evaluated or graded on this writing. But when you begin to do more formal writing, such as writing an essay for a class assignment, things become more complicated, and difficulties sometimes arise. In this section, we will discuss several common writing problems and suggest ways of dealing with them.

Choosing a Topic

Teachers frequently assign the topic for writing. However, there are times when you need to choose a topic on your own. There are also times when you are given a broad topic and you must narrow it down to one aspect that you can write about. At first this freedom of choice sounds wonderful. But students often discover that finding a good topic to write about can be difficult. This activity shows you an effective way to choose an appropriate essay topic.

1 Take about five minutes to write down four or five topics that interest you. Here are some examples of topics that other students have chosen:

> • Crime
> • My Trip to California
> • Immigration in the United States

2 Show your topics to a partner and explain why you chose each one. Then find out which of your topics your partner thinks is most interesting and why.

3 Based on the feedback from your partner and your own ideas, choose the topic you would like to work with.

4 Think about whether you need to narrow your topic down to make it more manageable and easier to develop. Here is how the topics listed above were narrowed down to more specific ones. An asterisk (*) indicates the topic the student finally chose to write about.

> • Crime
>   Crime in My City
>   Crime in My Neighborhood
>   *The Fear of Crime in My Neighborhood
>
> • My Trip to California
>   The Things I Like Best About California
>   Three Things I Do Not Like About California
>   *San Francisco vs. New York: Where Would You Prefer to
>   Live?
>
> • Immigration in the United States
>   The New Asian Immigrants
>   Korean Immigration in the United States
>   Korean Immigration: Advantages and Disadvantages
>   *Three Korean Immigrants: How They Feel About Life in
>   the United States

5 If you think you need to narrow down your topic, write a list in which you make your topic more specific, as was done in the examples above. (Note that the narrowing process may result in two or more equally good topics.) Then discuss with a partner or your teacher which of these narrower topics seems most appropriate.

6 Take about 15 to 20 minutes to write as much as you can about the topic you chose. If you discover after a few minutes that you have nothing more to say, pick another topic from your list and try again.

Adjusting to Different Purposes and Audiences

Understanding the purpose and audience for your writing can greatly influence what you say and how you say it. *Purpose* refers to the reason for writing – what you want the readers to do or think after they have finished reading. *Audience* means the intended reader(s) for a piece of writing. For example, the purpose of a letter of complaint to a department store might be to convince the store that it made a mistake on your bill. The audience would be the person who handles complaints for the store. The purpose of an essay for a literature class might be to analyze the psychological motivation of one of the characters in a short story. The audience for this type of essay is your instructor and often a group of your classmates. The activity that follows will help you to understand how audience and purpose influence what you write.

1 Do all three of the following pieces of writing:
   - Write a journal entry explaining what kind of person you are.
   - Write a short description of yourself to share with the class.
   - Write a one-page description of your personal background as part of a job application for a position as one of the following: a computer programmer, a high school teacher, or a nurse.

2 Write your intended purpose and audience at the bottom of each piece. For example, the audience for your journal entry might be yourself or your group, and its purpose might be "to reveal my deepest personal qualities."

3 Working in a small group, compare the purposes and audiences for which you wrote each piece. Then discuss the following questions:
   - Were the group members' purposes basically the same or different?
   - How did the different audiences influence what you said in each of the pieces of writing?
   - Which one was the hardest to write? Which was the easiest?

4 Have each student choose one of these pieces to read to the group. Then discuss the following questions: How effective was each piece at achieving the purpose stated by the writer? How was the writing influenced by the intended audience?

Dealing with Writer's Block

Writer's block is the inability to get your thoughts down on paper. Sooner or later, all writers – professionals as well as students – are faced with this troublesome problem. What keeps people from writing? Fear is part of the problem. What if my writing isn't good? What if I make mistakes? What if I fail? These kinds of fears can be distracting and stop you from doing your work. If you can figure out what it is that worries you, you may be able to overcome the fear and start writing. Sometimes personal problems interfere with writing. A quarrel with a friend or relative, the end of a love affair, an illness or death in the family, or too much work and not enough sleep can all contribute to writer's block. The one good thing about writer's block is that it is almost always temporary. Sooner or later, you will find yourself writing again. It is important to recognize that these ups and downs are a normal part of writing.

1 Read these comments by a writing instructor, two students, and a professional writer to find out what they do when they have difficulty writing. As you read, think about whether the experiences each of these people describes are similar to or different from your own.

Steven Haber, writing instructor and coauthor of this textbook:

I am probably the world's worst procrastinator. As much as I love writing, if I have to write something with a deadline, I almost always put it off until the last minute. I think the reason this happens is that before I start, every writing job seems enormous, impossible. I don't know where to begin. So before I start to write, I do other things, such as clean up my office, clear off my desk, drink a cup of coffee, turn on some soft music on the radio. Then, when I feel relaxed, I sit down at my desk and take a look at what I have to do. I tell myself that I only have to write a few pages. Surely I can write a few pages. Once I get started, it seems so much easier than I thought. Then I begin to enjoy it again.

Maria F. Barrueto, a student from Peru:

Sometimes having my blank page and pen ready to start what I expected to be an adventure or at least a trip is like being in front of a wall – a huge, tall, dark wall without any door or window to see through. First, I get the sensation of being so small, but as I think of what is waiting for me on the other side, and the great panorama that I can enjoy once I see it, that feeling changes. I start growing and growing, and without me realizing it, the wall has disappeared.

Pikwah Chan, a student from China:

If I can't think of something to write, I just won't write. I'll just take a break. I put my pen down, take a walk outdoors, or just do something else. I may totally forget what I am writing, or I may think about my subject in my leisure time, almost 90 percent sure that when I sit at my desk again, I can easily continue my writing. Sometimes the thinking is there, but it is subconscious. You should not ignore these kinds of impressions or feelings. They usually are important. They are just not really formed yet. When you give yourself time or release yourself from pressures, you will catch them easily.

Susan Sackett, novelist:

Writer's block. My fingers tremble at the mere sound of the words. My first reaction is denial, just as in any other crisis of life. I think that if I turn my back on the typewriter, maybe the whole problem will go away. All writers have their own cures, but mine is basic stubbornness. I do not allow myself the freedom of not writing until I start to get some ideas. If I did that, I'd never finish a book. So instead of giving up, I sit there, staring at the typewriter keys, even if it means I have nothing to show for that day's effort. My mind is free to wander, and eventually it takes a course along the lines of my work.

I never aim for perfection, especially on a first draft. I don't allow myself to agonize over a word that is lurking at the edge of my consciousness, nor do I bother with spelling or grammar. Details, I find, only get in the way of the story I'm writing, and they can always be taken care of later.

All I've really been saying is that writing requires work. After all, it's a craft, like any other, and if you don't allow yourself to give up on it, sooner or later you begin to see results.

2 Now write for 10 to 15 minutes about your own experiences with writer's block. In your writing, address each of these questions:

a Describe a time when you had trouble writing. What finally helped you to start writing?

b Which of the descriptions printed above seem most similar to your own methods of dealing with writer's block?

c What strategies do you use that are different from those described above?

d What advice would you give to a friend or relative who has trouble writing?

3 In a small group, share part of what you have written and discuss your ideas about writer's block. What different strategies do your group members use for coping with writer's block?

4 Have one group member report the results of your discussion to the class.

Doing Well on College Papers

Unfortunately, there is no set of foolproof rules to follow to get high grades on all your papers. How you approach a writing assignment depends on the specific course, the specific teacher, and the purpose of the assignment. In order to understand the problems students face on out-of-class writing assignments, we interviewed four students who were working on papers for different courses.

1 Read these excerpts from our interviews with students. Write a sentence or two below each excerpt that explains the main point(s) you think the student is making about how to do well on college papers.

Student A

For my history class I had to write a paper about the role of immigrant workers in building the Transcontinental Railroad. I did a lot of research about the Irish, the Chinese, and also Native American workers. But I didn't know how to organize all this information, so I went to my professor's office for a conference. The professor looked at my notes and said I had way too much information for a five-page paper. He said I should just focus on one of the groups. Since I'm originally from China, I decided to talk about how the Chinese helped to build the railroads. My professor thought that was a good idea.

---

a _did alot of research about the Irish, the chinese, and also Native American workers. And didn't know how to organize all this information, so Need focus a ___ idea_

Student B

When I was in high school, I always put off writing my papers until the last minute. But in my college writing class, we had to write in stages. First we talked about our ideas in groups. Then we wrote a rough draft, discussed it with a partner, and revised it. After that we wrote a second draft, got comments from the teacher, revised again, and wrote the final draft. Now when I write papers for my other courses, I try to do it the same way. If I'm having trouble, I talk with the professor or go to the Writing Center. This way of writing takes a lot more time, but it's more relaxing than my old way of trying to write the paper in one night. And my grades have gone up a lot.

---

b _This person is procrastinator, and talks about how is different between high school and college writing, and that is big change. And you have apprcenty to do first draft, then second, and final. for that way you will not have trouble to writing._

Student C

My assignment was to write an "informative essay" for my political science class. I had to pretend to be a member of the U.S. State Department writing a memorandum to the President about recent events in the Middle East. Most of my classmates found sources on the Internet or in the library, but I wanted to be more creative. Following foreign affairs is my hobby, and so I spent a lot of time finding unusual sources of information. First I contacted the Russian Mission to the United Nations to get their official statements on the Middle East. To get the opinions of the American Jewish population, I went to a large newsstand and located several Jewish publications. I even went to a meeting of one of these groups and talked to people about their opinions. I really got deeply into this subject. When I finally had to write the paper, it wasn't hard because I had been reading and talking about this subject for a long time.

c This person want to got deeply into this subject or information that, and to be more creative.

Student D

I had to write a paper about *The Great Gatsby* for my English class. I put off writing this paper because the book was very hard for me. The night before the paper was due, I was really scared. I decided to go on the Internet and see if I could find something to help me understand this book. There were a lot of Web sites, and I read some of the articles. They didn't really answer the question of our assignment: "Was Gatsby a materialist?" But I decided to use a few sentences from one of the Web sites in my introduction, just to get me started. When I got this paper back from my professor, she had written "See me" at the top of the page. She was pretty upset. She said that what I did was called plagiarism and it was like stealing someone else's words. She said I would have to write the whole paper over on a different topic. She also said if I ever did this again, I would get an F for the course.

d this person before tis/ther assignment due want to find information go to internet, and read some artical but didn't get any information to answer what they need. And her teach comments that was stealing someone else words.

2 Working with one or two other students, do your own informal interviews with students at your institution (not members of this class) about how to do well on out-of-class writing assignments. Follow these guidelines:

  a Write out a list of interview questions. Here are a few to get you started:

  - How do you feel about writing papers for college classes?

  - Can you describe a specific paper you had to write recently? What was the assignment? Did you have any problems writing the paper? How pleased were you with this paper when you turned it in? Were you satisfied with your professor's comments when you got the paper back? Why or why not? Were you satisfied with your grade? Why or why not?

  - What specific advice would you give new college students about how to do well on their out-of-class writing assignments?

  b Decide who will ask the questions and who will take notes.

  c Choose an interview site that is a common meeting place, such as the cafeteria or student union building.

  d When you get to your interview site, explain that you are doing an assignment for your English class and ask if the student has a few minutes to answer some questions about writing. Interview both native speakers of English and ESL students.

3 Discuss with your partner(s) the things that stand out for you from these interviews.

4 As a class, share what you learned from the interview excerpts you read in step 1 and your own interviews. Use these questions to guide your discussion.

  - Did any of your interviewees make points similar to those in the interview excerpts you read? What were they?

  - What did you learn that surprised you?

  - Were there any differences in the ways native speakers of English and ESL students approached out-of-class writing assignments? What were they?

  - How does what you have learned support what you already knew about being a successful writer?

A NOTE BEFORE YOU CONTINUE

Everyone who writes faces problems at one time or another. As you move into the next part of this book and begin to write essays, there may be times when you, too, will experience difficulties. But by working with your classmates and teacher and by using the resources in this book, you will discover that most writing problems have solutions.

As you continue in this course, you may notice some changes in your attitudes toward writing as well as in your writing itself. We encourage you to think about these changes and to assess your own progress. While grades and examination scores are certainly important, they are not the only way of measuring writing progress. It is equally important for you to evaluate your own writing and to think about which activities, strategies, and readings were useful in helping you to improve.

To help you assess your progress, we have provided surveys for you to fill out at the beginning, middle, and end of this course. The first survey follows this chapter. A midterm survey follows Chapter 4. A final survey follows Chapter 7.

Now fill out "Goals for This Course: A Beginning Survey" on page 24.

Goals for This Course
A Beginning Survey

YOUR NAME: .... DATE: ....

Write your answers to these questions in the spaces provided. Later you will compare your answers to this survey with your answers to the midterm and closing surveys.

1 What are your strengths as a writer: for example, creativity, ability to organize ideas, ability to express ideas clearly? List three of your strengths below, starting with the most important one. Explain these strengths by giving examples, if possible.

2 What do you find most difficult about writing: for example, getting ideas, organizing ideas, not knowing enough about the topic? List three problems you face in your writing, starting with the most serious. Explain these problems by giving examples, if possible.

3 Describe your writing process by answering the following questions: How do you usually approach an out-of-class writing assignment? Do you start early or put it off until the last minute? Do you write only one draft or revise your essay one or more times? Where do you go for help if you find a writing assignment difficult?

4 In what ways do you hope your writing will improve by the end of this course: for example, more confidence in writing, more ideas for writing, better organization, ability to write more quickly? List three ways in which you hope your writing will improve, and explain why these things are important to you as a writer.

5 What do you think will help you most to improve as a writer: for example, freewriting, getting feedback and advice from other students, revising your essays, conferences with your teacher? List three things that you think will help you to improve, and explain why you think these things will be helpful.

PART II
PERSONAL WRITING

| Experiences | Chapter 2 |

| People | Chapter 3 |

| Places | Chapter 4 |

Experiences

In this chapter, you will use writing to recall an experience from your own life. You might choose to write about the experience of learning something new or about the experience of a painful or frightening moment. Perhaps you will simply choose to write about something very ordinary. The reading selections in this chapter reflect a range of possibilities. It is not the experiences themselves that make this writing interesting. Rather, it is the way the writers have been able to show us how these moments were meaningful to them. By recording their experiences, these writers have opened up the private worlds of their lives.

READINGS

Learning How to Cook

Florence Cheung

In this simple story, Florence Cheung, a student from Hong Kong, tells of an ordinary childhood experience – learning to cook rice. Yet by her careful choice of details, Cheung also paints a picture of family respect and togetherness. Before you read, think of a time in your own childhood when you learned a new skill.

"Kit Wah! Kit Wah!" my mother was calling me. I was her eldest daughter. She was a thirty-three-year-old married woman, with four children, six, four, three, and two years old. 1

In the 1960s, every Chinese had to work very hard in order to earn his living in Hong Kong. My father worked twelve hours a day, but his salary was scanty. Thus, my mother had to bring up four of us and sew trousers at home. 2

"Mama, Mama!" 3

I came back from outside. The house was dark. For a moment, I could not see anything. Then I saw my mother sitting in front of her sewing machine. The spot lamp shone on the left side of her face. She picked up the unfinished pair of trousers and examined them carefully under the light. As I was four feet in height and fifty pounds in weight, I leaned onto the table of the sewing machine and talked to my mother. "Mama, did you hear me? Why did you call me?" 4

My mother moved her eyes away from the sewing machine and said, "It's time to cook. Switch the light on first." She yawned and stretched her arms. 5

Though people might think a child should play around, I started making beds in the morning at the age of four. Thus, I lifted a stool toward the wall and climbed on top of it to reach the switch, and put the light on. Now, I could see my mother's whole figure in the middle of the parlor. She responded to the light. 6

"Listen! I have to finish this piece of work tonight. You have to cook." 7

She rolled my sleeves up and tied the apron around my abdomen. I was so small that the apron covered my back as well. It looked like a long blue skirt. 8

"Put one full cup of rice into the inner pot of the electric rice cooker. Then wash the rice with water. Be careful!" 9

I followed her instructions. Her voice was still in my ears, "Be careful!" I crashed the pot into the sink. "Ah!" I cried out. All the rice was in the sink and the pot was empty. 10

I went back to my mother with the empty pot. My head was down. Instead of scolding me, my mother patted me on the back for admitting the fault. 11

"I heard what happened. Remove the dirty rice and try again! There is nothing that you cannot do. Even a rod of iron, you can make it into a fine, small needle!" my mother told me as she reached into her bottomless supply of Chinese maxims. 12

This time, I held the pot as tightly as possible. I washed the rice and poured the 13
water out carefully. This procedure was repeated several times. Then I measured
the depth of the rice with my middle finger, a trick that I had learned from my
mother, and put the same amount of water into the pot. I brought the pot back to
my mother. She did the same thing to measure the depth of the water.

"That's right! You're a smart girl. Remember to switch the electric cooker on." 14
She smiled for the first time that evening.

I checked to see that the small red light of the electric cooker was on. My heart 15
was lightened.

Later, my mother got up from her seat and went into the kitchen. When 16
she saw the steam coming out from the rice cooker, she was satisfied. Then she
taught me how to wash the white Chinese cabbage leaf by leaf and inspect for
any worms. I was told to wash them at least four times. My mother steamed the
fish with some ginger and spring onions. Then, she fried the vegetable while I set
the table.

"Mama, we smell something good! We're hungry!" My sister and brothers 17
came back from playing.

"Wash your hands first," my mother said. "Your sister cooked the rice 18
tonight."

My three-year-old brother rolled his sleeves up and pretended to wash the rice 19
with his hands. "Mama, I know how to cook."

When my mother saw the performance, she burst into laughter. We laughed, 20
too. "Next time, it will be your turn." She smiled down at him.

Lord, how I loved the first time that I cooked. 21

Reading 1   Reflecting on the Reading

1 Although this essay focuses on learning how to cook rice, we also learn a
   lot about the relationship between Cheung and her mother. Underline
   three details that reveal the nature of the relationship between mother and
   daughter. Discuss the details you chose with a partner or a small group.

2 Do you think Cheung is telling this story from a child's or an adult's point of
   view? Underline the evidence you find in the essay to support your opinion
   and then discuss your answer. How does the author's point of view influence
   the meaning of the essay?

3 Cheung often uses dialogue (direct quotations of a person's exact words)
   in this essay. Underline five direct quotations in the essay. Then discuss the
   following questions: Why do you think Cheung decided to use so many
   direct quotations? How would the essay be different if she had presented this
   information without using quotations?

4 We learn from the ending that Cheung was very proud of her accomplishment
   the first time she cooked rice for the family's supper. Before reading the
   essay, you were asked to think of a time in your own childhood when you
   learned a new skill. In your journal, freewrite about your memories of this
   accomplishment.

What Is It Like to Have an Empty Stomach?

Youssef Rami

In this essay, Youssef Rami, a student from Morocco, describes an important event in his spiritual life – his first experience of fasting. Before you read, think back to your own childhood. Can you remember a time when you decided to take on an adult responsibility? What were your reasons for this decision?

1   Ramadan is the holiest month in the Muslim year. In fact, it's the fourth pillar of Islam. All adult Muslims must fast from dawn to sunset every day of Ramadan. This means abstaining from eating, drinking, smoking, and conjugal relations during the hours of fasting. Travelers, the sick, and pregnant women can defer fasting during Ramadan and make up for it later. Fasting in a hot climate such as Morocco is quite difficult. Nevertheless, those who have to fast have developed a great deal of patience and self-control.

2   Going back to my childhood's best memories, I still recall my first day of fasting when I was only six years old. Of course, I was not supposed to fast since most children usually start fasting at the age of thirteen; however, since I was the only one among all my brothers and sisters who did not have to fast, I was very anxious and curious to experience the feeling of fasting for at least one day, so I decided to fast the following day.

3   "It is a great decision, Son," my father said. I smiled and promised to keep my word. At the same time, I ignored my mother's exhortation that I was too young to fast.

4   It was about 2:30 a.m. when my mother woke me up to eat our last repast that we could have before the sunrise. After I washed my hands and face, I sat at the table next to my father with a great feeling, knowing that I was allowed to eat as much as I could without being interrupted by my mother as usual, claiming that I eat too much.

5   After I finished my last meal, my father gave me some good advice. He said, "Kid, I want you to understand something very important." I looked at him and said, "What is it, Dad?" He replied, "Tomorrow is your first day of fasting. If you feel incapable of finishing the day, eat and break your fast and be honest about it, but never cheat because Allah is always watching you." I nodded my head and headed to bed.

6   The next morning, which was my first fasting day, was so terribly hot that I felt thirsty as soon as I got up. Yet I remembered that I could only rinse my mouth without letting a drop of water get into my throat. An hour later I was in school; of course, none of my friends was fasting, and that made it worse. They kept eating all kinds of fruits, candies, and cookies in front of me. At first I didn't care, but later, at lunch time, when everybody was enjoying his meal and I was the only one left with an empty stomach, so many ridiculous ideas came to my mind.

Fortunately, I remembered my father's last words, "Allah is watching you." So I found the courage to defeat all crazy and silly ideas.

During lunch time, I felt what it was like to have an empty stomach and not   7
be able to eat while food was next to me. I then knew how a poor person would feel if he was hungry and could not afford to feed himself or his family. I said to myself, "Maybe one of the many reasons why people have to fast is to experience what others feel."

My school sessions ended at 3 p.m., so I had about four and a half hours to   8
finish my day. I was very hungry, thirsty, and tired. As soon as I got home, I went to sleep. Honestly, the last hours of that day were the most difficult time I ever experienced in my childhood, and only now do I understand why I remained unruffled the whole day. During that day I learned how to resist my selfish desires, and I understood that self-control is very important for human beings.

The time of breaking our fast was 7:45. I was delighted that I had made it   9
successfully. The first thing that got to my mouth was a glass of water followed by some dates. This has been a traditional way to break the fasting throughout the Muslim world since the time of the prophet Muhammad. The first glass of water really rejuvenated me, and I felt refreshed. I was in a great bliss.

Now, when I go back to this childhood memory, I feel proud that I knew so   10
much.

Reading 2   *Reflecting on the Reading*

1 In paragraph 3, Rami states the different ways his mother and father reacted to his decision to fast. With a partner or small group, discuss how you would describe each parent's reaction. Why do you think the parents greeted Rami's decision differently?

2 In paragraph 5, Rami includes several direct quotations. Underline each of these quotations and, in the margin, write down who is speaking. Discuss whether you think these direct quotations are more effective than indirect speech (in which the author reports what was said but does not quote it directly).

3 Fasting during Ramadan is an important part of the spiritual life of Muslims. In other religions as well, the concept of self-denial (for example, by fasting or giving money to the poor) is considered important. Discuss whether you think we become better human beings by making sacrifices and doing without material things. Give reasons to support your opinion.

4 Before reading this essay, you were asked to think of a time in your childhood when you took on an adult responsibility. In your journal, freewrite about this experience from your own life.

A Teacher for a Day
Luisa Tiburcio

In this essay, the writer, a student from the Dominican Republic, describes the fear and excitement she experienced when her teacher asked her to teach the shorthand class while she was away. Before you read, think of an experience from your own life in which you felt both fear and excitement.

That morning was exciting to me because I had many projects and a lot of homework to do. The weather was hot like most other days. During my ten-minute break, I was talking with my friends when I heard a soft, beautiful voice pronouncing my name, "Luisa." At first I did not pay attention because everybody was talking. The classroom was too noisy. I heard my name again. I looked everywhere. Finally I found the person who was calling me. It was my shorthand teacher. Her name was Victoria Hichez, but I called her Vicky. I walked toward her, and I said, "I am sorry; I did not hear clearly the first time." She said to me, "Don't worry; it's okay." Then I asked her, "Why did you call me?" She said to me, "I need a favor from you. I won't be able to come this afternoon. Could you please replace me?"

That was a surprise for me because I was only sixteen years old. Then I said to myself quietly, "I am going to teach." I felt so happy because one of my dreams was to be a teacher. It came true when I was given the opportunity to teach people older than me, and at the same level of education. Even though I was afraid, I said yes to my teacher. Then she showed me the material that I had to teach. I understood everything well. After a hard day of school, I finished my usual schedule at 1:05 p.m. However, that afternoon I had to take over Vicky's shorthand class.

I lived in Santo Domingo, the capital of the Dominican Republic. My house was near the school, about a ten-minute walk. While I was walking home to have lunch, I was thinking about how I would teach. When I arrived at my house, I yelled: "Momma, Momma." My mother was in the kitchen. She came into the living room, where I was. She was nervous because she thought something bad had happened to me. But it had not. Then she asked: "Why did you call me like that?" And I said to her: "Momma, a great thing is happening to me." "What is it?" she asked. "Momma, I'm going to teach shorthand," I said to her.

3

While my mother set the table, I took a shower and dressed up. Then I ate fast because I had to be back in the school by 2:05 the same afternoon.

4

When I arrived back at school, I was nervous again. My hands were cold and sweating, and my heart was beating fast. When I got near the classroom, my heart was beating faster and faster. The zero hour had come. Before I passed through the classroom's door, I said to myself, "Hey, Luisa, you can do this, you know the material." Finally, I was in the classroom. At first I felt nervous again, but then I explained to the students, "I am in the twelfth grade. Please, if I make any mistakes, tell me." But I didn't make any errors.

5

I started to explain to the students that they should write the sounds they hear using the Spanish shorthand symbols. For example, I showed them the shorthand symbol for the word *padre* (father) and then asked them to translate the symbol into Spanish. They did that so well. They asked for some words that they were confused about. I explained because I was able to do that. Finally, everybody understood the lesson.

6

After I finished the class, I felt proud of myself because I handled the situation well, and one of my dreams had come true.

7

Reading 3 Reflecting on the Reading

1 Tiburcio experienced both fear and excitement as she prepared to teach the class for the first time. In the margin, put an *F* by any detail that indicates fear and an *E* by any detail that indicates excitement. Compare your choices with those of a partner or small group. Discuss why you think Tiburcio emphasized these conflicting emotions so much in this essay.

2 Tiburcio has organized her essay *chronologically* – in other words, according to when the events happened in time. Circle each word or phrase in the essay that refers to time. Discuss how these references to time helped you understand the essay.

3 Working with your partner or group, underline all the verbs in paragraph 1. What basic verb tense has Tiburcio chosen for her essay? Looking at all the paragraphs, find three examples of verbs that are not in this same basic verb tense. Why is a different verb tense needed for each of these examples?

4 At the end of the essay, Tiburcio says that she was proud of herself because "one of [her] dreams had come true." Think of an experience in which one of *your* dreams came true and freewrite in your journal about it.

To Be Alive Again

Jian Feng (Jimmy) Ye

In this essay, the author, a student from Canton, China, describes a frightening incident that occurred when he was a teenager. Before you read, think about whether you remember any frightening experiences from your own childhood or adolescence.

I am just a 21-year-old boy. I don't have a great range of life, but I have lived twice in this world. Don't you believe me? Okay, now I'm going to tell you my experience.   1

I should begin when I was 14 years old in high school in China. My father was a businessman, and my family was a middle-level family in China. I liked to ask my father to buy some gifts for me on his trips. In that period, China was not as rich as it is now. Many people, especially teenagers, worshipped the richest foreign countries, like the United States.   2

In my class, some classmates were gang members. They liked to rob people's expensive things. First these "friends" asked me slyly about my watch, "How much did you pay for it?" Actually, I never lied to people, so I just answered them quickly, "My father bought it in Hong Kong. I don't know how much he paid for it." When these people heard the words *Hong Kong*, their eyes kept a close watch on me. Then there was the silence of danger.   3

About 10 seconds later, they asked me to give my watch to them. I waved my hand and said, "Absolutely not." They looked at me as a cat looks at its food. But they knew that they were still in school, so they went away quietly.   4

In the next few days, I was afraid that these guys would come back again to ask me to give them my watch, but they didn't. So I felt more comfortable than on that confusing day. But frequently, life is not as safe as you might think.   5

One day, after I finished my night class, I rode my bicycle on the street. At that moment, I felt that the darkness on that narrow street was abnormal. Neon street lamps were only lit a little bit. There was the silence of darkness. Suddenly, I heard many footsteps behind me. These footsteps disturbed the silence of the darkness. I didn't have enough time to turn my head back to see what was going on. A big, strong hand caught my collar and pushed me to the ground. I didn't know exactly how many feet stepped on my body: my head, my face, my chest. . . . Then I couldn't feel anything. I was unconscious. I didn't have any feeling, like a dead person.   6

I didn't know how long I had been in a coma. I felt I was in a dark room. When I tried to open my eyes, I saw dimly that everything was white. I thought that maybe this was heaven. While I was trying to find out, I heard someone not far from me calling my name. Strenuously, I opened my eyes as wide as I could. I saw lights on the ceiling, trees outside the windows, and my parents standing by my bedside. I tried to use my hands to touch them to make sure that they were real. Unfortunately, my hands could not move. I was amazed at that moment.   7

My parents were still calling my name. I could feel them holding my hands, so I knew it was the real world. I hadn't died. It was difficult to open my mouth to say something. But at that moment, I saw my parents' eyes filling with tears. At the same moment, tears were starting to emerge from my eyes, too. My lips were trembling, and I spoke a few words, "Where . . . am . . . I?" After that, I didn't have any more energy. My father calmed down and told me that someone had found me on that narrow street. My nose and mouth were bleeding. Then that man who found me on the street called the police, and I was taken to the hospital. My parents told me that I had been in a coma for about two days. At that second, I told myself that I was alive again. Later, my father told me that my watch had been taken.

Nowadays, I still cannot forget about this "tour." I hate darkness and the   8
silence of the night because I don't want to lose my life again. Even if you have a lot of money and expensive things, you cannot have your life again. I will cherish my life.

Reading 4 Reflecting on the Reading

1 In this essay, Ye does a good job of providing enough background information to enable readers of various ages and nationalities to understand the significance of his experience. For example, he tells us that he is 21 years old now but was 14 at the time of this incident. Working with a partner, read through paragraphs 1–3 and find four other examples of important background information. Discuss how the essay would have been different if Ye had not provided this information. When you have finished, work with another pair of students and see whether they found different examples.

2 The dictionary defines *suspense* as a state of mental uncertainty usually accompanied by anxiety or fear. Reread the entire essay and underline sentences or parts of sentences that create suspense. Then discuss the examples you found with your partner.

3 At the end of the essay, Ye states: "I will cherish my life." Discuss what you think Ye means by *cherish*. Has there ever been a time in your own experience when you learned to cherish your life?

4 Before reading this essay, you were asked whether you could remember any frightening experiences from your own life. Now list in your journal four or five frightening experiences you still remember. Select one of these experiences and freewrite about it.

Exodus

Xiao Mei Sun

When asked to write about an experience from her past that she still remembered clearly, Xiao Mei Sun decided to explore a painful memory – the Cultural Revolution, which severely disrupted life in China from 1966 to 1976. As you read her essay, think about this question: Has your own life or that of a family member or friend ever been disrupted by a political or economic development beyond your control, such as a war or a depression?

1   I was standing by my desk looking for a book. When I pulled out the last drawer and searched down to the bottom of it, a small box appeared in front of me. I opened it and saw a set of keys inside. They looked familiar, but at the same time they were so strange. Holding the keys, some long-locked memories flooded into my mind, as if they had been released by the keys. I sank slowly into the chair. It was raining outside. The room was so quiet that I could hear the rain pattering on the windowpanes. My thoughts returned to another rainy day.

2   There were several knocks on my bedroom door. "Wake up, my dear," Mother's soft voice floated into my ears. "We need time to get everything done." I opened my eyes and muttered some sound to let her know I was awake. It was dim outside, though it was past daybreak. I turned my body; the hard "bed" beneath suddenly reminded me that I was sleeping on the floor. The only thing between me and the hard, cold boards was a thin blanket. I looked around the empty room and remembered that the day before we had sent most of our furniture and belongings to the Nanjing Railway Station, where they would be transferred to Paoying County – a poor, rural place where we were being forced to go. I heard Mother say something again and realized that I had to get up immediately. Suddenly, I loved the "bed" so much that I didn't want to leave. It seemed softer and warmer than the bed I used to sleep in. I clung to the floor as tears rolled down my face. I wished I could sleep there for the rest of my life instead of going to that strange place. I sighed deeply, wiped my face, and got up.

3   It was very cloudy, as if it would rain at any minute. "I hope it's not going to rain today," Mother addressed my father and me when she saw us step into the dining room. I joined my parents for breakfast around the small table – the only furniture left in the house. The air above the table was as heavy as the sky. "The cave men would never imagine that people in the twentieth century would sit on the floor to eat, would they?" Father said with a grin to me. He had a sense of humor at all times, which had never failed to make me laugh. But today the joke had no charm and tore my heart into pieces. Mother saw my despair and warned, "Mei, I'm superstitious. It's bad luck to see any water when we are going to have a long journey. I hope you understand that." I blinked my tears away and managed a smile. "There is just something in my eyes," said I. Then I left the room to pack my things.

As our bus was arriving at the railway station, some strange noises could be heard in the distance. I was wondering what they could be when the bus suddenly halted in front of the station. I got off and saw a band playing music. Surrounding the band, there were quite a few people holding some colorful banners with slogans on them that read: "Long Live the Cultural Revolution!" "Go to the Rural Areas and Receive Re-education from the Peasants!" "Carry Out Chairman Mao's Revolutionary Ideas Firmly!" Another crowd was also nearby chanting frantically with their arms in the air and their faces full of excitement.

4

Looking at these people, I suddenly felt angry. Since earlier this year – two years after the Great Cultural Revolution that had begun in 1966 – thousands of party bureaucrats and intellectuals, including most students and teachers of high school and college, had been banished to the countryside, to "learn from the people." After they came to the countryside, these intellectuals were ordered to do the hardest work in the fields, such as picking cotton or planting rice. They had to work every day from dawn to sunset, no matter how old they were or how bad their physical condition. Some of them even collapsed in the fields. The reason the party's leader had given was that these intellectuals were open to Western ideas and criticized the government's policies. They were too dangerous to stay in the cities. If they were punished physically, perhaps then they would learn how to keep their mouths shut. Today it was my family's turn. My parents were high school teachers. They had spent their lives educating the young generation. Many times when I had awakened at midnight, I had seen them still marking their students' papers or preparing for their classes. But now all those years of hard work had become the fatal reason they were being sent away. They shouldn't have been punished like this. The truly dangerous people were those gathered around the band. They helped the government confiscate our property, humiliate the intellectuals, and beat the innocent. They were chosen to stay only because they were labeled as the so-called working class and firm followers of Mao Tse-tung revolutionary lines. Now, at this critical moment of our lives, these "chosen people" were cheering for our bad luck and for their survival of this political disaster. Where was the justice?

5

I turned my head away in disgust and saw at the other side of the station a lot of people standing in small groups. Most of them were wiping their eyes and blowing their noses; some were hugging each other while they murmured; the young people were just looking at each other with their mouths half open, uttering no sound. The scene on the two sides of the railway station was so contradictory that if someone came from out of the country and saw this, he would be bewildered. On one side there were people, standing around the band, who were as cheerful as if they were waiting for Napoleon's Army to return in triumph, while across from them there were others who were as sad as if they had been exiled to Siberia in the reign of the Tsar. I felt a strong pain in my heart and was almost choked by the lump in my throat, but at the same time I was glad that no relatives and friends had come to see me and my family leave the city. This was not a happy exodus.

6

It was about ten o'clock now. The clouds were even heavier and moved very fast. I looked up but could not see the sun. People always praised the warm sunshine in early October. Where were its charm, brightness, and warmth today?

7

It seemed that the sun hid her face behind a cloud; she felt pain and shame at seeing the tragedy in the world. A whirlwind swept through the station and blew pieces of white paper from the ground. The paper danced in the air for a while, then dropped slowly again. A chill came through my skin and penetrated into my bones. I stood there with my mind thousands of miles away from the present, and was aware of nothing. The world around me was frozen. I thought about the happy times I had had with my teachers and friends in school; the books I had enjoyed so much in the libraries; the warm room I had spent most of my time in; the beautiful city where I had lived for all of my fourteen years. Those memories were so close to me that I could touch them and hold them. Though the world around me now was ice cold, I felt my heart begin to warm up, warm up. . . .

"Mei, get on the train." Mother's voice broke through the frozen world and woke me up. I was so deep in thought that I hadn't even noticed that people had started boarding. I moved slowly toward the train. The music and the sobs were louder. They mingled and hung in the air. The train was packed. I was standing by the door with my left foot on the platform and the other on the step of the train. It began to rain. The drops were so big and hard that they made my face hurt with each direct hit. I looked up again and prayed: "Mother said it was unlucky to see water today. Please stop, rain!" A sharp whistle pierced the air and I jumped. The sudden shrill noise silenced the whole world. People stopped sobbing and talking; the band even stopped playing. It was so quiet that I couldn't believe there were hundreds of people around. Another whistle sounded and the train started to move. The world came to life just as abruptly as it had ceased a few seconds ago. Father reached out his hand and pulled me in. The wheels moved very slowly, as though a gigantic monster were dragging its huge body unwillingly to another place. I rolled the window down and put my head outside. The heavy raindrops became a downpour. Oh, the heavens could no longer hold their tears and they finally cried out against the unfairness in the world. I watched sadly as the city and the platform were left behind. I repeated silently: "Bye, my school. Bye, my libraries. Bye, my city." Water was running down my face like a stream. I didn't know whether it was my tears or the rain. I reached my hand into my pocket and held the house keys tightly. I said loudly to the receding city: "I will come back; just wait for me. . . ." 8

A gleam of dim, soft light came through the windows and lighted up my room. I didn't know how long I had sat there or when tears had wet my face. I put the keys into the box and sighed heavily. Since the day I left my hometown, I had never gone back. Now I was in New York and I would never use the keys again, but they were still precious to me because they linked the happy memories of my childhood and the tragedy of my country. Closing the small box, I rose and approached the windows. The rain had already stopped. I opened the windows and inhaled the fresh, clean air greedily. The lights from the lampposts along the streets, mingled with the headlights of cars, were shining in the dark. The leaves of the trees were swaying in the gentle breeze. Oh, what a beautiful city! What a sweet night in this foreign land! My heart was melted and a smile rose on my face. . . . 9

1 There are many references to rain in this story. Underline all the references to rain that you find. Then discuss with a partner or small group which of the following things you think the rain symbolizes:

   a sadness

   b injustice

   c nature

   d bad luck

2 Paragraph 5 was not included in the first draft of this essay but was added later in response to a question from a reader. Reread paragraph 5. Discuss what you think the reader's question was. How does the information in paragraph 5 strengthen the essay as a whole?

3 Reread the first and last paragraphs of the essay. Discuss when and where they take place. What would have been lost if Sun had decided just to tell the story of her childhood experience directly and had omitted the first and last paragraphs?

4 Before reading this essay, you were asked to think about whether your own life or that of a family member or friend had ever been affected by a political or economic development beyond your control. Freewrite about this question in your journal.

Reading 6

The Photograph
Sha Sha Chen

In the following selection, Sha Sha Chen, a student from Taiwan, recalls a painful memory from her childhood in this story about a missing photograph. Was there ever a time in your own childhood when you were disappointed by someone you loved or trusted?

"Little Sister, Little Sister," my big sister whispers into my ear.   1
"Mm . . . ," I answer.   2
"I need to go to the bathroom," she whispers again.   3
"Go by yourself." I do not want to leave my sleep.   4
"I can't. It's so dark and quiet. I'm scared. Please get up and come with me.   5
Please!"

Her voice is like a frightened little kitty. I wait for her outside the bathroom,   6
which is on the same floor as my parents' bedroom and ours. As soon as she
finishes, we walk quietly back to our room, and right away I'm asleep again.

* * *

"Don't be ridiculous! There is no ghost in our house," I say to my big sister. 7
We are on our way home from school.

"Then how would you explain the missing photo of our father?" She is looking 8
at me; she seems puzzled.

"What's such a big deal about that?" I wince a little. 9

"Don't you think it's strange that the photo disappeared all by itself? Nobody 10
knows where it went."

"Well, it may be strange, but still, what has this got to do with a ghost?" 11

I move my eyes down to the sidewalk to avoid her eyes. 12

"I think it was a ghost who stole the photo of our father." 13

"Why would a ghost want a picture of our father?" I say, moving my eyes to 14
take a peep at my sister.

"I don't know, but Mother is very worried. She has gone to pray in a temple 15
this morning."

When my mother hears the rumbling sound of my father's motorcycle 16
approaching the door, she gives us a relieved smile. And I, as usual, take out the
pair of slippers that my father wears at home from the shoe cabinet and lay them
on the floor by the living room door.

"Put this on and keep it with you all the time," my mother says, showing my 17
father a red string with a square of red cloth hanging from the center. It is called
a *fu sen fu* in Chinese.

"What do I need this for?" my father frowns, refusing to take the *fu sen fu*. 18

My father is a man who doesn't believe in superstitions. He told us there are 19
no such things as ghosts. When he was in the military, his commander made him
stay overnight in a graveyard, and he did not see any ghosts.

"It is to protect you. Please wear it. Otherwise I can't rest for a minute," my 20
mother says.

"Nonsense," my father refuses firmly. 21

"Father, please wear it. Don't let us worry!" The voice comes from my big 22
sister.

"Don't be so superstitious. A missing photo doesn't mean I'm going to die." 23
My father is lighting up a cigarette.

A moment of silence follows. Neither my mother nor my sister utters a sound. 24
It seems to deepen their worry each time the missing photo is mentioned. And I
pretend to watch TV all through it.

* * *

It was a week before the photo had disappeared. I was at school one morning. 25
My best friend, Shu Yi, told me that my father had a girlfriend and she had seen
them together in a restaurant.

"You lie," I said, and made a face at her. 26

"I'm not. It was just last night. Didn't I tell you it was my mom's birthday, so 27
my dad was going to take us out to dinner?"

What Shu Yi said was true, but I still couldn't believe what she was telling 28
me.

"I saw your father's girlfriend. She was crying in the restaurant. They talked 29
and talked, and she cried."

My heart began to sink. For three nights I had not seen my father at the dinner 30
table. My mother said he was working late. Poor Mother.

That day, after school, I went home and asked my mother if Father was coming 31
home for dinner that night.

"No, he is working late again." 32

"When is Big Sister coming back?" I asked. My sister was on a school trip to 33
Taipei for a week.

"The day after tomorrow." 34

I left the kitchen, where my mother was cooking, and went into the living 35
room. I sat there angrily, not knowing what to do. Suddenly my eyes met my
father in the photo, which was framed and displayed behind a glass door of a wall
cabinet. I stood up on the sofa and let my hand reach for the photo. I separated
the photo from its frame and put the frame back in place. I came down from the
sofa, holding the picture in my hand, and went upstairs to my room. In my room,
I took up a big ink brush lying on the desk and wrote *wan ba dan** on the face of
my father in the photograph.

The doorbell rang the next morning, and there was my aunt's husband 36
standing at the door, asking to see my father. I let him in and went back to my
breakfast. In the meanwhile, from the conversation between my father and my
uncle, I realized that my aunt had run away from her husband and was living in a
hotel. My father had been seeing her after work for four days.

＊ ＊ ＊

Twenty years have passed since the photo of my father disappeared, and still, 37
my father keeps the *fu sen fu* in his wallet.

*wan ba dan: an insulting curse in Chinese

Reading 6 *Reflecting on the Reading*

1 The writer never tells us whether her father was actually having an affair with
her aunt. Underline three details from the story that suggest he might have
been having an affair. In a different color, underline three details that suggest
he might not have been having an affair. Discuss the details you found with a
partner or small group.

2 The little piece of cloth called a *fu sen fu* seems to be an important symbol
in this story. Discuss which of the following reasons might explain why the
father kept it in his wallet for 20 years:

  a He kept it because it reminded him of the love his family felt for him.

  b He kept it to remind him to be faithful to his wife.

  c He kept it because he believed it would protect him from harm.

  d He kept it because it reminded him of his girlfriend.

3 Look up the word *superstition* in the dictionary. With your partner or group, discuss which beliefs described in "The Photograph" could be considered superstitious. What are some superstitions from your own country or culture? Discuss how the superstitions you are familiar with are similar to or different from those in "The Photograph."

4 The fear of ghosts, monsters, and other scary things may seem silly to adults, but to children, such fears are very real. Some psychologists believe that fears of imaginary things are related to more realistic fears or problems in daily life. Think of some of the fears you had as a child or that you have observed in young children. In your journal, freewrite about these fears and how they might have been related to real-life problems.

TECHNIQUES WRITERS USE

Memory Chain

A memory chain is a technique writers use to remember stories from their own experience that can be used as material for writing. When you do a memory chain, you write down a word or phrase that comes into your mind, and then, in a process of free association, you write down other words as they occur to you. Later, you can use these details to develop an essay.

Task 2.1 *Analyze*

1 Read this memory chain by a student.

> *1973 – Good Friday – ten years old –*
> *swimming in the river – almost died.*

2 Now read the first draft of the essay the writer wrote based on her memory chain.

I Almost Died

In sum, life can hold both happiness and tragedy, and there often comes a moment or a day that you will never forget for the rest of your existence. I had this experience on the day I almost died.   1

In 1973, I was ten years old. I was living in a little town in my native country, Haiti. My neighbors, who were also my best friends, were playing together with me.   2

The date was on a Good Friday at about 2 o'clock in the afternoon. My friends and I sat together praying and singing some religious songs, as this was our custom on this holiday.   3

After one hour, we decided to go to the river and swim, before we went to church. We enjoyed swimming, and we would often go under   4

---

the water. When I came up for air, I saw my neighbor trying to save herself, but she didn't know how to swim. I went to try to save her, but I didn't know how to rescue a drowning person. The moment I got to her, she grabbed my neck, and there was nothing I could do about it. As soon as I realized what had happened, I tried to get out from under because she was dragging me down with her. All my efforts were in vain.

I must have lost consciousness then. A few minutes later, I heard 5 somebody talking to me. It was a woman's voice, and even now I can still picture her face. I saw in my mind a beautiful little town. The woman said to me, "My husband's not home. Can I help you?"

"No," I replied.   6

Again she asked, "Do you want to stay with me?"   7

"No, no," I told her.   8

"Do you want some tea?"   9

I nodded my head and said, "Yes."   10

I drank it. Then she asked, "Do you want to sit down for a 11 moment?"

I said, "Yes, I am tired. I miss my mother."   12

All this time, under the water, I had been hearing my friends crying, 13 "She's dead! She's dead!" I had only one question in my head: "Am I dead, or in a dream? Where am I?"

I don't know to this day how I got out of the river. I do remember 14 that I embarrassed one of my friends when I emotionally kissed her and said, "I don't know how, but I am still here." We prayed then, and we thanked God because I believe I was saved by God.

Two days later I explained my near-tragedy to my mother and my 15 friends. We wonderingly asked each other: "Are there other planets under the earth? Was what I had seen real?" I know that it wasn't a dream because it really happened to me. That is the story of the day I almost died.

3 Working with a partner or small group, reread the draft and circle each item that appeared in the writer's memory chain. Discuss how you think the memory chain helped the writer to write her essay.

Task 2.2 *Practice*

1 Write a memory chain of your own. Begin by writing a list of words or phrases. You may start by listing whatever objects happen to be in the room around you. Or you may just write whatever words come to your mind. Keep writing words until an idea or story begins to form. For example, you might write:

window, glass, broken, four years old,
hospital, stitches, my father's eyes, tears

2 Show your memory chain to a partner or small group and discuss it. Does it seem to be something you could write more about? Do you think it would be interesting to readers?

3 Begin to draft your story, concentrating on the ideas and details first, the grammar and spelling later.

4 After writing for 15 or 20 minutes, stop and share what you have written with your partner or group. The response you get will help you focus your writing and recall important details that readers will want to know.

5 Complete your draft and share it with your partner or group again. Keep your draft in your notebook, because you may decide to use ideas from it in your essay for this chapter.

Time Chunks

Students are frequently asked to write about relationships, problems, or experiences. Usually these narratives are set within a limited time frame. By deliberately expanding the time frame over the course of a lifetime and thinking of events as they happened during various time "chunks," we have the opportunity to identify patterns of growth and change that occurred over many years. For example, the following time-chunk outline traces the importance of reading in the life of Rebecca Mlynarczyk, one of the authors of this book:

Early childhood:	My mother read aloud to me every night. My father took me to the library once a week.
Preschool:	I learned how to read simple books by myself.
Elementary school:	I read lots of books from the library, especially biographies.
High school:	Many books were assigned for English courses. In the summers, I did lots of "pleasure reading."
College:	I majored in literature and wrote many analytical essays about my reading.
Adulthood:	I still read all the time – for work and for pleasure.

Task 2.3 Analyze

1 Read the following essay, written with the help of a time-chunk outline, in which a student traces her history of obesity and her struggle to overcome this problem. In the margin, mark the places where one time chunk ends and another begins.

Obesity: Life Problem?

Do you agree with me that obesity is a big problem for many people? I see many obese people every day. There are also articles in newspapers and magazines on how to lose weight. Some of those people go to doctors, eat special diets, or exercise, but this is not helpful for everyone. And this is my problem too.

I remember when I was a child, I was always plump. I was born a big baby, about twelve pounds. I had a good appetite too. I remember how we ate from one big plate. Our mother put a big plate on a chair and we all sat around that chair on our small chairs, took spoons, and started to eat. We ate very quickly. But at that time, I didn't feel that my being overweight was a problem.

When I started grammar school, my problem with obesity started too. Some of my classmates called me "thick," and I felt very bad. I remember once a boy called me "thick" so I called him "stupid." He punched me and I went home crying. The next day I complained to our teacher about him, and she punished him, keeping him one hour after school, so I had enough time to get home.

Later on, I was ashamed to tell the teacher if somebody was laughing at me. My classmates didn't make fun of me so often as we got older, but I still had problems in my mind. I was very ashamed when I had to undress for gym class. I felt that everyone was looking at me and laughing.

When I entered high school, my overweight problem caused me to have an inferiority complex. If I saw other girls with boyfriends and I didn't have one, I thought that I was not as attractive as they were because of my obesity.

I was seventeen when I decided to lose weight. I went on a serious diet. I had almost nothing to eat, and during three months of vacation, I lost almost twenty pounds. When I came back to school, I surprised my friends. Some of them asked me for a prescription for that fantastic diet. I was very proud of myself.

But I wasn't happy for long. In the dormitory where I lived, I started to eat regular meals. I also ate some extra food, which my mother always gave me when I came home for a weekend. Can you imagine that during one year I came back to my previous weight and gained another twenty pounds? After that I really broke down. And I stopped even thinking about a diet for the next few years.

Nothing changed with my obesity until two years ago. At that time I had some bad personal problems. I was very nervous, but I didn't give up. I found a new school, which I attended during the day. Some afternoons, Saturdays, and Sundays I worked. My day started at 7 a.m. and finished about midnight, sometimes later. And what happened with my weight? I lost about ten pounds in a few weeks, then more and more. And it occurred without any effort from me.

Then I met a really nice guy, who is now my boyfriend. He helped   9
me very much and encouraged me to lose weight. As a result, I
became a regular-size girl.

I have kept the same weight for about one year, but I have to pay   10
dearly for that. Ice cream and cookies I can only look at, but I can't
eat. Even at regular meals I sometimes eat only half the food on my
plate. And I also have another bad habit. I smoke cigarettes.

My problem with obesity isn't over and will probably not be for the   11
rest of my life. Even though I look good now, I have to think about
my diet all the time. However, I feel that I am now mature enough to
surmount that obstacle.

2 Make a time-chunk outline for "Obesity: Life Problem?" using the following categories: early childhood, elementary school, high school, two years ago, the present time.

3 Working with a partner, compare and discuss your two outlines. How were your outlines similar? How were they different?

Task 2.4 Practice

1 Choose a theme from your own life that has been important for many years, such as homework, a sport or game, watching TV, or smoking.

2 Complete the following time-chunk outline by writing one or two sentences for each stage about the significance of the theme in your life.

Early childhood: *Child*   *Chronologycal order*

Elementary school: *grammar school*

High school: → *boarding school?*

Two years ago: *Age 17*

The present: *dormiting*
    two years ago now

The future (try to predict):

time place a day

3 Use your time-chunk outline and freewrite about this theme in your life.

INTERNET SEARCH

Expanding Your Knowledge Base

One reason for using the Internet is to increase your understanding of subjects you have read about. The following activity will give you a chance to practice this skill by locating additional information on a topic related to one of the readings in this chapter.

Task 2.5 *Practice*

1 Working with a small group, choose one reading in this chapter that all of you enjoyed.

2 Each group member should work independently and do an Internet search to locate additional information on the topic of the reading.

Here are examples of Web browsers you can use:

Altavista.com	Lycos.com
Ask.com	Looksmart.com
Encarta.msn.com	Netscape.com
Google.com	Yahoo.com

Here are examples of keywords you can use to search for more information on topics in the essays:

Essay Title	Keywords for a Topic in the Essay
Learning How to Cook	garment industry Hong Kong 1960s
What Is It Like to Have an Empty Stomach?	fasting and Islam
A Teacher for a Day	Pitman shorthand
Exodus	China Cultural Revolution

3 Select one Web site containing information that adds to your understanding of the reading you chose. Print out a page or two from the Web site that you think your group members would find interesting. (If you do not have access to a printer, write a summary of what you read.)

4 Discuss the new information you found on the Internet with your group. In what ways does this information add to your understanding and enjoyment of the reading?

5 Select one group member to report to the class about what your group learned from this activity.

ESSAY ASSIGNMENT

Your assignment for this chapter is to write an essay in which you describe an experience that you remember clearly and that was important to you. Your purpose is to re-create this experience in writing so that it seems almost as real to the person reading your paper as it did when it happened to you. Think of your audience as interested classmates who would like to know more about you and your background.

Reread the writing you have already done for this chapter to see whether it gives you any ideas for this assignment.

Writing Tips

- **Write an opening that will capture the reader's attention.**
  In Reading 4, notice how Jimmy Ye immediately gets readers involved with his opening sentences: "I am just a 21-year-old boy. I don't have a great range of life, but I have lived twice in this world." In Reading 1, Florence Cheung achieves a similar effect by beginning with a direct quotation: "'Kit Wah! Kit Wah!' my mother was calling me." Readers are invited into these essays and want to know what will happen next.   → attention

- **If you have trouble writing your opening, write it later.**
  Often it is hard to write a good beginning section until you know what the rest of your essay will be like. Many writers actually skip the beginning and go back and fill it in later.

- **Include significant details to help your reader imagine the experience.**
  Include details that will re-create the experience. What was the weather like? How were people dressed? What did they say? For example, in Reading 2, Youssef Rami makes his first experience of fasting seem real by including this specific detail in paragraph 6: "Yet I remembered that I could only rinse my mouth without letting a drop of water get into my throat."

- **Choose verbs that describe the action effectively.**
  Verbs – the action words – are important in any piece of writing, but they are especially important when you are describing an experience. In Reading 5,

Xiao Mei Sun uses effective verbs to describe the scene at the railway station as she was being sent to the countryside: "A sharp whistle *pierced* the air and I *jumped*. The sudden shrill noise *silenced* the whole world." These sentences are much more effective than if she had written, "I *heard* a whistle, and then everything *got* quiet."

- **Do not just describe the experience. Explain – directly or indirectly – what you learned from it.** *more then three page*
  The experience you are describing may be as simple as learning how to cook rice or as dramatic as being forced to leave your home for an unknown destination. But whatever your experience is, it will mean more to the reader if you express what you learned from it or why it was important in your life. In Reading 1, Florence Cheung uses the indirect method when she ends her essay with the sentence: "Lord, how I loved the first time that I cooked." It is up to her readers to decide why she loved it so much. Or the meaning may be stated directly, as in Youssef Rami's essay when he ends by saying: "Now, when I go back to this childhood memory, I feel proud that I knew so much."

Writing Your First Draft

For all the essays you write, we encourage you to use the process of drafting. A draft is a rough or unfinished piece of writing. Remember that your first draft is not meant to be a polished essay but rather a start toward discovering what you want to say.

Now, keeping the writing tips in mind, write the first draft of your essay. As you are working on this first draft, do not slow yourself down by worrying about correct grammar and spelling; it is more important just to get your ideas down on paper so you have something to work with in later drafts.

REVISING YOUR ESSAY

Once you have put your ideas down on paper by completing the first draft, you can begin the revising process.

What Is Revising?

Revising involves carefully rereading your own essay (*revising* literally means *reseeing*) and thinking about how you can get your meaning across more successfully to your readers. Before you can revise effectively, you need to analyze the content, ideas, development, and organization of your essay. When writers revise, they ask themselves questions such as these:

- Is this really what I want to say?
- Have I included enough information?
- Am I repeating myself unnecessarily?
- Are my ideas clear?
- Is my paper organized so that the reader can follow the ideas easily?

The revising process is different from editing. In this book we use *editing* to mean the correction of grammar, spelling, and punctuation. We recommend that you delay editing until you have revised your essay through two or more drafts and feel satisfied with the content. It does not make sense to spend time carefully correcting the grammar and spelling of an essay if you are going to make major changes in content.

The main reason we suggest delaying the editing process, however, is that it slows writers down and stops them from concentrating on their ideas. Just imagine if, during a conversation, you had to stop and think about whether every word and sentence you said in English were correct. You would not be able to concentrate on what you were saying. The same principle applies to writing. This does not mean that correctness is not important. However, you should try to develop your ideas as completely as possible before you get involved in the more mechanical process of editing.

You will find that revising removes some of the pressure from writing. Knowing that you can take time later to improve your essay frees you for the real work of a first draft, getting your ideas down on paper.

Peer Response

Peer is an old English word meaning a person of the same age, of the same social position, or having the same abilities as other people in a group. Peer response from other people in your class can be an invaluable resource for getting feedback on your writing and ideas for improving it. However, you need to be able to trust your peers, to feel that you can take risks with your writing without fear of embarrassment. All criticism of your classmates' writing should be constructive – that is, it should focus on the positive and should be offered in a helpful spirit. There is a practical aspect to this advice as well. If your classmates tell you what they like about your writing, you can use this strength in other writing; if you did something once, you can do it again. On the other hand, if your classmates focus only on what they think you did wrong, you may feel confused the next time you write; you will know what you *should not* do, but not what you *should* do.

We have found that students can get valuable suggestions from their peers and that some students feel more comfortable talking with a classmate than with their teacher. Of course, teachers can give valuable feedback too, and peer response is not designed to replace the teacher.

At the beginning of your course, it is important to establish ground rules for giving peer response. Gradually, as you work with the other students in your class, you will develop a feeling of community – a sense that you are working together and helping one another with something important. Responding to other people's writing is a skill that takes practice. But as the course progresses, you should find yourself getting better at giving and receiving constructive criticism.

Work as a class and discuss the following ground rules. Do you agree with them? Would you like to suggest any additional rules?

Ground Rules for Peer Response

- No student should be forced to share a piece of writing that he or she considers too personal.
- Positive aspects should be discussed first, unless the writer specifically asks for help with problem areas.
- The writer should tell the other students what specific aspects of the writing to respond to – for example, the first paragraph or the conclusion.
- Students should never write on other students' papers without first getting the writer's permission. All comments should be given orally or written on a separate piece of paper.
- All comments offered by others are only suggestions. The writer remains in charge of his or her writing and decides whether to take the advice that was offered.

Oral Peer Response

One method of generating peer response is simply to talk about your essay with someone else. Oral peer response can be given effectively in a peer conference – a discussion among two or more students in which they give and receive comments about their writing. Peer conferences are an efficient and useful way of working on writing. However, they require discipline and responsibility to your fellow students. The following task will familiarize you with the process.

1 Work in groups of three. If possible, make enough copies of the essays for everyone in the group.

2 One student begins by reading his or her essay aloud.

3 Then the other students take turns answering the following questions. This works best if both responders answer question **a**, then move on to question **b**, and so on.

  a What was one detail that made this experience seem real to you?

  b Were there any places where you got confused? If so, where were they?

  c Reread the first paragraph of the essay. Do you think this is a good beginning? Does it make you feel like reading on? Explain.

  d What basic verb tense does the writer use? If the writer changes tense, is the tense change appropriate?

  e What would you like to know more about when the writer revises?

4 Repeat this process until you have discussed each group member's essay.

5 Discuss these questions with your group:

a What worked well in this oral response process?

b What problems did you encounter?

c What did you learn from the peer conference?

6 Share your answers to the questions in step 5 with the class.

Writing Your Second Draft

Taking into consideration the feedback you have received from your peers and your own ideas about how to improve your essay, write your second draft.

EDITING YOUR ESSAY

When you are satisfied with the content and organization of your essay, you can begin the process of editing.

What Is Editing?

Editing is the last phase of the writing process, in which writers try to ensure that grammar, spelling, and punctuation are as correct as possible. Accuracy in these areas is important because language errors can interfere with meaning or distract the reader from the ideas of the essay. Consider this comparison: if the seats on an airplane are torn and dirty or the food trays are broken, people will probably wonder whether the plane's engines are in a similar condition. The engines might be fine, but the impression given is that the airline does not care about proper maintenance. In the same way, if an essay is filled with errors in grammar, spelling, and punctuation, the reader may get the impression that the writer does not care very much about what he or she is saying.

All writers agree that editing is hard work, but if you want your writing to be accepted and taken seriously, accurate language is necessary. If you work at it, your writing will gradually become more and more correct.

In each chapter, before you edit your writing you will review a particular feature of English grammar that students often find difficult. Then you will complete a task in which you analyze its use in someone else's writing and another task in which you practice correct usage yourself. After this grammar review, you will edit your writing for grammar, spelling, and punctuation, making use of the technique of proofreading.

What Is Proofreading?

As writers edit their work, they use a reading process known as proofreading, which is very different from the usual type of reading that we do every day. Proofreading means reading your essay carefully so that you can find and correct any errors. Students often have difficulties with this process because they do not realize that proofreading differs from ordinary reading in two ways. First, proofreading focuses on correctness rather than meaning. Second,

 proofreading is much slower than normal reading. When you proofread, you have to slow your eyes down so that you can see each letter and punctuation mark. It is much easier and more efficient to proofread on paper than on a computer screen. If you are writing your essay on a computer, print out your essay and proofread it on paper.

Here are some strategies for effective proofreading. Experiment with these strategies and decide which ones work best for you.

- If you have the time, wait a few hours or days between reading your essay for content (the revising process) and beginning to proofread (the editing process).
- Hold a pencil under each word to force your eyes to see every letter, and read the essay aloud. Look carefully at the endings of words, since this is where most errors occur.
- Hold a ruler or piece of white paper under the line you are reading so that you can see only one line at a time.
- Start proofreading from the end of the essay, reading the last sentence first. Some people find that this helps them to concentrate on correctness rather than on meaning.
- Be sure to proofread, even if you have used your computer's spelling and grammar checks. The computer's checks will help you to find some – but not all – mistakes.
- Always proofread your essays more than once. Nobody catches all the errors the first time around. Each time you proofread your essay, check for a different type of error – for example, verb tense, punctuation, or the plural form of nouns.
- Based on your teacher's feedback, learn what types of errors you tend to make. When you proofread, make a special effort to look for these types of errors.

Grammar in Context: Using Verb Tenses Consistently

In this chapter, the grammar focus is on using verb tenses consistently. If necessary, review the basic verb tenses in English in the appropriate section of your grammar reference book or in an online grammar resource, such as Purdue University's Online Writing Lab, currently accessible at <http://owl.english. purdue.edu>. You may also want to review how to identify subjects and verbs.

Every main verb in a sentence has a tense. Basically, tense refers to time; in other words, it tells when something happened. The two most common tenses in English are the simple present and the simple past.

> **Examples**
> **Simple Present:** I *like* to write.
> **Simple Past:** When I was younger, I *liked* to write.

When writing about experiences that happened in the past, whether many years ago or only yesterday, most writers choose the simple past tense. Sometimes, however, writers describe past events in the present tense to create a sense of excitement and immediacy. Within any piece of writing, you should be consistent in your use of verb tenses; this *does not* mean that you can use only one tense in the entire piece, but it *does* mean that you should have a good reason for changing tenses.

Task 2.6 *Analyze*

1 Working with a partner, analyze the choice of verb tenses in "Learning How to Cook" (page 30). Underline all of the main verbs in paragraphs 1 through 6 except those that are within quotation marks. What is the basic verb tense of this essay? Why do you think the writer chose this tense?

2 With your partner, examine the choice of verb tenses in "The Photograph" (page 41) by filling in the chart below.

Segment	When Events Occurred (past or present)	Basic Verb Tense
Paragraphs 1–6		
Paragraphs 7–24		
Paragraphs 25–36		

3 What verb tenses does the writer use in the last segment, paragraph 37?

4 Discuss with your partner why you think the writer chose different tenses for different parts of the story. Was she consistent in her use of verb tenses within each of the four segments? Do you agree with the choices she made in selecting verb tenses? Why or why not?

Practice

1 Working with a partner, read these first few paragraphs of a student essay, which has some errors involving verb tenses.

In the Cyber Game Room

A few years ago, I had a best friend. His name is Eric Chan. He came from Hong Kong. He has light skin, big eyes. Maybe it's because he thinks a lot. His head looks really big, especially the upper part around his brain. And he has very straight hair, which stands up 3 inches on top of his head. 1

Back in the high school days, we spend a lot of time together. Usually this was after school at the "cyber game room." It is a room that has a lot of computers. So people pay money to play computer games or do stuff on the computer and the Internet. When we were in front of the computer, we became partners. He is a great teacher. He shows me how to play the game and give me examples like strategies about how to play. He give me his ideas, explain how to catch what's in the enemy's mind, and tells me how to make the enemy play my own game. He leads me into battles. We fight, we bleed, and we win. We never lost since we become experts. We were as good as all those professional gamers out there in the world. 2

When we stay in the "cyber game room," he always has a cigarette in his hand or mouth. He smokes a pack of cigarettes every day. He says, "Having a cigarette, I am 100% sure what I am doing," and "A cigarette is like a battery; it can recharge the energy for my body." So after a few times with him in the cyber game room, I start to learn how to smoke. 3

After two years of our friendship, things begin to cool down a little. We both meet the same girl. . . . 4

---

2 Discuss with your partner any places where you think verb tense corrections are needed. Then make the corrections.

3 Check your work using the Answer Key on page 257.

Editing Checklist

If you are writing your essay on a computer, remember to print out your revised essay and proofread it on paper.

☐ **First proofreading: verb tenses**

Analyze the verb tenses that you used in the first few paragraphs of your essay and decide which verb tense is the best one for most of the essay. Then analyze the verb tenses in the rest of your essay and make any needed corrections. Are there places where you are not sure which verb tense to use? If so, discuss your choices with a partner and decide which tense is most appropriate. Check (✓) the box when you have finished.

☐ **Second proofreading**

Proofread your essay a second time and correct any other errors of grammar, spelling, or punctuation that you find. Check (✓) the box when you have finished.

☐ **Third proofreading**

Print out or write a copy of your essay that includes the corrections you made in your first and second proofreading. Now proofread your essay a third time. Try to find and correct any errors that you missed. Then print out, or write in dark blue or black ink, the final draft of your essay. Check (✓) the box when you have finished.

Nothing is quite so interesting to most of us as other people, so they provide a natural subject to write about. In this chapter, the writing task is to write a character sketch. Just as an artist makes a sketch to reveal a person's appearance, a writer can reveal a person's character using words. As you read the student essays that follow, think about some of the important people in your own life and how you could use writing to help readers understand what they are like.

READINGS

My Grandmother

Hikaru Takahashi

In many parts of the world, families have always had a great deal of power to influence the lives of their children, especially daughters. In this essay, a student from Japan describes her grandmother's struggle to free herself from the strictness of her family and become an independent person. Before reading, think of someone you know who made an important decision that was in conflict with his or her parents' wishes.

1   She always has a little smile on her face in her portraits. Although she is smiling, there is a kind of severity and dignity about her. She passed away on a cold February morning eight years ago. When my father came to wake me up, I was seized with fear and began to shake, knowing what had happened. Yes, she had just passed away.

2   She is the one whom I respected the most. When I was a child, I was proud to show her wedding picture to my friends because everybody said that she was beautiful. However, for some reason she was keeping all the pictures of her youth away from me. She did not want me to show them to others, but I liked to look at them and always tried to find them.

3   She was from a prestigious family, and her parents were very strict with her. She went to a girls' high school in Taiwan and then returned to Japan to go to one of the most famous women's universities. She seemed to follow her parents' will and lived very happily.

4   It must have been very surprising to her parents when she told them she was going to quit school and become an actress. She chose to be a stage actress even though it would mean giving up everything she possessed: family, education, and wealth. Of course, her parents would not allow her to be an actress, but her strong will was not to be changed. Finally, she was kicked out of the family and went to acting school.

5   "I was very proud to go backstage and see her surrounded by lots of flowers from her fans," her brother told me. "She was a tall woman, so she played a lot of male roles."* In one of her stage pictures, her glaring eyes and tightly closed lips gave a manly impression. However, she finally did get married to my grandfather.

6   Actually, her parents arranged her marriage. At that time, nobody knew how much her marriage would change her life. She had been living a hopeful life, doing what she really wanted. But once she got married, she had to move to my grandfather's house in the countryside. She had to work in the field, a completely new experience for her. She had to get along with other women there who did not have any higher education and who devoted themselves only to hard work. She

*male roles: It is common for women to play male roles in the Japanese theater, and vice versa.

had to accustom herself to the life of the countryside. Still, she did not become a village woman who never cared about her appearance. "She always spruced herself up and was somehow different from us," one of her friends said.

She did not tell me how hard it was for her, but I noticed it a little later when I got older. I understood why she was keeping all those pictures of her youth away from me. She did not even want to remember the time when she was really happy. She had never shown her suffering to anyone. Her pride did not allow her to do so.

Her last days in the hospital were too painful to look at. She could not even breathe by herself because of cancer. Two small tubes were placed in her nose. She was a mere shadow of her former beautiful and strong self. However, she still had her pride as a stage actress and a woman from a prestigious family. Every morning in the hospital, she put make-up on her face and groomed her hair neatly. "She did not forget to be a woman up until her last moment," a nurse who had been taking care of her said.

In my memory, she is still living as a beautiful woman with severity. Her life was not happy all the time, but no other person knew how hard it was. Whenever I describe her life, I use the same expression: "She lived a very short and deep life, as many beautiful flowers do."

Reading 1   Reflecting on the Reading

1 Discuss with a partner or small group which of the following statements best describes your feelings about the grandmother's decision to become an actress:

   a It was a foolish decision because it offended her parents, and she suffered a lot because of that.

   b It was the right decision because she had a great talent and needed to discover who she really was.

   c The decision was neither right nor wrong. She gained as much as she lost.

2 One of the themes of this essay is the struggle to become an independent person. Underline details in the story that suggest the grandmother succeeded in becoming independent. In a different color, underline details that suggest she did not succeed. Compare your answers with your partner or group.

3 Throughout the essay, Takahashi quotes what other people (her great-uncle, a village woman, a nurse in the hospital) said about her grandmother. Find three direct quotations and discuss what each quotation reveals about the grandmother.

4 Before reading, you were asked to think of a situation in which someone you know challenged the authority of parents. In your journal, freewrite about this situation. Was the conflict eventually resolved? If so, describe how. Thinking back on the conflict, who do you think was right, the parents or their child?

My Mother

Eileen Peng

When asked to write an essay about a person, Eileen Peng, a student from China, knew immediately that she wanted to describe her mother. As you will see, Peng's mother is a major force in her life. After you have read the first four paragraphs of this essay, stop and do not read any further. At this point, what kind of person do you think Peng's mother is? Write down one or two words to describe the mother's character, and then finish reading the essay.

Her sound was usually heard before her appearance. A ten-minute walk would take her twenty minutes or more, not because she walked slowly, but because she often met so many friends on her way. 1

Once, while I played in my neighbor's home, his friend asked him about me. "Whose daughter is she?" 2

"She is hers," my neighbor said, and pointed at my house. "Her mother can ride a bicycle as if she were flying." 3

"Oh, I see. I know her," his friend said. 4

Yes, she is my mother. She is a very capable, lively woman, although she has less energy now than she used to. As an accountant for a market, she could do her work fast, could even finish another accountant's work. So her boss thought that one accountant was enough and sent the other one to another branch. 5

Although she had a full-time job, she was also a very good housewife: shopping, cooking, cleaning, sewing, taking care of four children's studies, and going to parents' meetings for us. My father? Except for working at the office, he usually either sat down before the TV or stayed behind the door of the bedroom. 6

My mother was the eldest daughter in her family. When she was only sixteen years old, in 1952, she was put in a sedan chair, was sent to my father's home, and became a wife. After becoming a wife, she insisted on studying in junior high school in order to finish her general education. My older sister and I were born while she was still in school. (Having children while in school was a very rare circumstance at that time in China.) 7

She had no more opportunity to take advanced study after graduating from junior high school. So she thought that her children were her hope, her future. "Study hard. Get honors for me," she often said to us. 8

My family was not living the affluent life. In many ways, my mother was quite thrifty, but in buying study supplies for children, she was very generous. I have been interested in painting since I was a child. My mother was my great supporter. 9

One day, she gave me a surprise. "I found a fine arts teacher for you. He is a teacher of the Fine Arts Academy of Canton. Let us go to see him," she said. 10

She sent me to that teacher's home to have my first lesson. This teacher was so important for me! He gave me a great deal of help. When I entered the Fine 11

Arts Academy of Canton as a freshman, my teacher said to me, "You have a great mother. Without her, you could not be a student of this school." Indeed, he was right.

Whenever my works appeared in newspapers or magazines, my mother was 12 proud of showing them to relatives and her friends. She was so happy that she had such a girl. She liked to talk to those parents who felt unhappy when they had a daughter but not a son. "Don't let it get you down. Daughters can do anything that sons can do. Look at my daughter, how well she has done."

In my junior year of art school, I revealed to her my idea that I hoped to go 13 abroad to continue my study. "Good. Try to do it!" she said. The following year, she helped me to do everything necessary for my application.

When I left for the United States, she gave all her possessions to me, including 14 her marriage portions – a golden necklace, earrings and wedding ring, and money. Oh, how hard to save that money! When I received those things from her hands, my eyes filled with tears.

I had a hard time after arriving in the United States, but I was determined to 15 "Study hard," as my mother said. I have to make a success of myself. I would never want to see the expression of disappointment on my mother's face if I failed.

Reading 2 *Reflecting on the Reading*

1 Look at the word or words you wrote to describe the mother's character after reading the first four paragraphs. Compare your answers with a partner or small group. Were you right about the kind of person Peng's mother is? What clues in the first four paragraphs helped you to make a guess about her character? If your guess was not correct, discuss whether you would advise Peng to change the beginning of her essay in any way.

2 Underline two examples of what other people say about Peng's mother. In a different color, underline two examples of the mother's own actions. Compare your choices with your partner or group and discuss what these specific details reveal about the mother's character.

3 In paragraph 12, Peng mentions the traditional Chinese belief that it is better to have a son than a daughter – a belief her mother did not accept. Many other cultures share this idea that it is better to have a son. Discuss how you and other members of your family feel about this issue.

4 In this essay, Peng shows that education is an important value to her mother. Think of a value you learned from your family (such as hard work, a sense of humor, respect for other people, hospitality to guests) and freewrite about it in your journal. Which family members in particular do you associate with this value? Try to include specific examples to illustrate how you learned the importance of this value.

Rosita

Gloria Cortes

Gloria Cortes, a student from Colombia, describes the painful relationship she had with her family's housekeeper. The two had conflicting views on religion, manners, and sexuality, creating many problems for Gloria when she was growing up. Before you begin reading, think of someone in your own life with whom you have had conflicts throughout your relationship.

1   When my mother went away, the first person Rosita turned to after clearing away her tears was me. She was surprised that I was standing there calm and without tears. She said to me, "This girl never cries and never feels anything. She is like a rock." From that moment on, Rosita saw me as heartless and immoral.

2   Rosita built up the idea that I was a hard young girl because she couldn't understand my thoughts. I was distant from everything that happened in the house. I never paid attention to the rigid moral values that she established and by which she harshly judged me because they didn't mean anything to me, and I was too naive to understand them. But there was one thing she didn't know. The day when my mother left, I locked myself in the bathroom and cried and cried. She never noticed.

3   Rosita had worked for us for three years when my mother left. In my mother's absence, she ran the house and raised us. She was a small, frail, light brown woman. When she smiled we could see the perfectly straight, white teeth of which she was so proud. She took delight in letting everyone see how beautiful they were. We giggled at this because we knew they were not real.

4   She was so proud of her thin waist, which she seemed to exaggerate by wearing tight belts. But at the same time, she had a large stomach that flowed over her belt and made her look pregnant. When she showed off her thin waist, she somehow was able to ignore her hanging belly.

5   Rosita's legs were short and full of thick veins like worms burrowing under her skin. They had formed, she said, from wearing tight garters. She said that her legs were smooth and beautifully shaped when she was younger. I can still see her in front of the mirror pulling up her dress to her thighs and showing us what had been, at one time, beautiful legs.

6   The household that Rosita managed contained my father, my two sisters, and me. As my oldest sister, Magda, was growing up, I curiously observed the changes in her body. One day when she was changing her clothes, Rosita saw me observing her and said, "What a malicious look this girl has! What are you looking at?"

7   I was very confused because I didn't know what was wrong with looking at my sister. I always took showers with my sisters and we slept together. From that moment on, however, whenever my sister dressed, she hid herself from me and we no longer shared the shower. I never understood that drastic change in my sister, but at the same time, I started to hide myself from her.

We lived in the outskirts of Bogotá, Colombia, in a three-story, red-brick house   8
with a big patio surrounded by rooms. My small, windowless room, located just
off my sister's room, was like a cool, dark, moist cave. One day I woke up in my
humid room and as I put my feet on the floor, I crushed a slimy slug. I screamed
so loud that Rosita heard me from the kitchen. She ran into my bedroom. I was
almost in tears as I told her what happened. She said, "Is that all? You yelled so
loud that I thought you saw a nude man."

I didn't know what to make of her response because I always saw males as my   9
equals and never thought there was anything to scream at if I saw one nude.

Rosita was a very religious woman who believed in a wrathful God and a   10
ubiquitous devil. She saw the devil's work everywhere except where her stern piety
kept him at bay.

Every Sunday we used to go to our neighborhood church. I never understood   11
the purpose of it, but I knew it was a place to see my friends. It occurred to me
that Sunday could be more fun if we went to the church on top of the mountain
because I could climb the mountain with my friends, playing as we went.

By the time we arrived at the church, the service would be almost over, and   12
we could resume our playing as we descended the mountain. The mountain was
in the outskirts of the city. We had to take a bus at 4:00 a.m. to get to the base of
the mountain, where we would begin our climb on foot. In the bus we were with
a lot of poor people, many of whom got off with us and climbed the mountain
on their knees to show their piety. When they arrived at the church, their knees
were red with blood.

Rosita soon found out that our excursion had little to do with sacrifice and   13
screamed at me for being evil. But again, I didn't know or understand why I was
evil. I didn't see why I should make myself a martyr by climbing the mountain on
my knees.

Most of my friends were little boys because young girls had the same ideas as   14
Rosita, and with the boys I could play freely without reserve. But soon Rosita said
that playing with boys was bad because they would touch me. She used to say that
prostitutes were touched by men, and that I should not make myself one. I never
understood what that meant because I never saw anything in the hands of my
friends that would change me into a prostitute, whatever that was.

A few years later, when it was time for my first communion, I decided against   15
having it because I could not bear confessing sins to a person who was just as
human as I, and who had probably sinned just as much as I. Rosita attributed my
refusal to the devil, who, she believed, had taken permanent hold of me.

A year later, Rosita left us. I did not cry.   16

1 Do you think Rosita is someone Cortes pities, hates, or both? Underline details to support your opinion. Discuss with a partner or small group how you feel about Rosita. Is she someone to be pitied or hated?

2 Underline four specific details in the essay that describe Rosita's physical appearance. Compare your choices with your partner or group and discuss how these physical details shape your understanding of Rosita's character.

3 Reread the last two paragraphs of the essay. Do you think this is an effective ending? Discuss the meaning of the last sentence, "I did not cry."

4 Before you read this essay, you were asked to think of a person with whom you have had conflicts. In your journal, freewrite about your relationship with this person. Include lots of specific details in your writing, as Cortes has done.

Reading 4

My Father

Intissar Haddiya

The author of this essay is a young woman who used In Our Own Words *in her English class in Morocco. In a letter to the authors, she explained that reading essays written by students from all over the world taught her "to appreciate the differences between cultures" and to understand the ways in which cultures have "different impacts over their people." In this essay, she describes the person she "loves and emulates most," her father. Before you read, think about the person who has had the greatest influence on your life.*

He speaks Arabic with a sharp southern accent. When he gives lectures in 1
the university, nobody seems to pay attention to that, because he uses a very
refined classical Arabic; but still he cannot express himself in his native language,
especially in a crowd, without making everyone think about his origins. Sometimes
he's asked whether he's from the south. He usually replies affirmatively, ready to
give details about the town he is from, exhibiting a proud twinkle in the eye. In
fact, pride is just one of the countless qualities I myself often use in describing
what I deeply feel toward him.

He is my father, a very special man indeed. Arabic isn't the only language he 2
speaks oddly. English, too, sounds as musical as a Latin American dialect coming
out from Dad's mouth. Whenever he speaks English abroad, there's always
somebody who asks, out of pure curiosity, whether he is from Chile or Bolivia.
Speaking languages with a noticeably strange accent is a characteristic that makes
Dad different from everyone else.

I love him; that's a fact. I love him because he is different from the others, 3
because he's my father, and because he loves me too.

Being a psychologist in a society in which psychology is still viewed as a useless waste of time that can easily turn into a luxury, my father has proved so far, to our family and close friends, that psychology can be helpful in lots of cases. I remember, some years ago, his being in charge of my seven-year-old cousin, who happened to be suffering from a language problem. Thanks to his fruitful advice, mainly based on convincing the child of his real aptitudes, my cousin gave up stuttering little by little. He also gained more confidence in himself. That was the first time I seriously considered my father as a hero. He is one indeed. He is ambitious, intellectual, and moral. He helped me to shape my own goals and ideals in my life. As a person who had a thoroughly hard-bitten life and grew up in tough circumstances, my father is the right person to know about the lack of a diverse range of opportunities. However, what is really heartwarming and worthy of consideration at the same time is that he does his best to provide me with as many chances as possible. He believes in my abilities and encourages me to make the best use of them.

In appearance, my father and I are extremely different. He is much darker than me, with lighter eyes and really different facial features. In addition to that, he seems too young to be my father. Both of us get truly upset at the comments usually coming from his own friends or my mother's, such as, "That's your daughter! Quite incredible!" Or again, "How can you be his daughter?"

Whatever others' reactions are – I admit that sometimes they are hurtful and painful – my father will ever remain the person I love and emulate the most in my life. However harsh and ruthless the hurdles I face in my life may be, there will certainly be a sharp southern Arabic intonation lingering down inside me, leading me to the right decisions.

Reading 4 Reflecting on the Reading

1 In this essay, Haddiya mentions several of her father's personal qualities, or character traits. For example, in paragraph 1, she shows that pride is one of his characteristics. Identify three other character traits of the father. Compare your choices with a partner or small group.

2 At the beginning of "My Father," Haddiya calls attention to her father's "sharp southern accent." Discuss why you think she decided to focus on her father's accent in the first paragraph.

3 In paragraph 4, Haddiya states that in her country "psychology is still viewed as a useless waste of time that can easily turn into a luxury." Discuss the meaning of this statement. How are psychology and psychologists viewed in your community or culture? Do you think psychology is useful?

4 Before reading this essay, you were asked to think about the person who has had the greatest influence on you. In your journal, freewrite about this person and the ways in which he or she has influenced your life.

My Friend Nafiz

Syed R. Saeed

In this essay, a student from Bangladesh focuses on a student in his high school who stood out because he was "the bravest, toughest, and strongest boy in the school." Before you read, think back on your own high school days. Which of your fellow students do you remember most clearly?

I have made many friends in my life. Many of them were not good because they turned out to be traitors, and some forgot me. Nafiz is a person whom I met at my high school in Brooklyn. The day when we first met, he came to me with a cigarette in his hand and asked me, "Is it true you're acting tough in school?" He did not go through any introduction. He was the bravest, toughest, and strongest boy in the school. He used to fight with people and was always in trouble. The reason I am writing about him is because he made a decision without anyone's advice that changed his lifestyle.

Readers might think that maybe Nafiz went to jail after his fights. That is true; he visited the jail a few times. I did not see him for a long time after he threatened me on the first day. I asked people about him. They said, "He is inside." "Inside" meant jail to them. The next time I met Nafiz, he accused me, "Boys are telling me that you are talking behind my back." I was angry and shouted at him, saying that he should not listen to people. He offered to fight me after school, and I told him if he thought fighting would solve the problem, I would fight. He was staring at me for a moment and said, "You think you are smart. I will let you go today. Be good."

He did not fight me after school, but he had a fight with a group of Pakistani people, which got him suspended for a couple of days. The funny part was that he became more and more famous whenever he was out of school for fighting. Students used to talk about him, saying that he carried a 6-inch knife, that he seemed like a man walking on the moon, that he walked like a man with one small leg. He used to move his hands while he talked, which seemed like he was talking to a deaf person. He never smiled, and his dark black eyes were searching for trouble. His tall, loose, baggy pants used to drag on the floor, and he did not care because that was his style. He wore a bracelet and headbands and earrings, which used to sparkle. Everybody knew his 5 foot, 3 inch figure and his light, round face. There were a lot of students who followed his way of life. Nafiz used to tell his followers, "If you wanna be proud, you got to prove that you know how to fight. Fight the right way, which makes you bright." His right way of fighting took him and his followers to jail for six months.

I was shocked, astonished, and surprised when I saw him after six months. He was totally changed. The way of walking, talking, and looking were all gone. His followers were much more surprised than I. "What happened?" everybody muttered. He did not fight, he attended all classes on time, and he did not talk to anybody. Later on, his best friends stood against him because they wanted the old "trouble guy" Nafiz.

One day I met him in the library and asked him the reason for being changed. At first, he did not want to say anything, but later he said, "If you think that I forgot how to fight, then you are wrong. I can still drag you on the floor, but I won't because I am not like before anymore. I have learned a lesson from being involved in all those fights." First I thought that he was punished hard in jail. But later I found the real reason. He had lost his mother when he was young. He lived with his father in his aunt's house. His father always told him to stop fighting and be a good boy, but Nafiz never listened. When Nafiz was in jail, his father went to visit him and told him to stop fighting after he bailed him out. But Nafiz shouted at him and told his father to leave. Later Nafiz heard that his father died on the same night from a heart attack. That day was their last meeting. Nafiz never saw his father's face again because he was not allowed to go to the funeral.

Now Nafiz is keeping his father's wish. He understands that there is no benefit in fighting. It creates more problems. He works in a store and goes to college. But he has no friends because he thinks that there is nobody who can be his friend. I meet him sometimes in his aunt's house, and we play music and talk about our future projects. He is energetic like before, brave, strong, but not tough. His eyes look at others with peace and cheer. "I will study and get a good job with a lot of money and show those kids that I am proud, not in fighting, but in doing the right thing, right way." He pauses and looks at the sky without blinking. I look at him and think that he is talking to his father in his imagination and saying, "I will keep your wish and make you proud of me." He blinks, and a drop of tear comes out. He looks at me. "What are you looking at? Let's go." He rubs his eye and gets up. We walk through the streets, and he talks about life. I smile and listen to what he says.

Every time I meet Nafiz, he advises me, "Listen to your parents. Don't be a fool like me." I can feel that he has a good heart in him. He is not like before. He is calm, decent, and always smiling. "We need to stand on our own feet and earn respect from people. Going to jail will not make anyone proud. We can be successful if we do the right thing in a right way." By leaving him, his father taught him a lesson that he will carry for the rest of his life.

7

Reading 5 **Reflecting on the Reading**

1 One of the techniques writers use to reveal character is to include what others say and think about the person they are describing. Find three examples of what other students say and think about Nafiz. Compare your examples with a partner or small group. Discuss how these examples add to your understanding of Nafiz's character.

2 In paragraph 3, Saeed gives a vivid description of Nafiz's appearance. Underline four specific details that help you to visualize Nafiz. Or, if you prefer, you can draw a picture of Nafiz based on the details in this paragraph. Compare your details or drawing with your partner or group.

3 The student who wrote this essay is also a filmmaker, and his description of Nafiz in some ways reads like a movie script. Imagine that you are a filmmaker. Decide how you would divide Nafiz's life into five or six scenes. Present your choices to a small group and explain why you chose them. Choose one student from the group to present his or her choices to the class.

4 This essay tells the story of a person who changed his entire way of life. Think of a person you know who has changed in a dramatic way, and freewrite about that person in your journal. What caused the person to change? If you can't think of a person from your own experience, write about a character in a movie you have seen or a book you have read.

Reading 6

Teacher, It's Nice to Meet You, Too

Ruby Ibañez

Ruby Ibañez taught English as a Second Language and trained teachers in a refugee camp in the Philippines during the early 1980s. At that time, people from Kampuchea (formerly Cambodia) were forced to flee their homeland to escape political persecution, in which many people – possibly millions – lost their lives. Although this essay was written by Ibañez, it is told in the voice of a Cambodian refugee who was learning English in the camp and preparing to emigrate to the United States. Before reading, think about whether anyone you know has had to leave his or her country as a refugee.

Hello! I'm one of the twenty students in your class. I come every day. I sit here and smile and I laugh and I try to talk your English, which you always say will be "my" language.

As I sit here I wonder if you, my teacher, are able to tell when I am sinking in spirit and ready to quit this incredible task. I walked a thousand miles, dear teacher, before I met you. Sitting here listening to you and struggling to hold this pencil seems to be my "present." I want to tell you, though, that I, too, am a person of the past.

When I say that my name is Sombath, I want to tell you also that back in my village, I had a mind of my own. I could reason. I could argue. I could lead. My neighbors respected me. There was much value to my name, teacher, no matter how strange it may sound to your ears.

You ask, "Where are you from?" I was born in a land of fields and rivers and hills where people lived in a rich tradition of life and oneness. My heart overflows with pride and possession of that beautiful land, that place of my ancestors. Yet with all this that I want to share with you, all I can mutter is I came from Cambodia. I'm Khmer. I'm not even sure I can say these words right or make you understand that, deep inside, I know what you are asking.

"How old are you?" I want to cry and laugh whenever you go around asking that. I want so very much to say, I'm old, older than all the dying faces I have left behind, older than the hungry hands I have pushed aside, older than the shouts of fear and terror I have closed my ears to, older than the world, maybe. And certainly much older than you. Help me, my teacher. I have yet to know the days of the week or the twelve months of the year.

Now I see you smiling. I know you are thinking of my groans and sighs whenever I have to say "house" and it comes out "how" instead. I think many times that maybe I was born with the wrong tongue and the wrong set of teeth. Back in my village, I was smarter than most of my neighbors. Teacher, I tremble with fear now over words like *chicken* and *kitchen*.

Now you laugh. I know why. I do not make sense with the few English words I try to say. I seem like a child because I only say childlike things in your English. But I am an adult, and I know much that I cannot yet express. This I think is funny and sad at the same time. Many times the confusion is painful. But do not feel sad, dear teacher. I wish very much to learn all the things that you are offering me, to keep them in my heart, and to make them a part of me. However, there was this life I have lived through and now the thoughts of days I have yet to face. Between my efforts to say "How are you?" and "I am fine, thank you" come uncontrollable emotions of loneliness, anger, and uncertainty. So have patience with me, my teacher, when you see me sulking and frowning, looking outside the classroom or near to crying.

Please go on with your enthusiasm, your eagerness, and your high spirit. Deep inside me, I am moved that someone will still give me so much importance. Keep that smile when I keep forgetting the words you taught me yesterday and cannot remember those I learned last week.

Give me a gentle voice to ease the frustration, humiliation, and shame when I just cannot communicate *refrigerator, emergency,* or *appointment*. For you, my teacher, they are little words, but for me they are like monsters to fight. Pat me on the shoulder once in a while and help my tense body and trembling hands to write *A B C* and *1 2 3*.

Continue to reward me with a warm "good" or "very good" when I have finally   10
pronounced "church" correctly after one hundred "shurshes." Flatter me by attempting to speak a phrase or two from my language and I will end up laughing with you.

I am one of the students in your class. I came today, and tomorrow I will come   11
again. I smile and laugh and try to talk your English, which you say will become my language.

Reading 6 *Reflecting on the Reading*

1 This essay was written both for students of English and for English teachers. Place an *S* next to any of the following messages that seem to be directed toward students. Place a *T* next to any messages that seem to be directed toward teachers. Then discuss your answers with a partner or small group.

.... **a** Try not to judge people by their present circumstances.

.... **b** If you keep trying hard enough, you will eventually get what you want.

.... **c** People need encouragement in order to succeed.

.... **d** Be patient in everything you do.

2 Ibañez wrote this essay in the first person, as if her student Sombath were telling his own story directly to the reader. Discuss why you think she decided to use this approach. How would the essay have been different if she had used the more traditional approach of describing Sombath in the third person?

3 Look up the following words in the dictionary. Then discuss which word best describes Sombath's feelings about learning English. Give specific evidence from the essay to support your opinion.

a ambivalence

b confusion

c frustration

d enthusiasm

4 In your journal, freewrite about someone you know or someone you have heard about who survived a dangerous situation such as a war, a natural disaster, or a serious accident. How was his or her life similar to Sombath's? How was it different?

TECHNIQUES WRITERS USE

People Watching

The essays you read for this chapter show the variety of details that can contribute to an effective character sketch. Always try to be a careful observer of the people you see interacting around you. The activities in this section will help you to sharpen your powers of observation and think of imaginative ways to write about a person's character.

Task 3.1 Analyze

1 Read the following description of an old man from a student essay in Chapter 5. Underline the specific details that help you to imagine what this old man is like.

From "One of Us"
by Ahmet Erdogan

He was an old man. His white beard had darkened with the grime. 1
He looked in my eyes with his own blue eyes, which hardly opened because of sleeplessness. His dark, dirty face – unwashed maybe for weeks – became red for a moment. He bit his lip, which was almost lost under his mustache and beard. Then, taking his head between his hands, he tried to go back to sleep.

The crowd on the train walked off at the second stop. I was watching 2
the old man. His shoes were worn out. He had covered his legs up to the knees with tatters. The darkened skin of his knees could be seen through a hole in his pants. With a strange feeling, I stood up from my seat and sat just across from him. At his left on the seat there was a big bag which was full of remnants of food and other things. When the train stopped suddenly, he awoke and some of the food in the bag spread over the seat. The old man put the food back in the bag with special care. Then he took the remnant of a hamburger with his right hand and shoved his mustache away from his mouth with his left hand. Just as he had bitten into the hamburger, he felt me watching him. That aged, wrinkled face had become red with a childish shame.

---

2 In a small group, compare the details you underlined. Discuss what you learn about this man from reading about his physical appearance. What do you learn from the description of his clothing? What do you learn from his reaction to being observed by the writer? Decide on two or three adjectives that describe what this man is like.

1 Go to a convenient place where there are plenty of people to observe, such as the waiting room of the local bus station, a park where children play, or your college cafeteria.

2 For the first few minutes, observe all the people you see. Then select one person to observe more carefully for ten to fifteen minutes. Try not to let the person know that you are observing him or her.

3 As soon after the observation period as possible, freewrite for 20 to 30 minutes about what you observed. Answer some or all of these questions:

- What did the person look like – size, facial expression, clothing, and so on?
- What was the person doing?
- Was there anything unusual about him or her?
- Did you hear the person say anything? If so, you might want to include some direct quotations.
- Was the person interacting with other people? If so, try to describe this interaction.

4 Compare the results of your observation in a small group. Tell why you chose to observe this particular person, and share your freewriting.

Making Metaphors

A metaphor is an expression in which one thing is described in terms of another. For example: "He has a *heart of stone*," "A tree is a *home*," "Her face is an *open book*," "He is the *brother of the rain*." (Metaphors do not include the words *like* or *as*. For example, "She is as beautiful as a flower" is *not* a metaphor; it is a simile. Similes are discussed in "Reflecting on the Reading," on page 95.)

Metaphors can inspire rich images, memories, and emotions. When metaphors are used effectively, the implied comparisons create new and deeper meanings in the reader's mind.

Task 3.3 *Analyze*

1 Read the following short essay, in which the metaphor of rain reminded a student of a mysterious relationship with a man from her past. Like much imaginative writing, its meanings can be understood in many ways.

Rain

    It is the rain that forces me to think about him. This kind of weather   1
makes me so lazy that I don't want to do anything but hold my chin
up, look out at the rain, and listen to it. It is strange to say that the rain
reminds me of him, but I can't help it. He is the brother of the rain.

    He acted like the rain – for days with the same speed without any   2
interruption, like a big shower. The rain plays a music that has a quiet
harmony; he has a voice just like that. It used to make me fall asleep.
The rain has movement like his, not too fast but comfortable to walk
with. Having a conversation with him while walking is the same as
now, sitting in a chair next to a window by myself.

    Sometimes he made me feel that if he was not next to me, he did   3
not even exist. Rarely did he and I sit face to face. Mostly I was always
the one who made noise and he was the one who always listened.
Sometimes when he said something, he took off his glasses.

    Well, the man with medium height and light weight with heavy,   4
dark black-rimmed glasses did not impress me much. After all, my
memory of him is not so exciting. The interesting thing is that weather
like this reminds me of him for some reason.

    But now, this rain, which reminds me of him, talks all day long   5
and I am listening to it. It looks as if it will never stop, as if it does not
care whether or not I want it to stop. Probably I will regret that there
was no stop in the days of raining, just like him, who never showed
me his disturbed time.

---

2 Working with a partner or small group, discuss the following questions:

  a What do you think the writer's relationship was with the person she is
    writing about? What line(s) in the essay support your opinion?

b What do you think the writer means by "He is the brother of the rain"?

c In your opinion, which of the following words best describes the writer's feelings toward this man: *love, hate, boredom, excitement*? Point out specific lines in the essay to support your ideas.

3 Write two or three sentences that describe your reaction to this imaginative essay that makes use of metaphor. Is the writer's use of metaphor effective? How does it make you feel? What does it make you think about? Share your writing with your partner or group.

Task 3.4 *Practice*

1 Write a metaphor about a person you know.

> **Examples**
> My mother is a sunny day.
> My father's hands are steel.
> My niece is an icy waterfall.
> My boyfriend is a tree.

2 Discuss your sentence with your partner or group. Why did you think of this particular metaphor? In what ways is the person like the thing you chose?

3 Use this metaphor as the basis of a piece of writing. Push yourself to develop the metaphor as fully as possible.

4 When you have finished, exchange papers with your partner or group members. Read and discuss each other's writing.

INTERNET SEARCH

Locating Biographical Information

The Internet is a wonderful way of quickly locating information about people's lives. The following activity gives you a chance to practice this type of research.

Task 3.5 *Practice*

1 Think of a well-known person, living or dead, whom you would like to learn more about. Check with your teacher to be sure your choice is appropriate.

> **Examples**
> - Toussaint L'Ouverture, leader of the Haitian slave revolt at the end of the eighteenth century
> - Marie Curie, first woman to win the Nobel Prize for physics
> - Mahatma Gandhi, leader of nonviolent resistance in India

2 Type the person's name into your preferred Web browser (for example, Google.com, Encarta.msn.com, Yahoo.com).

3 Choose two or three Web sites that seem helpful and read through the information you find.

4 Print out a picture of the person and find answers to the following questions.

  a When and where was the person born? How would you describe the person's childhood or early life?

  b What accomplishment or event caused this person to become famous?

  c What was one thing you learned about this person that surprised you?

  d If you were asked to write a brief biography of this person, what three personal characteristics would you emphasize?

> **Examples**
> courage, determination, creativity

5 Discuss the results of your Internet search with a small group. What did you learn about the person you researched? What did you learn about doing an Internet search?

ESSAY ASSIGNMENT

Your assignment for this chapter is to write a character sketch, a descriptive essay in which you reveal a person's character. Your purpose in writing should be to reveal some important truths about the person's character. Think of your audience as an interested and perceptive reader, but one who has never met the person being described.

Give details of the appearance and actions of the person you are writing about and use metaphors and imaginative language in your writing. This will help the person you are describing to come alive for your audience. Remember that it is not enough simply to describe. You should also explain to the reader why you think the person is the way he or she is and why this person is important to you.

Reread the writing you have already done for this chapter to see whether it gives you ideas for this assignment.

Writing Tips

- **Describe the person's appearance.**
  Often a person's outward appearance – looks, facial expression, clothing – reflects something significant about his or her character. Skilled writers describe a person's physical appearance as a means of revealing character. Here are a few of the many revealing details Syed Saeed provides about his friend Nafiz in Reading 5: "He used to move his hands while he talked, which seemed like he was talking to a deaf person. He never smiled, and his dark black eyes were searching for trouble." As you begin work on your first draft, try to picture the person you are writing about. Is there anything significant about the person's appearance?

- **Quote what the person says.**
  One of the most important ways we learn about people is by listening to what they say. And good writers know that including a person's exact words in the form of direct quotations is one of the most effective ways of revealing character. In Reading 2, Eileen Peng quotes some of her mother's memorable sayings, such as "Study hard. Get honors for me." By quoting her mother's actual words, Peng reveals her mother's values and character. What are some of the typical sayings of the person you plan to write about?

- **Describe what the person does.**
  "Actions speak louder than words," according to an old saying, and it is true that sometimes people say one thing but do another. For instance, in Reading 3, Rosita constantly talks about piety and religion but is actually cruel in her behavior toward Gloria. When writing about people, we need to describe what they do as a way of revealing something about their character.

- **Tell what others say and think about the person.**
  The opinions of other people are also important in analyzing someone's character. Often we come to understand someone better as a result of what others say and think about that person. For example, in Reading 1, Hikaru Takahashi quotes what other people have said about her grandmother in order to make her portrait detailed and convincing. Think about the person you plan to describe. What can we learn about this person's character from the way other people react to him or her?

Writing Your First Draft

Now, keeping the writing tips in mind, write the first draft of your essay. As you are working on this first draft, do not slow yourself down by worrying about correct grammar and spelling; it is more important just to get your ideas down on paper so you have something to work with in later drafts.

REVISING YOUR ESSAY

Once you have put your ideas down on paper by completing the first draft, you can begin the revising process.

Written Peer Response

The previous chapter included instructions for oral peer response. Another useful form of peer response is through written comments. You exchange essays with a partner, read your partner's essay carefully, and respond in writing. At the end of this chapter and at the end of each of the remaining chapters, we provide a "Peer Response Form." These forms include questions for you to answer in order to help you focus your comments. After responding in writing, it is helpful to exchange your response forms and discuss them in a peer conference. The following task will give you a chance to practice giving effective written peer response.

1 Read this first draft of a student essay describing a person.

My Friend Marek (first draft)

His name is Marek. I know him since we were 5 years old. I consider him as my best friend. He's a tall boy and likes to wear nice sport clothes. He too does much sport, he does every available for him kind of sport, but socker is his favorite. When we were in grammar school he used to be the captain of our class team. It was interesting to observe how extremaly emotionaly involved he was in the game. He didn't play socker for fun only – he played to win. If our team was loosing scores, he was getting mad, he was doing more than his best to help it; if nothing changed for better he started to cry. Sport is for him the source of fun, emotions, his inner experiences which are for him important ingredients to his spiritual life. But it isn't the only part of his spiritual life. He love to read. When he was a young boy, his mother worrying about his eyes tried to stop him from reading so much. In answer for his mother's restrictions he used to close himself in the bathroom and continued reading there. He knows much about history and it makes him a real pleasure to have such knowledge about history. The thing what the other people notice and what irritates many of them is his behavior. He always tries to make something what

---

interfere with the environment. When all others are grave he laughs and when others laugh he is serious. He expresses his thoughts loudly and very often doesn't care about the fact that someone or a group of people can get mad with him. If he is conserned about it he says it. He likes to tell jokes and to make jokes alone or together with his friends.

Those who know Marek longer know that he is a person whom you can count on. It would be painful for him if someone got the reason to tell him: "Marek, you didn't keep your word." He is a kind of person who is not easy to know about his character much after meeting him a few times or knowing him a short period of time. His real character is hidden deep inside him behind jokes. 2

2 Fill out the "Practice Peer Response Form" on page 88. As you respond to this student's first draft, focus on the ideas rather than the grammar and spelling. Point out only those mistakes that interfere with understanding. Then have a peer conference with a partner or small group to compare your answers.

3 Now read the second draft of the essay, which the student wrote after receiving responses from his peers and teacher.

Marek (second draft)

His name is Marek Kubik. I met him for the first time when we were both five years old. My father was working with his father. Once my parents took me to visit his family. Marek was taking a bath when his father introduced him to me. We spent the evening playing with the fancy toys he got from his uncle from Scotland. 1

He was my first friend who lived on the other side of town, and I couldn't visit him too often. All my other friends lived in my neighborhood, and I could see them every day. 2

Now he's a tall boy with a blond shock of hair. He still lives in Poland, and because of political reasons, he feels sorry that he didn't leave Poland when he had the chance to do so, a few years ago. 3

He loves sports. Soccer is his favorite. We were in grammar school until the age of fifteen, and at that time he used to be the captain of our soccer team. It was interesting to observe how extremely emotionally involved he was in the game. I can remember one of our games on a summer afternoon. We were playing just for fun against another team from our school. Unfortunately, our team was losing. He tried to do more than his best to make things go better. When he realized that we had no chance to win, he started to cry. He didn't play soccer only for fun – he played to win. Sport was always for him a source of fun, emotions, inner experiences, which are important ingredients in his spiritual life. 4

He also loves to read. When he was still in grammar school, his 5
mother, worrying about his eyes, tried to stop him from reading so
much. In answer to his mother's restrictions, he used to close himself
in the bathroom, reading there. Henryk Sienkiewicz was his favorite
author. He especially liked Sienkiewicz's "Trilogy," a set of six large
books telling interesting romantic stories based on true events from
Polish history of the seventeenth century. Polish high school students
are supposed to know this piece of work. Marek read it twice when
he was still in grammar school. Then he used to demonstrate the way
Polish knights fought against the Swedish enemy. He used a wooden
stick as a sword. Marek knows much about Polish history of the
sixteenth, seventeenth, and eighteenth centuries, and he really enjoys
possessing this knowledge.

My friend loves to joke. Many people are irritated with his behavior. 6
He always tries to be different from the majority: when all others are
grave, he often starts to laugh; when others laugh, he doesn't, unless
he's in the company of his good friends.

He always expresses his thoughts openly and doesn't care about 7
the fact that other people may get angry at him. When we were in high
school in Poland, many students were complaining about the medical
care in our school. Someone said to one of our teachers that he could
hardly ever get to see the doctor because when the doctor happened
to be in his surgery, too many people needed to see him at the same
time. The teacher was embarrassed but tried to make us not forget
about the benefits of living in the "socialist paradise," where no one
has to pay for medical care. Hearing this, Marek didn't hesitate to tell
her that he would prefer to pay and be treated like a human being. The
Communist teacher was so surprised with the answer that she didn't
say anything more.

Those who have known Marek for a long time know that he is 8
a person whom you can count on. It would be most painful for him
if someone had a reason to tell him: "Marek, you didn't keep your
word."

You can't know much about his character if you've known him 9
only for a short period of time. You have to wait a long time to get the
chance to talk seriously to him. When you are patient enough, you can
learn about his precious values. His real character is hidden behind
jokes, which for most people seem to be stupid ones. I don't belong to
this group. I recognize him as my best friend.

4 Discuss your answers to the following questions with your partner or group:

   a What changes did the writer make in this revised essay? Explain how each of these changes affects your understanding of the essay.

   b Compare the paragraphing of the two drafts and analyze how the writer changed the essay's organization. Write a sentence expressing the main idea of each of the nine paragraphs of the revised essay. (Your list will be a sentence outline of the essay.) Are the paragraphs arranged in a logical order?

   c Compare the endings of the two drafts. In your opinion, which one is a more effective ending for the essay? Why?

   d Did your "Practice Peer Response Form" include suggestions that the writer used in his second draft? What advice would you give to this writer if he decided to revise his essay one more time?

Responding to Your Peers

1 Working with a partner or a group of three, exchange and read the first drafts of your essays. If possible, make copies for every student in your group. If that is not possible, you can either read the essay aloud to the group or exchange drafts and read them silently.

2 Fill out a copy of the "Peer Response Form" on page 90 for each of the first drafts you read. Focus on the ideas rather than the grammar and spelling. Point out only those mistakes that interfere with understanding.

3 Using the peer response forms you have filled out as the basis for your discussion, have a peer conference to discuss your first drafts.

Writing Your Second Draft

Taking into consideration the feedback you have received from your peers and your own ideas about how to improve your essay, write your second draft.

EDITING YOUR ESSAY

When you are satisfied with the content and organization of your essay, you can begin the process of editing.

Grammar in Context: Understanding Sentence Boundaries

In speaking, we rely on nonverbal signals such as pauses and intonation to indicate where one idea ends and another one begins. In writing, we use punctuation and capital letters to show these things. Without punctuation, it would be difficult, if not impossible, to understand a writer's meaning.

Proofreading your essay to be sure that your sentences are punctuated correctly is an important part of the editing process. The tasks that follow will give you a chance to check your understanding of where sentences begin and end. If you are unsure of how to punctuate the sentences in the tasks, or if you want more information on this topic, review the appropriate section in your grammar reference book or in an online grammar resource, such as Purdue University's Online Writing Lab, currently accessible at <http://owl.english.purdue.edu>.

Clauses

All sentences in English are made up of clauses. There are two types of clauses, independent and dependent.

An *independent clause* is a group of words that contains a main verb and a subject that goes with that verb. An independent clause can stand alone as a complete sentence.

> **Examples**
> My mother was an excellent housewife.
> My mother wanted the best for her children.

A *dependent clause* also has a subject and a verb, but it cannot stand alone as a sentence either because it begins with a *subordinating conjunction* (for example: *although* or *because*) or with a *relative pronoun* (for example: *that* or *which*).

> **Examples**
> although she had a full-time job
> which is why she did so much for us

In order to be part of a complete sentence, a dependent clause must be joined to an independent clause with the correct punctuation.

Sentence Patterns

To punctuate sentences correctly, it is useful to understand the four sentence patterns of English. These example sentences are based on "My Mother" (page 62). The main verbs are underlined twice, the main subjects are underlined once, and the conjunctions and transition words are circled.

1 A **simple sentence** consists of one independent clause.

> **Example**
> *independent clause*
> My mother is a very capable, lively woman.
> *independent clause*
> She sent me to that teacher's home to have my first lesson.

2 A **compound sentence** consists of an independent clause joined to another independent clause with a comma (,) and one of the coordinating conjunctions: *and, but, or, nor, for, so, yet.* An independent clause may also be joined to another independent clause by a semicolon (;) and is sometimes followed by a transitional word or phrase – such as *furthermore, in addition, however,* or *therefore* – and a comma.

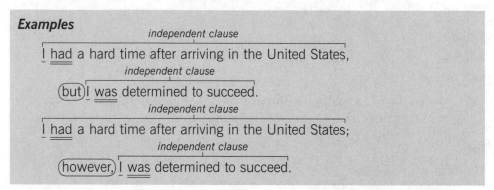

3 A **complex sentence** consists of an independent clause joined to a dependent clause. The dependent clause can come at the beginning of the sentence, in which case it is followed by a comma; or the dependent clause can come at the end of the sentence, in which case no comma is necessary. A complex sentence contains either a subordinating conjunction (such as *after, although, because, before, if, since,* or *when*) or a relative pronoun (such as *that, which, who,* or *whom*).

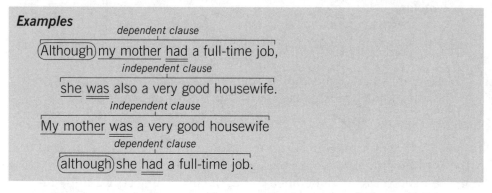

4 A **compound/complex sentence** consists of at least three clauses, two of which are joined with a coordinating conjunction and one of which contains a subordinating conjunction or a relative pronoun. Follow the punctuation rules for compound and complex sentences (see above).

Example

independent clause

I had a hard time after arriving in the United States,

independent clause   dependent clause

(but) I was determined to "Study hard," (as) my mother said.

Task 3.6 *Analyze*

1 All punctuation has been removed from the paragraph below from a student essay. Work in a small group and have one group member read the paragraph aloud. As you listen, try to decide where the periods and commas should go.

A Woman I Admire

I met her at a park near Chinatown she was an old healthy Chinese lady I thought she had a wealthy family and a happy life since we both spoke the same dialect we didn't have any trouble understanding each other after we had met a couple of times I learned that she got married when she was only fifteen her husband left his family in China for Singapore and then for the United States five months later they did not meet each other again until she came here twenty-eight years later when she was forty-three years old unfortunately they did not have any children she is living alone in this country now

---

2 Working with your group members, add the proper punctuation and capital letters. Discuss what helped you decide how to punctuate this paragraph.

3 Check your work using the Answer Key on page 258.

Task 3.7 *Practice*

1 Read the student essay below, which contains several punctuation errors involving sentence boundaries.

2 Working with a partner, correct the errors. If you are not sure how a particular sentence should be punctuated, underline the subject(s) once and the verb(s) twice and circle any conjunctions and transitional words or phrases. Then decide whether the sentence is simple, compound, complex, or compound/complex. Based on your decisions, punctuate the sentences appropriately.

The Third Day Behind the Wheel

When I was twenty-one, I got my first driver's license. Living in the   1
suburbs of New Orleans. I was forced to drive a car in order to get from
one place to another. At the place I lived, called Violet, nobody dared
to cross the street on foot.

Before I took the road test. I had driven for two hours at a shopping   2
mall parking lot. On the day after I got my license, I was already
forcing my eight-year-old Ventura to fly seventy miles per hour on a
two-way highway.

The next day I decided to check the Ventura's speed ability, I took her on a divided highway with two lanes going in each direction. In the middle was neutral ground full of potholes. On both sides along the highway were ditches filled with snakes, mud, and water. In the distance, the skeletons of dead trees greeted the haunted travelers.

It was the beginning of dusk. When I passed the Judge Perez Bridge and accelerated to ninety-six miles per hour. When the car wasn't going any faster; I had a glimmering thought of slowing down. Suddenly, the Ventura started bouncing from side to side and went off the road to the left. First I noticed the headlights of oncoming cars, so I was preparing myself mentally for a head-on collision. A second later, however, I had a panorama of eternal wetness and started subconsciously to press the brakes with all my might, the idea of dying in a swamp somehow didn't fit me. The Ventura was still turning, she made another cycle and a half and stopped, to my surprise. It took me a few deep breaths to recover my full awareness, but soon I was back on the highway again.

3 Check your work using the Answer Key on page 258.

Editing Checklist

If you are writing your essay on a computer, remember to print out your revised essay and proofread it on paper.

☐ **First proofreading: sentence boundaries**
Check the punctuation within and at the ends of your sentences. First, read your essay aloud, paying attention to places where you pause naturally. Often, pauses within a sentence will indicate where the punctuation, such as a comma(,) or a semicolon(;), should go. At the end of every complete sentence you should have a period (.), a question mark (?), or an exclamation point (!). Be careful, however, not to overuse the exclamation point or the semicolon. Check (✔) the box when you have finished.

☐ **Second proofreading**
Proofread your essay a second time and correct any other errors of grammar, spelling, or punctuation that you find. Check (✔) the box when you have finished.

☐ **Third proofreading**
Print out or write a copy of your essay that includes the corrections you made in your first and second proofreading. Now proofread your essay a third time. Try to find and correct any errors that you missed. Then print out, or write in dark blue or black ink, the final draft of your essay. Check (✔) the box when you have finished.

Practice Peer Response Form
Writing About People

WRITER'S NAME: *Andrzej Zganiacz*   READER'S NAME: ....

DATE: ....

Focus on the ideas in the essay rather than the grammar and spelling. Point out only those mistakes that interfere with understanding.

1 What do you like about this essay?

2 What one word would you choose to describe Marek's character? What specific information in the draft caused you to choose this word?

3 List any places where you do not understand the writer's meaning. He will need to clarify these things when he revises.

Photocopiable   © Cambridge University Press

4 What do you notice about the organization of the essay? For example, is the number of paragraphs appropriate? How could the writer improve the organization of the essay?

5 What would you like to know more about?

6 Who do you think would be interested in reading this essay? In other words, who do you think is the writer's intended audience?

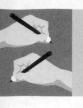

Peer Response Form

Writing About People

WRITER'S NAME: .... READER'S NAME: ....

DATE: ....

Focus on the ideas in the essay rather than the grammar and spelling. Discuss only those mistakes that interfere with understanding.

1 Write one sentence to sum up what this person is like.

2 List three details from the essay that support your sentence in step 1.

3 Put a check (✓) next to each of the methods below (a–d) that the writer uses to reveal the person's character. For each method that you checked, give one example from the essay. (Most essays will probably not use all four methods.)

☐ What the person looks like

☐ What the person says

☐ What the person does

☐ What other people say about the person

4 Were there any things in this essay that you did not understand? If so, what were they?

5 Why do you think the writer chose to describe this particular person?

6 Write one or two questions about the person described in this essay that you would like the writer to answer in the next draft.

In this chapter, you will write an essay in which you describe a place that has been important in your life. In the reading selections that follow, many of the writers reveal their love for a special place, often a place from their childhood. They also express a sense of belonging to a particular place where they feel most at home, most at peace. But in some of these student essays there is a feeling of loss as well; the writers now live far away from these special places. As you work in this chapter, you will have the opportunity to think and write about your own places – places from the past or from the present.

READINGS

The Tree of My Secrets

Amalfi Richard

In this essay, a student from the Dominican Republic describes a childhood in which she moved often and lived with many different relatives. During these changes, she was comforted by the presence of a special tree, which came to represent the roots of her childhood. As you read, think about whether there was a special place in your childhood that, like the tree described in this essay, provided a sense of comfort and safety.

1   In my childhood memories, I have many favorite places, but I will write about the one that I prefer. It is the tree of my secrets. I began my journey in the Dominican Republic with my tree, and it was there at the end of my journey.

2   A long time ago, when I was a young child, my parents decided to travel to the United States to get better opportunities and enhance the quality of our family's life. My parents left me in the Dominican Republic, and I lived in different family members' houses. When I first came to live with Uncle Pipe Sosa and my godmother, Ramona, in 1981, the tree was young like I was. At the age of four, I started to enjoy the company of my tree. I played around it with my two younger sisters, neighbors, and friends. Then my godmother and my uncle decided to sell the house and move to a big empty place.

3   They made a big pool in the new house, and there were two walls that served as a division between the pool area and the terrace. These walls were painted with magic – a variety of cute fishes, blue water, sunshine, and beautiful seashells – all of which were reflected in the deep water of the pool. The strong rain in May produced a big, strange noise when it crashed into the pool's water. This gave me a fabulous feeling of peace, because I felt as if the rainstorm transported me far away from many changes. But at the same time, it brought me memories of my parents. At that moment, I experienced feelings of emptiness, just as I had when my parents had left me. The truth was that I could be distracted, but I couldn't forget everything that had happened. I loved to spend hours meditating in front of the pool. It was as if I was living between the present, which was the pool, and the past, which was the memories of my parents when they had left me in my country. It was like the taste of a lemon, like the roses and the thorns.

4   After seven years, my godmother died. Therefore, I had to move again. At that moment, I was twelve years old, and I moved to my grandmother's house. She was a widow and had six other grandchildren with her as well as her own family. Life was difficult in my grandmother's house. I had no privileges, less space, and there were too many people. So she couldn't let me stay.

5   Then the same thing occurred. I had to move again, but this time I found one good thing. I met my tree again when I went to live with Aunt Luz, because her

house was right next to my uncle's and godmother's old house. Aunt Luz took me in because we all agreed that we could help each other. She had a little baby boy, and she thought I could take care of the baby after school and help with the chores in the house. At night, when there wasn't electricity and the tropical weather obliged the community to go outside of the house, Aunt Luz and I spent hours around the tree. I had missed my tree, but it hadn't changed a lot. It was still bigger than I was.

My tree was always there throughout my life to witness my most important steps. When I was sick, there were some of the tree's leaves to make tea. At midday there was orange juice to drink from my tree. The Catholic school that I attended for twelve years was located in front of my tree. Also, my best friend, Noelia, and my boyfriend, Cristobal, lived near the tree in the same neighborhood as I did. On September 9, 1989, my tree testified when I got my first kiss.

My tree was what had made me lucky ever since the time my parents had left me. On February 26, 1992, an elegant van was waiting for me in front of my tree. On this day I had white and pink flowers that matched the long, beautiful white dress I wore for my wedding. My tree was there just as the father is in the church to give the bride to the hands of her fiancé. The tree looked triumphant to see how happy I was on my wedding day. The air produced friendly movements in the tree's leaves that made me smile when I felt its fresh breezes, which were, for me, like a hug.

To conclude, I want to say that in each house I found one special place, but never like my tree. I think this is because in my tree I found someone to share the most special steps of my life. The tree was there at the beginning and the end of my journey in the Dominican Republic. It was the roots of my whole life and made me feel that I was not alone.

Reading 1   Reflecting on the Reading

1 While reading this essay, you were asked to think of a place where you went to find comfort and safety when you were a child. Discuss this place with a partner. How your place similar to the tree described in Richard's essay? How was it different?

2 Richard uses the literary technique of *personification*, describing her special tree as if it were a person. For example, in paragraph 2, she says, "I started to enjoy the company of my tree." And in paragraph 6, she says that the tree was always there "to witness my most important steps." Underline all the other examples of personification in the essay. Compare your answers with your partner or a small group and discuss why you think Richard used personification in describing the tree.

3 Another literary device that Richard uses in this essay is the *simile*. In similes, writers use the words *as* or *like* to describe one thing in terms of something else. For example, at the end of paragraph 3, Richard describes her emotions when she thinks about her parents as being "like the taste of a lemon, like

the roses and the thorns." Discuss the following questions: What different meanings do you get from these comparisons? How do these similes help you to understand the writer's situation?

4 In paragraph 3, Richard describes the conflicting emotions she experienced during the May rainstorms. She felt a sense of peace because these storms "transported" her away from the many changes in her life, but at the same time she remembered the sadness of being separated from her parents. Think about places in your own life where you experienced conflicting emotions. In your journal, list two or three of these places. Then choose one, and freewrite about it.

The Home of My Childhood

Volkan Cinozgumus

In this essay, a student from Turkey reminisces about the favorite place of his youth, a small marina in his hometown where he spent happy times with his friends. Before you read, think about the places from your own childhood that you associate with happy memories.

1   I know how difficult it is to describe a place to other people if they've never seen it before. But I don't believe you'll have a hard time to picture it after I tell you the secret world of a harbor. Actually, it's not a harbor; it's only a marina that is located in Iskenderun, a small city in Turkey that has a big economic role in the country with its harbors and factories. But what I like best about Iskenderun is that it's the home of my childhood.

2   My friends and I had only one thing to do before the sun went down in that city: fish. Fishing was almost our daily duty, and we were hooked on it. It's funny, but whenever I see a boat in a movie that takes place in a harbor, the smell of fish comes to my nose and takes me to my little marina.

3   You must have seen marinas like this on TV many times. The small boats were tied to each other very tightly so as not to get scattered by big hurricanes. Two lighthouses stood right by the water at both ends of the seawall. I remember buying very fresh bread to catch the fish. There was a bakery right next to the entrance of the marina, where delicious smelling bread was sold. But I wouldn't let my friends eat the bread because the purpose of going to the marina was catching fish, not feeding my friends. I still remember how the bread made me hungry, but when I thought of eating the fish that I would catch with that bread, I stopped my stomach.

4   Once, I remember, I was trying to get out of a small boat that was shaken by waves. I had two bags in my hands, which were full of fish, so I couldn't use my hands. I put one of my feet on the ground where my friends were standing and pushed myself toward them. Suddenly the rope that held the boat broke off, and I

2

lost my balance. So as you could guess, I found myself in the water. All my friends were laughing at me because we were going there to have some fun, and what happened to me was very funny and enough to make them laugh.

One more funny thing I remember happened to me and my friends when we were really hot and tried to cool off a little bit. We took our clothes off and put swimsuits on, and we left all of our clothes on the sand. Right after we got into the water, the cops showed up and asked us to get out of the water because we were not allowed to swim there. Of course, we were so scared, and we decided not to obey their orders. And also we were making fun of them because we knew they had their uniforms on and they wouldn't come to get us. But what they did was, they took all of our clothes that were on the sand and left us there in our swimming suits. After we were sure that they were not coming back, we got out of the water and walked down to our houses with our swimming suits on. I remember that people who witnessed this scene laughed so much.

In this marina, which I haven't visited since high school, my childhood is buried. Even though I haven't been there for almost six years, I still remember the smell of fish and that bread.

5

6

Reading 2   Reflecting on the Reading

1 Good writers often make their descriptions seem real by appealing to their readers' senses of sight, hearing, taste, touch, and smell. For example, in paragraph 2, Cinozgumus writes that "whenever I see a boat in a movie that is taking place in a harbor, the smell of fish comes to my nose and takes me to my little marina." Underline each place where Cinozgumus appeals to one of the five senses and write in the margin which sense is involved. Compare your answers with a partner or small group. Discuss the ways in which these sensory details added to your enjoyment of the essay.

2 Throughout this essay, Cinozgumus speaks to his reader directly. For example, in the first two sentences, he draws the reader into the story by saying, "I know how difficult it is to describe a place to other people if they've never seen it before. But I don't believe you'll have a hard time to picture it after I tell you the secret world of a harbor." Underline every place where the writer speaks to the reader as if he were having a conversation. Discuss how the effect of the essay on the reader would have been different if the writer had not addressed his reader directly.

3 Discuss why you think the marina was such an important place for Cinozgumus. Think of as many reasons as possible.

4 What place would you choose as "the home of your childhood"? Would it be a house, a neighborhood, a school, or some special place where you went with your friends? In your journal, freewrite about that place.

The Coldest Winter of Beijing

Jian Wei

In this essay, a Chinese student describes his visit to Tiananmen Square, a famous historical site in the capital of China. After leaving the tomb of Mao Tse-tung, the powerful chairman of the Chinese Communist Party, Wei begins to revise his thinking about this important political leader. Before reading, think about a political leader who has been influential in your life.

A shiver ran over my body. There was a nip in the air. I suddenly remembered it was already the end of the year 1989.

1

The sun was nearly down. Shafts of light covered the empty Tiananmen Square, full silent, as if the Square were exhausted. There were only several teams of armed policemen, tiny and lonely in the empty vastness of the Square. From June 4, 1989, the bloody end of the greatest demonstration of the People's Republic of China, the Square had been closed for many months, and had just re-opened. The bicycles drifted off, almost silent, and the buses ghosted past. Stopping to look in the Square was not permitted for the residents of Beijing. The Tiananmen (the Gate of Heavenly Peace) stood in the cold weather as a witness to the violent changes making up China's history and as a warning that the Communist Party still had absolute power in China. The red flags on the wall waved in the wind like hairs swaying on an old man's head.

2

I stood for a while looking for someone who could take a picture for me. But very few tourists stood in the Square. Before entering, the tourists had to pass through two sentry posts. They had to show the ID cards that they carried every day, and official proof that they were "good elements." Many people didn't come into the Square because they didn't have such proof.

3

For a while, no one passed me. I found some people waiting in line before the Chairman Mao Memorial Hall, so I decided to go there and ask someone to help.

4

When a young man was taking a picture of me, a plainclothes policeman called to us, "Hey, wait in line." "Why?" I asked. He came near and stared at me. His skin was black and rough, and his eyes were red. Obviously, the sharp wind of Beijing had caused it. In a harsh and imperious voice, he said, "Wait in line if you want to see Chairman Mao." Then he pointed at the bag I carried: "Deposit your bag." I noticed he was carrying a walkie-talkie, maybe also a gun under his clothes, and I did not ask the second "why." I suspected that his mission was to prevent a bomb scare. Later I found some policemen searching people's handbags and warning them not to take pictures or speak in the hall.

5

When I was walking into the hall, a big marble screen with Mao's writing caught my eye. Mao was a good poet in his early life. I appreciated one of his early poems. When he wrote it, he was a young man and China was an isolated country, struggling to stand up. The dreamy poem went like this:

6

Alone I stand in the autumn cold
And watch the river northward flowing
Past the Orange Island shore.
And myriad hills are all
Tier upon tier of crimsoned woods.
On the broad stream, intensely blue,
Hundreds of bustling barges float;
Eagles strike at the lofty air,
Fish hover among the shallows;
Millions of creatures under this freezing sky are
Striving for freedom.
In this immensity, deeply pondering,
I ask the great earth and boundless blue
Who are the masters?

Later Mao became the great dictator of China and remained in power until his   7
death. He became a famous idol, and his photographs and portraits were hung in
every corner of the country. He was the god of China.

Just then, some policemen hurried us. Through a dim passage we entered the   8
central room. Holding our breath, we looked carefully at Mao's dead body through
a glass screen. He lay in a crystal coffin far from us. Flowers circled him, and a red
party flag covered his whole body. Four armed soldiers stood at the corners. The
bayonets cast some glittering reflections on their young faces.

At that moment, the remaining little motion of Mao's wit died in me. There   9
is a famous old proverb: "When the moon is fullest, it begins to wane; when it is
darkest, it begins to grow." Now the glories of Mao's wealth and power had turned
into passing smoke.

Light from unknown places shone on Mao's face, but it was too strong. It was   10
hard to recognize his familiar face from so far away. I felt that his face looked
wooden and not so real in the coffin. The air was blended with mystery and
tension, which now seemed to grow and grow.

I heard a man murmuring when we got out, "Is he real?" I also had my doubts.   11
For the few seconds that I was in the room, what had I seen? I took a deep breath.
It felt good to walk in the fresh air again, although the air was much colder than
inside. I took out an old portrait of Mao from my pocket. But it was not bright
in the Square. The moon was just peeping over the horizon. I held the picture in
the light. It was too old, somewhat crinkled, faded. Just when my eyes focused on
Mao's face, a strange wind passed by, circling, and carried the picture through my
fingers, whistling, like someone's sigh. I extended my hand to try to hold it. But it
was too late. It had gone with the west wind. The picture was caught in the light
that spilled like fog from the Memorial Hall's windows, and waving, rocking, it
vanished in the dark.

1 Reread the first paragraph of this essay. Discuss with a partner or small group which of the following words best describes the mood or atmosphere Wei creates in this paragraph:

a happiness   b fear   c uneasiness   d excitement

Does this mood continue throughout the essay, or does the mood change at some point?

2 This essay includes many details that relate to the senses of sight, hearing, taste, touch, or smell. For example, in paragraph 2, Wei mentions "shafts of light" (sight) and describes the Square as "full silent" (hearing). Underline every place where Wei refers to one of the five senses; each time, write in the margin which of the five senses is involved. Discuss the effect these details have on you as a reader.

3 Discuss the ending of the essay. In the last paragraph, Wei describes taking a portrait of Mao out of his pocket. Then he creates an eerie mood when he says that "a strange wind passed by, circling, and carried the picture through my fingers, whistling, like someone's sigh." What do you think the picture of Mao symbolizes? Do you think the wind really carried the picture away, as Wei describes? Or did Wei make this up to provide an effective ending for his essay? Give reasons to support your opinion.

4 At one time, Mao Tse-tung was a hero to millions of Chinese, yet since his death in 1976, many people, like the writer of this essay, have become disillusioned with their former hero. Who are some of your own heroes? Have any of these heroes disappointed you? Freewrite about this question and then discuss your writing with a partner.

Reading 4

Community Culture

Tatyana Sokolovskaya

In the essay that follows, a student from Ukraine describes her new communities – the neighborhood in which she lives and the place she visits when she needs to "feel at home." Before you read, think about the place you visit when you want to reconnect with your past and feel at home.

My family and I have been living in the United States for almost five years. It is   1
not long, but at the same time it isn't a short period of time for immigrants. Since we arrived in New York, we have found out that it is a very big and nice city. Our city includes a lot of ethnic and precious cultural values. People came and are still coming to the United States from countries all over the world. Each one of the immigrants is bringing his/her own culture and lifestyle to this new place.

I remember once when my family and I went outside in the morning, we were surprised. It was Sunday on Flatbush Avenue in Brooklyn. There were a lot of African-American people around. Most of them were dressed up in very nice, colorful clothes – green, yellow, white, brown, and red. I had never in my life seen such a big number of black people in one place. At first, we felt scared because we were the only white people among them. But very soon our feelings dispersed when we saw a lot of smiles on their kind faces. Later on we found out that the church that was located in our neighborhood was a religious center where African-American people gathered every Sunday.

Today my family members know almost all of those people, and very often our children play together. I explain to my children that we live in an area where black people are the dominant ethnic group. They also know that New York is a very big city, and next to us there could be people from Spanish or Jewish or Italian ethnic backgrounds. Each of those groups has its own community, where people live, gather, and follow their religion and cultural traditions. Every community has its own stores, where they sell all kinds of plants, fruit, and food that are popular and known by people from their native countries.

My family and I are a part of the Russian community in the Brighton Beach section of Brooklyn. We go there very often for many reasons. For example, if I really miss my country, relatives, language, food, or people, I can always find those things there, in Brighton Beach. There are two Russian theaters, many restaurants, agencies, and stores that sell delicious food and expensive European clothes. This is a really good place, where my family and I can feel at home. I remember clearly one summer day last year. My children and I went to a food store that was located in Brighton Beach. As usual, we decided what we had to buy. We were talking in Ukrainian, which is our native language. Two men were standing right next to us in the checkout line. I had a big watermelon because it was very hot and my children were thirsty. Also, I had two cabbages for salads. One of those men questioned me, "Could you tell me approximately how much those vegetables cost?" "About ten dollars," I answered. "It is very expensive," he said. "In our country maybe we could buy twenty watermelons with ten dollars." I was pleasantly surprised for a few seconds by his question and the language he used. He was speaking in Ukrainian. But shortly after, I learned more about them.

Those men had been in New York for three hours. They had just arrived from the airport and came to that store to buy some food. They didn't have any idea about the prices and measurement here. I explained that in the United States people don't weigh food in kilograms as in Europe. Here people weigh in pounds.

It turned out that those men were artists of the big dramatic theater from Ukraine. They came from Kiev to New York for two weeks to give concerts to the Russian immigrants in the area. If anybody could understand my feeling when I heard them speaking in my native language! The beauty of the Ukrainian language was simply indescribable. At the time we were speaking, I felt as if I was in my parents' garden with a lot of cherry and apple trees near our small house. The grass was very soft and green under my feet; the birds were singing, and the fresh air smelled like dew. Then I simply raised my head, closed my eyes, and forgot for a few seconds about America, New York, Brighton Beach. I was home.

We citizens of New York are very lucky that our city has places where every immigrant can go and feel at home. These places help many people to feel connected to groups of people with similar backgrounds. And this link really works. People can gather in these special places for any reason and at any time – at the time of success or in a tragic time.

Reading 4 Reflecting on the Reading

1 Why do you think Sokolovskaya decided to include the first three paragraphs in an essay that is primarily about the Russian community? Consider the following options, and discuss your opinion with a small group.

 a She wanted to emphasize the importance of community for all ethnic groups, not just her own.

 b She wanted to prove that she is not prejudiced against the African Americans who live near her.

 c She wanted her readers to understand the cultural diversity that exists in Brooklyn.

 d She wanted to show how hard she is trying to adjust to life in America.

2 In paragraph 5, Sokolovskaya describes the deep emotions she felt when she heard the two strangers speaking in her native language. Discuss whether you like the way the writer describes her feelings. Have you ever experienced similar feelings when you hear people speaking in your native language or dialect?

3 Reread the last paragraph of this essay and discuss what it means to you. How effective is this paragraph as a conclusion for the essay? Does the essay seem finished, or do you want to know a little more? Share your group's reactions with the class.

4 Before reading the essay, you were asked to think about the place you visit when you want to reconnect with your past and feel at home. In your journal, complete the following sentence: "When I want to feel at home, I go to . . ." Use this sentence as the beginning of a piece of freewriting.

A Village from the Past

Zhanna Kayumova

Even though the trip described in this essay took place many years ago, the writer, a student from Ukraine, clearly remembers this visit to her grandparents' village, where she experienced a very different way of life. Before you read, think about whether you have ever visited a place where everything seemed new and strange to you.

Dear Reader, 1

I would like to share my memory about an episode from my childhood. I 2
remember I was an eleven-year-old girl when my mother sent me and my aunt to
visit my grandparents for vacation. The village where they lived was in Ukraine,
but far away from the city, near the forest. My aunt and I took the bus to get there,
but in the middle of the journey we switched to a horse and carriage.

I even remember that the horse looked very skinny and tired, and she pulled 3
us very slowly through the dark forest. For me it seemed like something new that
I never experienced. That is why I started to pay attention to everything. In the
dark, everything looked different to me, especially the trees. They were so high,
with huge trunks and the biggest leaves.

Also I recognized the sounds of owls, which gave me a terrible feeling. And the 4
smell of the air was fresh like after the rain. We rode through the forest without
any conversation. The driver was falling asleep, but when he felt that the horse
was going slowly, he punched her with his leg, and we would continue on our way.
Later, when we got to my grandparents' house, I was so tired that I went to bed
very soon.

In the room where I slept, I felt like I had come to another century. First of 5
all, the bed frame was made from iron instead of wood, which was very unusual
for me. However, I had a soft mattress pad stuffed with feathers, and it was really
comfortable. I loved this feather bed, and I think I will never forget it.

Second, in this room my grandma had a lot of icons in each corner, and this 6
confused me. Each of those icons represented a different person. But the icon
with Jesus Christ scared me the most. His look seemed very stern to me. Later,
when I told my grandma about my worries, she said, "He is watching you to make
sure that you are not going to do bad things, but if you do, he will punish you." I
wanted to ask her more and more about it, but I did not.

My grandparents' house was small and pretty old, with only a few rooms and 7
without any fancy furniture. They had a black-and-white TV and a big chest in the
corner. Later, I tried to explain to my grandmother that in a big city nobody used
a chest like this anymore. She said that in this chest she kept a lot of important
things and many pictures of her family. I was too little to ask her to show me those
pictures, but the time has passed, and I feel really sad that I didn't have a chance
to see them. Now I feel like I missed something. Maybe my grandma's personal
life or something else that was important for her.

I forgot to mention that the house was not too far from the river. That river 8
was like the soul of this village. Often my grandma and I went to the river to enjoy
the beautiful view. We liked to watch the boats and the fishermen. We saw a lot
of lights across the water, and we knew that some other world was over there, with
people who had a different lifestyle, unknown to us. I remember that my grandma
used to touch my hair very gently, and I felt her warm hands, her very quiet voice.
I saved this memory because I really felt relaxed and secure.

During the week, this place was pretty quiet; we could even hear the sounds 9
of frogs and reeds. However, on the weekends, it was a different story. A lot of
people came to the bank of the river. Usually, the old people and kids enjoyed their
sandwiches, and the young couples sat around a campfire, playing the guitar and
singing songs that I had never heard before.

The atmosphere around me, compared to the big city, was different. It was 10
warm and relaxing, without stressful situations. People seemed more peaceful and
happy. Even though those people didn't have an easy life, they seemed more calm
and friendly. They knew how to enjoy life.

Reading 5   Reflecting on the Reading

1 In describing the trip to her grandparents' house, Kayumova mentions many
details. Underline five of these details. Then compare the details you found
with a small group. Discuss what kind of mood or atmosphere these details
create.

2 In paragraph 7, Kayumova explains that because she was so young, she
wasn't interested in the family pictures and other treasures her grandmother
kept in the big chest. Looking back as an adult, she says, "Now I feel like I
missed something." Think of a particular photograph that means a lot to
you because it is connected with your family's past. If possible, bring the
photograph to class. Discuss the photograph with your group. What do you
"see" when you look at this picture? What do your group members "see"? Is
it different from what you see? If so, why?

3 Kayumova writes this story from the perspective of an adult looking back
on her childhood, but she also includes the reactions of her younger self.
Underline places in which the writer describes a child's reaction to what was
happening and write a C in the margin. In a different color, underline places
in which she is writing as an adult and write an A in the margin. Discuss your
choices. Then discuss how the essay would have been different if Kayumova
had written everything from a child's point of view.

4 In paragraph 2, Kayumova writes that because everything seemed new and
strange, she "started to pay attention to everything." Before reading this
essay, you were asked to think of whether you had ever visited a place where
everything seemed new and strange to you. Freewrite about this place in your
journal. What details did you pay attention to in this new place? Why do you
still remember this place so clearly?

New Horizon of Beauty

Sumiko Masaki

In this essay, a Japanese student tells of a visit to a small church in France – a visit that changed her outlook on life. Before you read, think of a place that has changed your own life in some way.

It was early summer in the south of France. My husband and I were staying at a small hotel near the beach in Nice. Opening the window of my room, I could look out over the sea, whose face changed according to the time of day or night. At this time of year, the darkness does not arrive until after eleven o'clock. People can enjoy the sensitive change of the color of the sky for more than four hours in the evening.

I love beauty – the color of the sky, the calm sea, the flowers in a Japanese poem – but I always felt that it included something sad. I had been a kind of pessimist since my aunt's death ten years before. She was a beautiful lady, like a white rose. When she was in the hospital called the Cancer Center, one day she asked me to bring her white roses, which she loved very much but nobody gave her because white flowers are not considered appropriate. One week after that, she passed away with those roses. I could not understand why a wonderful person like her had to die young. But after that, I lost still more – two grandmothers. When I recovered from my great sorrow, I had to face new sadness. These happenings made me a person who thinks that a sunshine day must change to a rainy day. I came to believe that there is no happiness which never ends and there is no beauty which has no limit.

The day was sunny. The morning sky and sea were truly blue. The bright 3
sunlight of southern France made everything vivid. I strolled along the beach
with my husband. It was a beautiful and happy time, but I could not enjoy it
completely because of my thought that sadness always comes after joy.

We had planned a trip to Vence to see a chapel decorated by Matisse, an artist 4
whom my husband admired very much. Vence was about a thirty-minute drive
from Nice. As we drove into the town of Vence, we could see the small brick houses
with their brown roofs. We went up along the road through the peaceful village,
looking for the church. Our guidebook said that Matisse had designed the stained
glass, the tile work on the walls, and even the priest's vestments. He worked for a
sister in that church, because she had taken care of him and comforted him when
he was very ill. It was one of the greatest works of Matisse's last years.

Although the church was on top of a hill, we nearly missed it because it was 5
small. There was a small wooden sign on a fence which only said, "Chapelle
décorée par Matisse." I was just a little disappointed. While we were standing at
the entrance, two sisters invited us to come in. The door was opened.

At first, I could see stained glass in front of me. It was at the corner of the 6
white stairs leading to the chapel. It was the simplest glass I have ever seen. The
color was only white and blue, and the motif was a dolphin and a star, which a
child might draw. It was so lovely that it made me smile. We went down the stairs
and came into the chapel.

Chapel? I was surprised by the warm atmosphere and the light coming through 7
two big stained-glass windows. I have never seen such a bright chapel. There was
no confession room, authoritarianism, or heavy atmosphere. It was small, like one
room of a kindergarten. We could be children in this room. Sunshine through the
stained glass dyed the white floor yellow, green, and blue. The design of the glass
was some kind of plant or seaweed. But I felt that they were flowers of joy.

There were three walls covered with white ceramic tiles on which Matisse had 8
drawn three scenes using only black lines. One was a big priest wearing a cape.
Another was flowers and the Virgin Mary embracing a baby. The third one was the
scene of the Resurrection. What simple and genuine pictures! I was struck by a
strong emotion. Although I am not a Christian, the pictures spoke to the deepest
place in my heart. They showed me that I must be a child in front of God and
I must enjoy my happiness. I cried in my mind sitting in the small chair in the
beautiful church. At that time a candle of my heart was lighted.

My husband and I strolled along the beach that evening. The sky was sensitive 9
orange, like a picture by an impressionist painter. The sea was like a piece of
golden cloth. I felt the warmth through the arm of my husband. I was pleased that
I had found a new horizon. For years I had been a person lacking in moral courage.
I had been afraid of making my heart uncovered. I had forgotten the smile of
children. But now I could truly enjoy the air of southern France, because I could
return to the genuine child in front of great beauty. I closed my eyes and breathed
deeply. At that time I saw the flowers of joy drawn by Matisse shimmering on the
golden waves of my mind.

1 In this essay, Masaki "paints" with words to create visual images. Underline three visual images that she creates. Then discuss with a partner or small group how these images relate to the ideas being expressed. Why do you think Masaki chose to include so many visual images?

2 Underline all of the references to children in paragraphs 6–9. Then discuss why you think Masaki refers to children so often. How do children relate to Masaki's main idea?

3 In paragraph 2, Masaki says, "I had been a kind of pessimist since my aunt's death ten years before." Look up the definitions of *pessimist* and *optimist* in the dictionary and discuss the meaning of these words with your partner or group. Then think of two people you know, one who is a pessimist and another who is an optimist. Explain how these two people might react to the same event. Do you know of anyone who, like Masaki, has changed from being one type of person to being the other type? If so, describe the person's change and discuss what caused it.

4 Before reading this essay, you were asked to think of a place in your own life that had changed you in some way. Freewrite about this place in your journal. What do you remember about this place most clearly? When you picture yourself in this place, are you alone or with someone else? What was there about this place that caused you to change?

TECHNIQUES WRITERS USE

Appealing to All the Senses

When asked to write a description, student writers often rely almost entirely on the sense of sight. Yet professional writers appeal to all the different senses – touch, hearing, smell, taste, *and* sight – in order to make the places they are describing seem real to the reader. Appealing to all five senses is one of the most important techniques writers use.

Task 4.1   *Analyze*

1 Read the following description written by a student. Underline each sensory detail and write in the margin which of the five senses the writer is appealing to.

Subway

    I close my eyes trying to imagine that I am not here. I have no   1
idea how many times I have been in the same awful train, reading
the same ads, watching the most horrendous people and their routine
attitudes. Today I believe that I have been doing it for centuries.

> I open my eyes, noticing that I hate their smells. I hate the shocking   2
> perfume of an old woman because it is cheap and too strong. I hate
> the smell of the fresh-printed newspapers and the wet second-hand
> coats that people wear on rainy days.
>
> I close my eyes and pretend that I'm sleeping because I don't know   3
> where to direct my eyes anymore. I'm tired of seeing what surrounds
> me inevitably on this daily trip to the city. Now everything is dark.
> I start experiencing a different sensation, the sound of the train. Its
> repetitious noise to which I have become addicted is methodical; I
> could say that it almost hypnotizes me. The time passes by and I feel
> that people are looking at me. I feel uncomfortable and finally I'm
> dying to see what's going on in the car.
>
> When I open my eyes again, I realize that I have missed my stop.   4

2 Compare the details you found with a small group and discuss which of the senses the writer used.

3 When the writer closed his eyes, what was the effect on his other senses? Point to specific details in the reading to prove your point.

Task 4.2 *Practice*

1 Think of a place where you could go to practice using your senses, and go there either by yourself or with a partner

2 Close your eyes for a few minutes. Then open them and write down all the information you gathered using only the senses of hearing, smell, touch, and taste. Do not use any information that you got from the sense of sight.

3 Reread what you have written and add any new details that you think of.

4 Share the results of this experiment with a small group.

Using Memories from the Past

A writer's memories of experiences, people, and places from the past are rich sources of material for writing. Often writers use words to re-create places they can't visit again in reality. As you begin to write about a place from the past, memories you haven't thought about for many years often come flooding back into your mind.

Task 4.3 *Analyze*

1 Read the following description of a place from the past that was written by a student from Turkey.

> **Miserable**
>
> When I was ten years old, I went to my village to visit my 1
> grandmother with my family. My brothers and I were really happy
> because we did not know what was waiting for us there.
>
> We took the bus to get to the village. After two hours, we got off 2
> the bus and I asked my mother if we were in the village. She said that
> we had to walk the rest of the way because there was no road to the
> village. We walked into a forest that was very steep.
>
> There was no electricity in the village. My grandmother was using a 3
> kerosene lamp to illuminate her home. She had a radio, but she could
> only listen to one station that gave only news.
>
> The first night, we could not sleep because of grasshoppers. My 4
> grandmother said, "They are harmless; there is nothing to be scared
> of." But the grasshoppers were making a lot of noise.
>
> In the village, the houses were not very close together. My 5
> grandmother and her neighbors were using a different method
> for communicating with each other. This method was called bird
> language. They were singing to each other like birds. The first time I
> heard it, I did not understand what they were doing. But they could
> understand each other.
>
> Two weeks later, we went back to Istanbul. My brothers and I 6
> thanked our parents for moving to the city. We were glad not to live in
> the miserable village.

2 Working with a partner or small group, underline all the sensory details
(sight, sound, smell, touch, taste) in the essay. Using a different color,
underline words, phrases, or sentences that reveal the writer's emotions about
the place.

3 Discuss whether you agree with the writer that the village was a "miserable"
place. Why or why not?

Task 4.4 Practice

1 Think of a place from your past that was important to you for some reason –
for example, a special place from your childhood, a workplace, or a place
where you went with friends.

2 Make a brief list of details to describe the place, using the categories below.
(You can also use taste as a category, if it applies to your place.)

    sight   sound   smell   touch

3 Show your list to a partner and talk about what this place was like.

4 Freewrite about this place from your past in your journal. Create your impression of this place by *showing* rather than *telling* the reader what it was like. A good example of *showing* rather than *telling* is in paragraph 6 of "New Horizon of Beauty," in which Sumiko Masaki writes, "The color [of the stained glass] was only white and blue, and the motif was a dolphin and a star, which a child might draw." With this specific description, Masaki *shows* readers the stained glass, rather than *telling* readers that the designs were childlike and innocent.

INTERNET SEARCH

Finding Your Hometown on the World Wide Web

Writers often rely on their memories when writing about a place. But sometimes they need to do research to find additional information. In the following activity, you will practice doing research about a familiar place – the town where you lived as a child.

Task 4.5 *Practice*

1 Go to an Internet search engine, such as Yahoo.com, Netscape.com, or Google.com, and do a search using the name of your hometown (the town where you grew up) as the keyword for your search. If your hometown does not come up, use the name of the nearest major city as the keyword. Try to find information about at least four of the items listed below. For larger cities, you will be able to find information about all of the items.
   - The year your town was established
   - Who first settled your town
   - Any historical events that happened there
   - The current population
   - The major industries or employers in the area
   - Any points of interest or attractions

2 Using the information from your Internet search, write a one- to two-page description of your hometown to share with a partner from your class who has never visited your town.

3 Exchange papers with your partner and read each other's descriptions. Write three questions about information you would like to know that was not included in your partner's description. For example, "How long did you live there?" "Why did you leave your hometown?"

4 Discuss the questions you wrote for step 3 with your partner. Then tell your partner whether you learned anything about your hometown that you didn't know before or anything that surprised you. If you are not living in your

hometown now, discuss how the town where you live now is different from your hometown.

5 Share with your partner any new things you learned about searching the Internet.

ESSAY ASSIGNMENT

Your assignment for this chapter is to write an essay about a place that has meaning for you. Think of your audience as interested classmates who have never visited the place you are describing. The purpose of this essay is to describe the place so clearly that it seems real and to reveal your feelings about the place.

Reread the writing you have already done for this chapter to see whether it gives you ideas for this assignment.

Writing Tips

- **Include significant details that will help your reader imagine the place.**
  Develop the habit of observing and recordings details. The secret to describing a place vividly is to include significant details that will help readers to re-create the place in their own minds. For example, in Reading 6, Sumiko Masaki writes: "I was surprised by the warm atmosphere and the light coming through two big stained-glass windows. I have never seen such a bright chapel. . . . There were three walls covered with white ceramic tiles on which Matisse had drawn three scenes using only black lines." Masaki's careful choice of details helps us to feel present at the scene.

- **Use information from the five senses.**
  Remember to include information from as many of the senses as possible: sight, sound, smell, touch, and taste. For example, in Reading 1, Amalfi Richard evokes sight, sound, taste, and touch in the following description: "These walls were painted with magic – a variety of cute fishes, blue water, sunshine, and beautiful seashells – all of which were reflected in the deep water of the pool. The strong rain in May produced a big, strange noise when it crashed into the pool's water. . . . It was as if I was living between the present, which was the pool, and the past, which was the memories of my parents when they had left me in my country. It was like the taste of a lemon, like the roses and the thorns."

- **Convey the mood or atmosphere of the place.**
  Is the place you are describing happy or sad, peaceful or tense? Use details in your writing that will create an impression of the mood or atmosphere of the place in the reader's mind. In Reading 3, for example, Jian Wei evokes a mood of fear and foreboding near the beginning of his essay: "The sun was nearly down. Shafts of light covered the empty Tiananmen Square, full silent, as if the Square were exhausted."

- **Reveal why the place is important to you.**
  This does not mean that you should tell the reader directly by saying, "I chose to write about this place because . . ." But it does mean that after reading the essay, the reader should understand why it was important for you to write about this place. For example, in Reading 4, Tatyana Sokolovskaya explains the significance that a Russian neighborhood in New York City has for her when she says, "Then I simply raised my head, closed my eyes, and forgot for a few seconds about America, New York, Brighton Beach. I was home."

Writing Your First Draft

Now, keeping the writing tips in mind, write the first draft of your essay. Remember that you can also use personification and similes in your writing. These were discussed in "Reading 1: Reflecting on the Reading," steps 2 and 3, on page 95. As you are working on this first draft, do not slow yourself down by worrying about correct grammar and spelling; it is more important just to get your ideas down on paper so you have something to work with in later drafts.

REVISING YOUR ESSAY

Once you have put your ideas down on paper by completing the first draft, you can begin the revising process.

Giving More Helpful Peer Response

Giving honest and constructive peer response is a skill that must be learned through practice. As with every other skill, there is usually a period of trial and error at the beginning. It is important to understand that giving really helpful peer response takes time. It may take an hour or more for you and your partner to read each other's papers, answer the questions on the "Peer Response Form," and then discuss these answers thoroughly in your peer conference. But if you keep practicing, you will see positive results of the peer response process in your writing.

1 Read "Peer Response Form A," below, and "Peer Response Form B," on page 114.

Peer Response Form A
Writing About Places

WRITER'S NAME: *Student X*   READER'S NAME: *Student A*

DATE: *February 15, 2005*

1 What did you like best about this essay? Be as specific as possible.

I liked everything. It was good.

2 Did the writer describe the place clearly? List any parts that were not clear to you.

It was pretty clear.

3 Did the writer appeal to the different senses? List two sensory details that you especially liked.

He said the station was silent.

4 How would you describe the mood or the atmosphere of this place?

I think this is a peaceful place.

5 Why do you think the writer chose to write about this place?

I really don't know. Maybe it reminds him of home.

6 How could the writer improve this paper when he or she revises? Make only one suggestion.

Correct the grammar and spelling errors.

Peer Response Form B
Writing About Places

WRITER'S NAME: *Student X*　　　READER'S NAME: *Student B*

DATE: *February 15, 2005*

1 What did you like best about this essay? Be as specific as possible.

I liked the way Ai Ming used his imagination in this essay. I'm not sure, but I think this station wasn't real. I think Ai Ming just imagined it from looking at a picture when he was a little boy. Kids often imagine things like this.

2 Did the writer describe the place clearly? List any parts that were not clear to you.

I'm sorry, but I don't think this essay was very clear. In paragraph 2, it sounds more like the station was real. Was this place real or imaginary? He should try to be more clear in the second draft. Think about how to show the reader what parts are real and what parts are imaginary. Also, I didn't really understand what he meant in paragraph 1 when he said, "I knew this station from a picture and my own imagine." I'm not sure what he meant at the end of the essay when he said, "but his still remembers there have a little station in his way."

3 Did the writer appeal to the different senses? List two sensory details that you especially liked.

He did this a little bit. For example, he said that the station was "silent" and "quiet." But I think he could add more sensory details when he revises.

4 How would you describe the mood or the atmosphere of this place?

I would say the mood of this place was mysterious.

5 Why do you think the writer chose to write about this place?

Even though this place is probably imaginary, it must be important to the writer because he chose it for his essay. At the end he says he still remembers the little station. Why?

6 How could the writer improve this paper when he or she revises? Make only one suggestion.

I think the writer needs to add more details. Maybe he should explain why this place is so important. I know I was only supposed to make one suggestion, but he really needs to work on the grammar and spelling.

2 Discuss the following questions in a small group:

a Which of the two peer responders liked the essay more? What evidence can you give to support your opinion?

b Which peer responder gave more specific answers to the questions? Give an example of an answer that you feel is specific.

c Did either of the peer responders give any answers that were not constructive? If so, what were they?

d Did either of the peer responders give any answers that would embarrass or offend the writer? If so, what were they?

e Which of the two peer responses would be more useful in helping to revise, A or B? Why? Give an example of a comment that would be helpful in revising and one that would not be helpful.

Responding to Your Peers

1 Working with a partner or in a group of three, exchange and read the first drafts of your essays.

2 Fill out a copy of the "Peer Response Form" on page 120 for each of the first drafts you read. Focus on the ideas rather than the grammar and spelling. Point out only those mistakes that interfere with understanding.

3 Using the completed peer response forms as the basis for your discussion, have a peer conference to discuss your first drafts.

Writing Your Second Draft

Taking into consideration the feedback you have received from your peers and your own ideas about how to improve your essay, write your second draft.

EDITING YOUR ESSAY

When you are satisfied with the content and organization of your essay, you can begin the process of editing.

Grammar in Context: Using the Plural Form of Nouns

Using the plural form of nouns correctly is something that students often have difficulty with. The tasks that follow will give you a chance to check your understanding of when a noun should be used in its plural form. If you find this aspect of English grammar confusing or if you want more information on the topic, review the appropriate section in your grammar reference book or in an online grammar resource such as Purdue University's Online Writing Lab, currently accessible at <http://owl.english.purdue.edu>.

Some nonnative speakers of English are unsure about when a noun should be used in its plural form because in their native language the endings of nouns do not change to indicate the plural form. As an example, try translating these sentences into another language.

> She gave me a **book**. (singular form of the noun)
> She gave me three **books**. (plural form of the noun)

Did you need to make any changes in the word for *book* in the second sentence to show that it was plural? If so, how did the word change? In English, the majority of nouns are regular and become plural by the addition of *-s* or *-es*. For example: *book* becomes *books*. (There are some irregular nouns that do not become plural by adding *-s* or *-es*. Check your grammar reference for a list of these irregular nouns.)

If you are unsure when to use plural forms, it is helpful to look for key words that always signal the need for a plural noun: for example, expressions like *a few*, *several*, *many*, and any number larger than one. The expressions *one of the* and *all of the* also signal the plural.

Examples

a few girl**s**	*many* subject**s**	*one of the* student**s**
several computer**s**	*four* professor**s**	*all of the* book**s**

Task 4.6 *Analyze*

1 Read the first two paragraphs from "The Tree of My Secrets," by Amalfi Richard, below. Underline each of the nouns you find, and above the noun write S (for singular) or P (for plural). For this task, do not underline proper nouns such as *Dominican Republic* or *Uncle Pipe Sosa* or pronouns such as *I*, *my*, or *it*.

> In my childhood memories, I have many favorite places, but I will   1
> write about the one that I prefer. It is the tree of my secrets. I began
> my journey in the Dominican Republic with my tree, and it was there
> at the end of my journey.
>
> A long time ago, when I was a young child, my parents decided   2
> to travel to the United States to get better opportunities and enhance
> the quality of our family's life. My parents left me in the Dominican
> Republic, and I lived in different family members' houses. When I first
> came to live with Uncle Pipe Sosa and my godmother, Ramona, in
> 1981, the tree was young like I was. At the age of four, I started to
> enjoy the company of my tree. I played around it with my two younger
> sisters, neighbors, and friends. Then my godmother and my uncle
> decided to sell the house and move to a big empty place.

2 Discuss with a partner why the writer chose either the singular or the plural form for each of these nouns.

3 Check your work using the Answer Key on page 259.

Practice

1 Read the following student essay, which contains 14 errors involving the choice between the singular or plural form of nouns. Then, working with a partner, find and correct the errors. Discuss the reason for each change that you make.

I Was a "Little Devil"

In the summer of 1980, I had to attend a chemistry class because 1
my father thought I was doing poorly in it. I admired karate very much at
the time, but my father always gave me good reasons not to take lesson.
Therefore, instead of going to chemistry class, I skipped school and took
karate at a little school nearby, without my father's permission.

After I had taken a few lesson, I became one of the most annoying 2
kid in the neighborhood. I always made plan for us (our kid gang) to
fight with the other kids on the surrounding block. This was one of
the game that we enjoyed most. But as you may guess, every wild
start must have an end. In my case, this was how I ended my karate
lesson.

One day when I got out of my karate lesson, two of my friend and 3
I were all excited because the next day would be the big contest to go
a step higher in karate. Suddenly I bumped into somebody. When I
looked up, it was a guy who was around my age, but by appearance
stronger than me. However, I didn't notice that, but stood up and started
a fight with him. Even though he said "Sorry" many time and asked
me to forgive him, I didn't. We took off our shoe and started. The kid
surrounding us were cheering, and their yelling made me even more
excited. I was winning for the first several minutes, but my strength left
me as the fight went on. Finally, the guy punched me so hard that he
completely knocked me down. I sat on the ground with bruise on my
body and a bloody nose. He came over, looked at me, and asked: "Are
you okay? I didn't want to fight, but you insisted. I'm sorry." After that
he left. I was sitting on the ground feeling like a total fool.

On my way home, I didn't cry out loud, but tear kept rolling down 4
my face. After crying, I began to laugh about my stupidity and decided
to give up physical fighting for the rest of my life. That was the end of
my karate lesson.

---

2 Check your work using the Answer Key on page 259.

Editing Checklist

If you are writing your essay on a computer, remember to print out your revised essay and proofread it on paper.

☐ **First proofreading: singular and plural forms of nouns**
Proofread your essay and make any corrections necessary in the use of the singular or plural forms of nouns. Check (✔) the box when you have finished.

☐ **Second proofreading**
Proofread your essay a second time and correct any other errors of grammar, spelling, or punctuation that you find. Check (✔) the box when you have finished.

☐ **Third proofreading**
Print out or write a copy of your essay that includes the corrections you made in your first and second proofreading. Now proofread your essay a third time. Try to find and correct any errors that you missed. Then print out, or write in dark blue or black ink, the final draft of your essay. Check (✔) the box when you have finished.

A NOTE BEFORE YOU CONTINUE

In Part II of this book, the essays you have written have been based primarily on your own life – the experiences, people, and places that have meant the most to you personally. As you move into Part III, you will begin to write more formal essays in which you explore and analyze the ideas of others.

Now that you have finished your work in Part II, take the time to reflect on your progress as a writer by filling out "Assessing Your Progress: A Midterm Survey" on page 122.

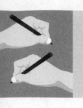

Peer Response Form
Writing About Places

WRITER'S NAME: .... READER'S NAME: ....

DATE: ....

Focus on the ideas in the essay rather than the grammar and spelling. Discuss only those mistakes that interfere with understanding.

1 What did you like best about this essay? Be as specific as possible.

2 Did the writer describe the place clearly? List any parts that were not clear to you.

3 Did the writer appeal to the different senses? List two sensory details that you especially liked.

Photocopiable   © Cambridge University Press

4 How would you describe the mood or the atmosphere of this place?

5 Why do you think the writer chose to write about this place?

6 How could the writer improve this essay when he or she revises? Make only one suggestion.

Assessing Your Progress
A Midterm Survey

YOUR NAME: .... DATE: ....

Reread your responses to "A Beginning Survey" on page 24. Then answer the questions below. Later you will compare your answers to "A Beginning Survey" and this survey with your answers to "A Closing Survey."

1 How satisfied are you with the course as it has been presented so far? Explain.

2 What one activity has been the most helpful for you? Some possible answers might be small-group discussions, freewriting, reading, and peer conferences. Identify the activity and explain why you think it has helped you.

3 What one activity has been the least helpful? Identify the activity and explain why you did not find it helpful.

Photocopiable   © Cambridge University Press

4 Review your writing and check to see whether you have done all the assignments so far. If you have not turned in some of the assigned work, list the missing assignment(s) below and write down the date(s) when you expect to hand in this work to your teacher.

5 Which of the essays that you have written so far do you feel is your best one?

Title of essay: ....

How did you get the ideas for this essay? How many drafts did you write? In your opinion, what are the strong points of this essay? Which parts could use more work? Did you enjoy writing this essay? Why or why not?

6 How would you describe your attitude toward writing at this time in comparison to your attitude at the beginning of the course?

PART III
MORE FORMAL WRITING

Oral History
Writing Based on Interviews

Chapter
5

Families in Transition
Writing Based on Reading

Chapter
6

Issues of Identity
Writing Based on Research

Chapter
7

Oral History

Writing Based on Interviews

The process of interviewing people to learn about their lives and times is a form of historical research known as oral history. In this chapter, which provides a transition between personal and more formal writing, you will read a variety of essays, all of which are based on interviews. As in all formal writing situations, the writer must develop generalizations and support them with specific evidence. In your essay for this chapter, the evidence will come from an interview that you conduct. But the processes needed to incorporate this material into your essay – direct quotation, paraphrase, summary, and analysis – are the same ones you will use in Chapters 6 and 7 as you write essays based on written sources.

READINGS

A Reward from Buddha

Zhong Chen

The interview assignment gave Zhong Chen, a student from China, an opportunity to have a long conversation with a respected member of his family, his 92-year-old great-uncle. Before you read, think about the elders in your own family. Is there an older relative you would like to interview?

1   Entering this traditional living room furnished with old-fashioned Chinese furniture, such as a redwood sofa and chairs decorated with colorful shells, I seemed to come back to my hometown and couldn't help feeling comfortable. I looked at the bleached wall on which some Chinese calligraphy and old photographs were hung. This apartment, located in Manhattan, is the home of my great-uncle, who emigrated to the United States forty-eight years ago during World War II. Now he is ninety-two years old.

2   In order not to disturb my uncle's afternoon nap, I walked to the window over the plush carpet in silence. As I looked out through the soft white curtains, I noticed the contrast between this peaceful Chinese room and the noisy American street eleven floors below. It made me curious about my uncle's extraordinary experience – about his life in China, his immigration to America, and how he dealt with the contrast between the two countries.

3   "Oh, Zhong Zhong [my nickname], I am really glad to see you," my uncle said with strong dialect as he walked briskly out of his bedroom. "Have you been here long?"

4   "I didn't want to bother you. Did you have a nice nap?"

5   "Just like every day. Now my life has become nonsense without working and challenge. Have a seat!"

6   We sat down. With a distinctive movement, he took an old wood frame from the center of the shelf and began to wipe off imaginary dust. In the frame there was a precious certificate praising his service in the American Navy during World War II.

7   "Why do you emphasize this certificate so much?" I asked.

8   "Actually, I never got any certificate in my life except this one. You know, I didn't receive any formal education. Even though I can't understand each word in this certificate, I know its real meaning," he said, and then looked around the room. Compared with the small house of his childhood, the room was like a paradise.

9   He began to remember. My great-uncle was born in a small village in 1902. At that time, China was still ruled by the Qing Dynasty. Most of the people suffered from poverty caused by constant civil war, especially in the underdeveloped remote countryside, where my great-uncle lived. As a result, he had to struggle for food and clothes in order to survive.

During his childhood, he lived with his parents, two brothers, and three sisters 10 in a small wood house with no windows, which was on the verge of collapse. They all depended on their father's low salary and frequently had to endure hunger.

My great-uncle never owned any toys. Instead, he had to play with mud. When 11 he was seven years old, he should have started school, but there was no school in his village, and his parents couldn't afford to send him away to a nearby village to study.

He remembered it sadly: "At that time I was very anxious to go to school, 12 but I couldn't. When I saw my friends carrying their book bags, I envied them and said, 'Ah, so you must study hard now, really study hard since you have the opportunity.'"

At age nine, my great-uncle was already regarded as a man because his father 13 had died of disease, and his mother couldn't manage alone. As the eldest son, my great-uncle had to find a job to support the family. Finally he found work as an apprentice in a tobacco store. His job was to polish approximately two hundred pipes every day. It was such hard work for a nine-year-old boy that his fingers were swollen day and night. Still, he didn't give up. On the contrary, he was delighted that he could earn nearly ten yuan a month to support his poor family.

"Hard work can create a better life," he often says. "The more you work, the 14 more you gain."

When my great-uncle became a teenager, he began to worry about his future. 15 Poverty and painful experience had made him decide to be a successful man who depended only on himself. Having worked at a boring job for three years, he realized he could learn nothing more in the tobacco store. He didn't want to spend his whole life there. He hoped to leave the small village and explore the outside world. Finally he decided to go to the modern city to learn a skill. However, he didn't have enough money. At his mother's urging, he swallowed his pride and asked for his uncle's help. His uncle, a wealthy merchant in their village, had scorned his father many years ago. Afterward, they didn't communicate any more.

"When I went to his house to ask for help, he showed his scowling face and 16 refused me without mercy," my great-uncle said. "At that time, I realized that the only one who could help me was myself." His words impressed me. Even though he was an old man, what he said was full of energy and vitality.

Before long, he found a job in a shipping company. Although it was hard work, 17 he was excited to be a sailor and learned a lot working on domestic cruise ships. But soon World War II broke out, and he was hired by an American shipping company that transported weapons all over the world. His family advised him not to accept this dangerous job. Nevertheless, he refused to give up the opportunity.

On the ship, he began to learn English from Americans. "I just tried my best 18 and memorized every word they told me. For example, when they pointed to a chair, I would keep repeating *chair, chair.*" Gradually, he was able to talk with Americans freely.

I was interested in his experience in the war: "Were you ever afraid?" 19

"Generally not. But one night in Denmark, more than ten bombers attacked 20 the port. Flames brightened the whole sky. We just sat in the dark cabin and kept silent. I prayed for Buddha to bless me. Eventually we were lucky to escape. I think my life was a reward from Buddha."

After World War II, my great-uncle arrived in the United States and made up his mind to stay. "I began to love this country the first time I saw her." 21

Because he had served in the American Navy, he was naturalized as a U.S. citizen. In New York City, he began his new American life working as a chef in a Chinese restaurant. In contrast to his previous job, this one seemed easier. Ten years later, he opened his own restaurant and began to earn a lot of money. He was completely satisfied with his life in America. 22

"Do you think of yourself as an American or a Chinese?" I asked. 23

"Me? I think I'm a Chinese," he answered with hesitation. "Although I have lived in America for a long time, there are all Chinese thoughts in my deep mind after all. To this day, I still keep the Chinese lifestyle and customs. As soon as you see this room, you can feel it, right? And, I was honest and loyal when I communicated with other people here. I made a great effort to show how a Chinese immigrant should be." 24

We had talked for more than two hours. It was already dusk outside. I looked out the window. The sun was starting to set, though the sunshine was still dazzling and splendid. 25

Reading 1   Reflecting on the Reading

1 Do you think the great-uncle believes that his success was a "reward from Buddha," or do you think he believes that he earned his success through his own hard work? Underline parts of the essay that support your opinion. Then discuss your answer with a partner or small group.

2 Sometimes the setting for an interview is significant. Chen conducted this interview in his great-uncle's apartment, and he chose to mention several features of the apartment and its furnishings in his essay. Underline four of these features. Discuss why you think Chen included them. What do they reveal about the great-uncle's personal values?

3 In an essay based on an interview, a writer must combine direct quotations (the exact words of the interviewee or interviewer), indirect quotations (the writer's paraphrase of what was said), and the writer's own analysis. Working with a partner, analyze Chen's use of direct quotations in this essay by answering the following questions:

   a Put a check mark (✓) in the margin next to every paragraph that contains a direct quotation. Of the 25 paragraphs in the essay, how many include direct quotations? About what percentage of the essay do the paragraphs with direct quotations represent?

   b Next to each of the paragraphs that contains a direct quotation, put a U if the quotation is from the great-uncle or a C if the quotation is from the writer, Zhong Chen. Of the direct quotations in the essay, about what percentage are quotations from the great-uncle and what percentage are from Chen?

c Notice that the paragraphs with direct quotations are not all grouped together in the essay. Look at the sections that appear between the quotations. For each of these sections, analyze and discuss Chen's purpose for including it.

d Taking into consideration your answers to a, b, and c, how would you describe the way in which Chen has mixed direct quotations, indirect quotations, and his own analysis in this essay?

4 In your journal, write down the name of the oldest living member of your family. Then think of a story you know about this person and write it quickly, putting in all the details you can remember.

Reading 2

Unfinished Interview

Tatyana Dyachenko

Tatyana Dyachenko, a student from Ukraine, had always wanted to know more about her mother's experiences as a child during World War II. An interview assignment provided the chance for Dyachenko to ask about her mother's childhood during World War II, a conversation that led to a deeper understanding of her mother's character and values. As you read, think of someone you know who has lived through a war or other violent situation.

All my conscious life I remember my mother as working: knitting, embroidering, or sewing. She could do several jobs at the same time. Her hands – always busy. Her eyes – always slipping around for "what else to do." 1

At the time I visited her for an interview, she was busy as always. First of all, she asked me her usual question: "Have you already had your breakfast?" (or dinner, or lunch, depending on the time of day). This question always has opened each of our meetings. And it doesn't matter whether the answer is yes or no, she'll serve me a meal. The most important thing for my mother is to keep her children satisfied. 2

When she put everything on the table, I asked her to sit down and said, "I'm going to interview you." She laughed. "Me? I'm not a movie star." Then I said, "Mom, I need your help. I'm going to write an essay." She asked, "What's it about?" I answered that I was going to write an essay about her life. My mother said, "I'm not a famous person. There is nothing to write about me." "I'll try to find something," I said. "You just sit down, please, for twenty minutes." 3

The first question I asked was about her childhood. My mother was born in 1930, in the city of Kiev. Her childhood was very short because of World War II. When the war started, she was ten years old. Her father was killed at the beginning of the war; her mother died from starvation in Bukhara, Uzbekistan, 4 where the family was evacuated. And my mother was left with her four-year-old sister. In her ten years, life had turned her into an adult person; she became the mother for her sister.

Then they were evacuated to Irkutsk, Siberia. When I asked her how two little girls could survive in the severe conditions of that land, my mother refused to answer this question. She said, "My children don't have to know anything like this." She stood up and began to clean the table. "Twenty minutes haven't passed yet," I said. "Could you sit down, please, and tell me more about the war in your life." But the answer she shouted was sharp: "That's all about it."

I knew she wouldn't say anything more, but I tried again. "OK, answer me, please, the last question. What was most terrifying for you during the war? You were only ten years old. I mean, were you afraid of bombs exploding, or were you afraid of death around you?" I was surprised by her answer. She said that she wasn't afraid of explosions or death, fires or cries. When my mother saw my astonished eyes, she explained, "It wasn't because I was a brave girl, but because when you see tragedy, horror, and ruin, death and tears all around you every day, every hour, you get accustomed to these awful things. It is terrible, but it is true. But, of course, there was one thing that I was afraid of most of all." "What was that?" My mother read this question in my eyes. She looked at me (I was almost finished eating her homemade cookies and drinking some tea) and said, "Starvation." I froze with an open mouth, unable to swallow the bite of cookie. My mother continued, "I experienced the terrible feeling of starvation. There was nothing to eat. I wanted to eat all the time. I wanted to eat when I went to sleep and when I got up. I woke up at night because I wanted to eat. I got crazy from it. When I'd found something to eat, I gave it to my little sister." Here, my mother saw my expression (still with a piece of cookie that stuck in my throat) and cried to me, "How many times have I told you, don't ask me questions about it! My children do not have to know these things!" And she went to the living room.

I understood that she wouldn't say anything more. My interview wasn't finished, but I knew that was the end. My mother was already knitting in the living room. She always knits when she gets nervous because it calms her down. I stayed in the kitchen. Suddenly I recollected one thing from my childhood. Like most children, I very often whined about meals: "I don't want to eat. I'm not hungry." But my mother would say, "You'll eat everything that I give you. There is no question about it!" Sometimes I sat at the table for one hour or more to eat my meal, which became cold and not tasty. But my mother wouldn't let me go until I finished. I cried and ate my meal with my tears. And now, in the kitchen, I learned in less than twenty minutes that it was because somewhere, in the past, my dear mother cried and ate just her tears without any meal. I understood why every time we meet or call each other, her first question is "Have you already eaten something today?"

It is impossible to write about a person's life in a few pages. Just one episode of my mother's life took several pages. Of course, she has a lot to tell, but she doesn't like to talk about herself. I just want to add that my mother tried to build all her castles in the air for her children, my brother and me. When I look at her rough, overworked hands, I understand why my hands are soft and smooth. When I look at her wrinkled face, I understand why I look young. She found her happiness in her children's lives, and I will try not to let her down. I'll try to be happy for her and for me.

When I was about to leave that day, I asked my mother the last question, "What do you want most of all?" She said, "To see my children smiling, happy, and never knowing what war is." We kissed goodbye, and I went home.

9

Reading 2 *Reflecting on the Reading*

1 Write one sentence that describes the overall meaning of this essay. Share your sentence with a partner or small group. Then discuss the similarities and differences you found in the meaning of the essay.

2 Dyachenko includes many details related to eating or food. Underline each reference to food in the essay. Then compare your answers with your partner or group members and discuss why you think she included so many of these references.

3 It is important to learn the skill of introducing direct quotations in ways that set a context for the reader and make the quotations relevant to the ideas in your essay. For example, in paragraph 2, Dyachenko introduces her mother's question ("Have you already had your breakfast?") with these words: "First of all, she asked me her usual question: . . ." Working with a partner, analyze the skill of introducing quotations in the following way:

a Underline two places where Dyachenko introduces a direct quotation of something her mother said during the interview.

b In a different color, underline one place where Dyachenko quotes from memory something that her mother said in the past.

c Discuss each place you underlined. What is gained by introducing the quotations as Dyachenko has done in this essay?

4 In her essay, Dyachenko explains how she grew to understand her mother's behavior better as a result of this interview. Think about your own parents. Is there anything about their behavior that you did not understand when you were a child but have come to understand now that you are older? Freewrite about this question in your journal.

My First Interview

Larisa Zubataya

In this essay, a student from Russia investigates a subject of great interest to her personally – prejudice against people of other racial or ethnic groups. As a Jew, Zubataya had experienced discrimination in her native country, and she was eager to learn more about the position of Jews in the United States. This conversation with an American-born Jew gave her the chance to discover the answers to some of her questions. As you read this essay, think about people you know who have been discriminated against.

I first met Irving in a happy, but at the same time, difficult period of my life. 1
My family came to America from Russia, escaping from national prejudice against us as second-rate persons because we are Jews. We immigrated to a community where we could be accepted as equals. On the other hand, I experienced what Americans call "culture shock." I lost my ease of communication and my professional experience because we arrived in a society with a different language. I met Irving and continued to see him every Sunday in the Jewish Center, where he works as a volunteer helping newcomers adapt to a new environment and understand their new country, its culture, and its citizens.

Fate presented me with another chance to meet Irving the next year. 2
Accidentally, I met him in the computer laboratory at my college. This old man is enrolled in a special college program to learn about the computer.

I chose Irving for my interview because he is an American-born wise man. Thus, 3
I could get sensible answers to my questions. I had experienced discrimination as a Jew in Russia, and I wanted to know an American's point of view on this problem.

I began my interview with a question that worries me: "What do you think 4
about prejudice?" He replied, "I think that pre-judging people is an ignorant and horrible thing. One is not born with prejudice. It has to be learned. If children were taught from their early years to accept people of different colors, customs, and religions, the world would be a better place." I was listening to him, and I agreed with his position.

Prejudice is always dangerous if it is against people of a different color of skin, a 5
different religion, or a different social status. I remember my dismay when I heard in a job interview in my former country: "This is not Israel! We cannot take a Jew to work in our research center!"

Irving's mother's family came from Riga in Russia in 1888 to find a better life 6
in America. His father's family also came here in 1888; they came originally from Spain to England and then to South Carolina. Thus, Irving grew up, was educated, and worked in the United States. He grew up during the Great Depression and attended Brooklyn College at night for seven years while he worked during the

day. He was a chemist for most of his life. He is the father of three children and has one granddaughter. Irving is an observant Jew and a supporter of Israel.

I asked Irving whether he had ever experienced discrimination or prejudice as an American Jew. He sighed, then answered me, "I experienced prejudice several times in my life, especially when applying for a job when someone of another religion told me of her misconceptions about Judaism. Fortunately, it was possible for me to change her negative viewpoint to a positive one."

Irving continued: "I feel fortunate to have been living as a Jew in America all my life. I have never been seriously discriminated against in college or in my profession." He added that he has always been very proud of his Jewish heritage, proud also of the great strides Jews have made in science, art, literature, and music. Although Jews in America are a very small part of the population, their achievements greatly outweigh their numbers.

I noticed a similar pattern in Russian society, where fewer than 1 percent are Jews, but a high proportion of Jews are scientists, engineers, and technicians. However, they are forced to hide their Jewishness. Jews cannot observe traditions in Russia. A circumcision was done for my fifteen-year-old son only here, in America. I expect that those prohibitions have influenced the Russian Jews' mentality. Thus, I asked, "Do you see a difference between American and Russian Jews?" He answered, "I see many differences between American and Russian Jews, and I believe that I know the reasons for these differences. I agree with you that in Russia Jews are made to feel ashamed of the label 'zhid.'* Russian Jews know nothing about Jewish history. It was against the law to circumcise a male child or have a Jewish marriage ceremony. Here in America a Jew has the privilege of choosing whether he wants to observe his traditions or not."

I was full of questions: "Why the Jews? Why were these people who never constituted more than a small minority singled out as scapegoats in Russia?" His answer was full of wisdom and understanding, "It is always necessary to have a scapegoat; it relieves people of the responsibility of taking the blame for their own problems and mistakes. The Jews in Russia have always been disliked and treated badly. Perhaps it is because they excelled in all fields. They worked hard to become educated and performed well in whatever positions they held."

During the interview, Irving, his wife, and I were sitting at a table in their comfortable, small apartment. I asked questions about his attitude toward the new immigrants, about the advantages and disadvantages he sees for America. Because I am an immigrant, I've received assistance to come to America. I thank Americans for this help and feel sorry because it takes money from American taxpayers. Irving smiled, then answered, "America is a country of immigrants. The only native-born Americans are the American Indians. This country has welcomed the oppressed and the persecuted since its inception. If you study American history, the arts and sciences and social institutions of this country, you will find that people who settled here from every country in the world added to the greatness of America. I am sure that some Russian immigrants will contribute in a positive way to this country."

*zhid: an insulting name for a Jewish person

I enjoyed meeting with Irving and his wife. I received full and truly interesting
answers to my questions. And I had a comfortable and relaxed feeling, as if I were
in my grandmother's house.

As we parted, Irving said, "Larisa, you made the right choice to come to
America. You are making many efforts to achieve your goal and to improve your
English. My wife and I will be happy to help you. We invite you, when you have
time, to come visit us. Take care! Be happy!"

Reading 3 Reflecting on the Reading

1 Questions provide the foundation for every successful interview. Working
with a partner, reread the essay and underline each question Zubataya
asked. Put a *D* next to every question that is a *direct quotation* enclosed
in quotation marks. Put an *I* next to every question that is expressed as an
indirect quotation without quotation marks, such as *I asked Irving where he
was born.* Now practice changing direct into indirect quotations by rewriting
two of the direct-quotation questions as indirect quotations. Then compare
your answers with another pair of students.

> **Example**
> **Direct quotation:** "What do you think about prejudice?"
> **Indirect quotation:** I asked Irving what he thought about prejudice.

2 In paragraph 4, Irving states, "One is not born with prejudice. It has to be
learned." Do you agree with this statement? With your partner or a small
group, discuss some of the ways in which children learn to be prejudiced
against people who are different from them in some way.

3 Think of a topic that interests you in the same way that prejudice interested
Zubataya. Write down your topic and write five questions about this topic.
Then write the name (or names) of people you could interview to find out
answers to your questions. Share these notes with your partner or group and
see whether they have any suggestions about people you could interview.

4 In paragraph 10, Irving says, "It is always necessary to have a scapegoat;
it relieves people of the responsibility of taking the blame for their own
problems and mistakes." Look up the word *scapegoat* in the dictionary
and discuss its meaning with your partner or group. Then freewrite in
your journal about any people or groups you know about who have been
scapegoats.

Interview with Andrei

Young Ja Lee

Young Ja Lee, a student from Korea, interviewed a Russian man she had met in a previous English course. She decided to focus her interview on a common problem experienced by older immigrants – the difficult adjustments involved when people give up the prestigious jobs they held in their native countries and have to work in low-level jobs in the new country. As you read this essay, think about whether you know anyone who reminds you of Andrei.

1 I often see many immigrants in the United States who used to hold highly professional jobs in their native countries but now make their living by working in low-skilled fields. These jobs are far from their once prestigious professions.

2 Andrei (not his real name) is a Russian native who was born and raised in Siberia. He went to college and became a metallurgical engineer. He worked for the Siberia Railroad Company for many years. Then he immigrated to the United States. At that time he was in his early fifties. Since his immigration to this country, he has been working as a cleaning man.

3 I asked him how he liked his present job. He sighed, then answered with a strong Russian accent, "I don't like the job. Doesn't have any interest. I can't talk to people about art, literature, or anything. No discussion about intellectual things!" He shook his head with a slight motion of resignation.

4 He tried to find a job as an engineer in the railroad construction and maintenance fields only to learn that the railroad business in the United States was history for bygone days. He said, "Nobody construct railroad in this country. I had a very interesting job in Russia. I loved it. So much activity in my job. I was in-charge metallurgical engineer of the railroad company covering from the Pacific Ocean to Lake Baikal." He added that Lake Baikal was the coldest area in Siberia. And he lived near this lake.

5 When he graduated from high school, he didn't want to go to engineering school at all. "I wanted to study languages. But I was forced to go to engineering school by my parents." He added, "Because in Soviet Union, you make more money and have more opportunities in society. When I first got a job as an engineer, my salary was three times more than my sister's. Do you know she was a professor in the university at that time?" He was content with his job and enjoyed his high salary. He was happy that he had listened to his parents' advice.

6 I asked him why he gave in to his parents. He smiled, saying, "In my country, children were and are raised to respect their elders. That's why, even though I wanted to study languages, I listened to my parents and their advice. In the United States young people don't have much respect toward their elders like parents, old people, or teachers. It's sad. I think this is a serious problem. Old people are much wiser and know what is the best for the young ones."

I pointed out that a cleaning job wasn't highly regarded socially. I asked, "Do you feel uncomfortable to tell your friends, especially Russians, what you do for a living now?" He replied quickly with a slight tinge of impatience, "I never make any secret. Doesn't matter who they are. All my friends, actors and scientists, when they ask me, I tell them without hesitation. For the time being, I have to do something. The real shame is being lazy and don't do nothing. I believe in hard labor." 7

"Hard labor!" he repeated. Then, in my imagination, I drew a picture of Andrei wearing a fur coat, a fur hat, and a pair of fur boots working in snow-covered Siberia filled with arctic wind, constructing the endless railroad over the bare horizon. It must have been hard labor physically. But for this very intelligent man working as a cleaning man, it must be hard labor emotionally. "Do you miss your old job?" I asked. "Yes, I do. Sometimes, a lot," he quietly answered. 8

Since there wasn't any hope of working as an engineer for the railroad as long as he lived in the United States, I asked him whether he planned to keep his present job as a lifelong occupation. He leaned his chest toward the table. His voice became sharp. He stared at me for a couple of seconds. Then he declared, "No! No! No! Never!! Young, if someone tells me today that I would be a cleaning man the rest of my life, I'll draw all my money from the bank, spend them all, then I'll commit suicide!" His voice and his eyes revealed his misery, which he had never spoken of before, and at the same time displayed his determination to get out of his present situation. 9

He speaks four languages very fluently besides his mother tongue, Russian: German, Slovak, Polish, and English. He is studying at Hunter College, majoring in Russian and Slavic languages. He had always wanted to study languages, even when he was a young boy. Now as a middle-aged man, he is pursuing his lifelong wish. I remember the two beautiful short essays which he wrote in our English class. They were so well written they became the professor's collection items. He said, "I want to become a translator in United Nations in international committee. Also I look forward to be a teacher of Russian literature." 10

Now it was time for him to go to work, the night shift. He studies during the day and works at night. He headed for the subway. The air was cold. But still the crisp October sunlight was falling on his back. Suddenly I felt that he was lonely and homesick right at that moment. I called out, "Andrei!" He looked back. I put my thumbs up. "You will make it!" I shouted. He grinned and waved. Then he disappeared into the crowd. 11

Reading 4   Reflecting on the Reading

1 Find one direct quotation from Andrei that tells something important about his attitude toward his present job. Discuss with a partner or small group what readers learn from Andrei's own words that they might not have understood if Lee had expressed these things indirectly, that is, in *her* words.

2 In this essay, Lee reports on Andrei's nonverbal reactions to her questions. In paragraph 3, for example, she tells us that after saying what he did not like

about his job as a cleaning man, "He shook his head with a slight motion of resignation." Underline two other examples of places in the essay where Lee describes Andrei's nonverbal communication – tone of voice, facial expression, body language, and so on. For each example, discuss what these details tell us about Andrei.

3 Reread the concluding paragraph of the essay. Discuss why you think Lee decided to end her essay this way. Do you like this ending? Why or why not?

4 In paragraph 8, Lee focuses on Andrei's phrase *hard labor* and talks about two kinds of hard labor, physical and emotional. In your journal, write a definition for each of these two kinds of labor. Give examples from your own life or the experiences of people you know to illustrate both types of hard labor.

One of Us
Ahmet Erdogan

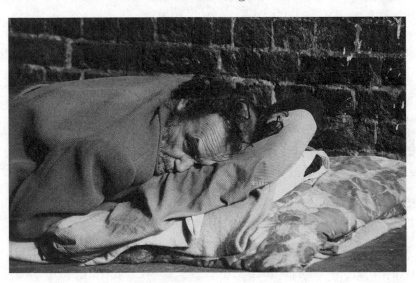

In this essay, a student from Turkey reveals how a chance encounter with a homeless man led to a deeper understanding of the problem of homelessness – and of the society in which we live. Before you begin to read, think about some possible meanings of the title, "One of Us."

When we see a filthy man in torn clothing sleeping on a street corner, we look at him with contempt or with pity. These people are called "homeless." There are very few who worry about what these people, whose bones only meet the warmth in summer, do in winter. Although they live in a city with millions of other people, they are forsaken and lonely. Some of them talk to themselves. Others tell their thoughts and feelings with their eyes. Nobody asks them their thoughts. If they

1

are interviewed by a reporter, he broadcasts or publishes distorted truths. And by doing so, he reinforces the prejudice of the rest of the society about the homeless people.

Once I had this prejudice, false-consciousness, and it isolated me from society. Now, I can see that it also isolated me from myself. When I first saw him, I wasn't aware of this fact.

It was a cold winter evening. I had pulled my hat down over my ears, covered my face with a scarf, and put on my thick overcoat. But I still felt the bitter cold. I walked down into the subway. When the train came, the crowd pushed to get inside. I knew there wouldn't be an empty seat. But I was tired, and, with hope, my eyes looked for a place to sit. On my right there were seats for at least four people. I sat joyfully. Not one minute had passed when I raised my head with a feeling that all eyes were concentrated on me. I looked at my clothes. There wasn't anything strange about them. I soon became involved with the thoughts on my mind. This time my thoughts were broken off with a weight on my left shoulder. He was an old man. His white beard had darkened with the grime. He looked in my eyes with his own blue eyes, which hardly opened because of sleeplessness. His dark, dirty face – unwashed maybe for weeks – became red for a moment. He bit his lip, which was almost lost under his mustache and beard. Then, taking his head between his hands, he tried to go back to sleep.

The crowd on the train walked off at the second stop. I was watching the old man. His shoes were worn out. He had covered his legs up to the knees with tatters. The darkened skin of his knees could be seen through a hole in his pants. With a strange feeling, I stood up from my seat and sat just across from him. At his left on the seat there was a big bag which was full of remnants of food and other things. When the train stopped suddenly, he awoke and some of the food in the bag spread over the seat. The old man put the food back in the bag with special care. Then he took the remnant of a hamburger with his right hand and shoved his mustache away from his mouth with his left hand. Just as he had bitten into the hamburger, he felt me watching him. That aged, wrinkled face had become red with a childish shame. After he had barely swallowed the food in his mouth, he wiped his mustache with his hand. He tore a piece of paper, rolled it thickly like a cigarette. He took the rolled paper between his lips and started to search his pockets. After a while, he gave up the search. He took the rolled paper between two fingers, looked at it with hopeless eyes, and threw it down on the floor. And again he went back to his thoughts. I took my cigarettes and matches out of my pocket. He raised his head and started to look at my face with strange eyes. "Take, Uncle," I said. "I think you want to smoke. I know how difficult it is sometimes not having a cigarette." He was just looking at me strangely. "I already have decided to quit smoking. Since I don't need this anymore. . . ." Then he smiled, took the pack, and lighted a cigarette with his shaking hands.

"Isn't it forbidden to smoke here?" I asked.

"Yes, but this is my home. If I go out, I freeze," he replied. And he continued to talk after each drag. "They call us bums. No one likes us. They look at us as if we are animals, though animals don't suffer in this country. They are fed with special food. Did you ever see a dog with a nice sweater on, little boots on his feet?"

He extinguished his cigarette and continued, "They say we are lazy. We are not working, not because we don't want to but because we couldn't find a job. . . ." 7

His head between his hands, he just stared ahead, and continued, "You know, my son, many years ago we didn't have this much unemployment. Then there was no fear of being laid off. . . ." His hands fell away from his head. It was easy to see the anger in his face. For a while he forgot my being there as he stared ahead. And probably many thoughts, memories were reflecting on his mind. "You know, my son, if there are a lot of hungry people who are willing to work even for nothing, there is no need to pay you more." While he was telling this, he closed his eyes and continued. "They didn't bring those people here to save them or to help them. On the contrary, they brought them here to make both them and us slaves for them. A new slavery." He opened his eyes, but he couldn't bear the lights and closed them again. He raised his head heavily while starting to talk again, "The fear of being laid off makes us slaves. But they are not contented with this. They destroyed everything, anything good." 8

Then he stopped his talking. That anger appeared in his face. Suddenly he opened his eyes. Sheltering his eyes with his hands, he continued to talk: "How can I take a shower? Where? If I take, I freeze. I don't have anything to put on. Look, you have a hat on your head, a coat, and for sure a nest to sleep." 9

My face had become red. I felt this and a pain deep inside of me. I wanted to say something but I couldn't move my tongue in my mouth, as if it were swollen. Then I asked in order to change the subject, "Uncle, you are always saying 'they.' Who are 'they'?" 10

Fearfully he looked over his left and then his right shoulder. And again he took his head between his hands and stared. His lips had sealed, as if he were troubled. After a short silence he continued slowly, "You know, in many neighborhoods the apartments were set on fire, purposefully. If you take a walk through these streets, you will see hundreds of such apartments." I had already missed my station, and we had come to the last stop. 11

On the way back he kept talking. He had been taken into a mental hospital. As he said, first he was happy about that but after living there a couple of months he couldn't stand – in his words – "the animal trainers," and he escaped. He feeds himself with the remnants of food from big hotels such as the Plaza and the Sheraton, which, according to him, in one day throw away food with which thousands of homeless people could be fed. When we came back to the stop where I was to get off, he said, "We lost the loving respect and trust, my son, because they wanted it so, but now I am happy because I learned that there are still men who have not been robotized. . . ." He had not finished his words, yet I got off. As the train pulled away, he kept on talking. 12

On my way home and for the rest of the night, all this talk reflected on my mind. He was a man, one of us. The only difference was that he was one of the victims of "they." And the number of these victims is increasing. This means that one day I too may be a victim of "they." My mind was confused. But I had learned one thing: that he and the people like him do not deserve to be blamed, to be looked down on. It should be "they." "They" are the cause of this unprecedented hunger and suffering, so "they" should be blamed, not the homeless people. 13

1 Discuss with a partner or small group what you think Erdogan's purpose is in the first two paragraphs. Why does he wait until paragraph 3 to introduce the homeless man who is the focus of most of the essay? How would the essay have been different if Erdogan had omitted the first two paragraphs?

2 Reread paragraph 4. Discuss which of the following words best describes the writer's feelings about the homeless man, as portrayed in this paragraph. Then discuss which words describe your own feelings about the homeless man.

a disgusted **b** sympathetic **c** curious **d** hostile

3 Discuss Erdogan's purpose in writing this essay. What did he want his readers to do or think? Do you feel he succeeded in achieving his purpose? Explain.

4 Both the homeless man and the writer refer to "they" throughout the essay. In your opinion, who is being referred to by "they"? Do you agree that "they" are the ones to blame for the suffering of the poor and homeless? Freewrite about your answers to these questions in your journal.

Reading 6 **Professional Writing**

An Immigrant's First Day on the Job

Saravanan Rangaswamy

From *September 11: An Oral History*

Dean E. Murphy

Murphy, a reporter for the New York Times, *covered the aftermath of the terrorist attacks that occurred in the United States on September 11, 2001. Eventually, he published a book – an oral history – containing the stories of people he had interviewed for this assignment. The selection that follows, which is reprinted from Murphy's book, is the dramatic first-person account of Saravanan Rangaswamy, an immigrant from India who was scheduled to begin a new job on September 11 at a company located on the 40th floor of Number 1, World Trade Center. Before you read this story, think about your own experiences on that historic day.*

It was my first day so I thought I would get there early. I was excited to work on a project in the World Trade Center, which was a famous landmark. It had been fun being in the tower for my interview. They said my start time was nine a.m., but I was inside the building by 8:15. I told the security people in the lobby that I was new and that they should contact my boss on the 40th floor for clearance to let me in. They called upstairs, but there was no one there. So they left a message for my boss to call the lobby.

There were about ten security people there screening everyone coming into the building. I stood there and watched everyone as they arrived for work. I had a food bar with me, so I munched that. But no phone call came. I guess my boss wasn't expecting me so early. That was okay. I waited patiently. One of the security guards explained to me that they could not let me upstairs until they got the word from my boss. Eventually, I would get my own ID and could pass through the scanner, but today I would have to wait.

I had been standing there about a half hour when I heard a huge blast. I thought a bomb had gone off. Immediately, everyone around me started running toward the doors. I just followed them. I heard one of the elevators come crashing down at full speed. There was another big noise and then smoke everywhere. I had managed to get into the revolving door just before the thick black smoke reached me. I had only been at the World Trade Center twice before – once to visit the observation floor and once for my job interview ten days earlier – so I didn't know my way around. I just followed the crowd. In less than a minute, I was about 50 yards from the building, where I stopped and tried to figure out what had just happened.

There were a lot of us gathering on the street outside. Someone next to me said that an airplane had hit the building. When I looked up, I saw a huge hole in the side of the building with smoke coming out, but no sign of an airplane. There was debris falling everywhere. Most of it was paper but there were also big chunks of things I could not make out. I saw something like a huge container falling and it landed about 50 yards down the road from me in a big group of people.

I really didn't feel afraid, though. I was outside and far from the burning building. That feeling changed when I spotted people falling. That was the most horrible thing I had ever seen. The crowd around me started waving at the top of the building. Some people near me were crying. When I looked, I saw three or four bodies falling from the sky. They were landing right next to the building. That was a difficult thing to see right in front of my eyes. I had been outside two or three minutes, when I said to myself: Let me leave this place.

I took four or five steps through the crowd when my world went blank. The 6
next nineteen hours passed in a flash. I woke up at four o'clock the next morning
in a bed at Bellevue Hospital. I had undergone four and a half hours of surgery on
my skull the day before. My hair had been shaved and I had an incision from the
top of my cranium to just above my left eyebrow. I had nuts and bolts and a metal
plate inside. I had cerebral lacerations from a broken bone. The doctors told me
I was lucky. A piece of the bone was pointing closely toward my brain. Any closer,
and who knows what might have happened. I wouldn't be able to open my left eye
for a week. But, most importantly, I was alive and recovering well.

I had absolutely no recollection of what had happened, but I found out very 7
quickly that it was part of a very big event. I had a cell phone with me. It had
35 messages from my wife and from friends who knew I was going to the World
Trade Center for work that morning. I gave my number at home to a nurse and she
called my wife for me. But Sripriya was not there. During the nineteen hours I had
been unconscious, she had been frantically searching for me. At that moment, she
was in Jersey City with three or four friends trying to find a way into Manhattan.
A friend was staying at our house, answered the phone and immediately called my
wife on a cell phone to let her know where I was.

They were a little surprised to hear the name of the hospital. Bellevue was 8
one of the many hospitals and police stations they had called asking about me.
As it turned out, the hospital had my name reversed. My wife was asking for
Mr. Saravanan Rangaswamy. But I was somehow registered as Mr. Rangaswamy
Saravanan. I am not sure how that happened, but the many traditions involving
Indian names can be confusing for Americans. For example, my wife's last name is
my first name, which probably added to the confusion when she called inquiring
about me.

My wife got into Manhattan that afternoon and we had a very happy reunion. 9
I needed to stay in the hospital for eight days. I was so thankful for the care I
received. Everyone was so nice to me. I was soon able to piece together what had
happened during my nineteen hours of unconsciousness. Something fell from the
sky that morning and hit me on the head. When I fell to the ground bleeding,
someone pulled me inside a shop and the shopkeeper called the police. The police
loaded me in an ambulance, which took me to Beekman Hospital. But they looked
at my injuries there and said they couldn't do anything for me, that I had to go
to Bellevue. A doctor there actually got behind the wheel of the ambulance and
drove me to Bellevue. Seven minutes after I got to Bellevue, they started the
surgery.

I feel I am lucky and I thank God for saving my life. I have responsibilities 10
to my family and I have a lot of things I want to do with my life. I am glad God
saved me. Even so, I went through a rough time. Lehman Brothers was very nice
and held my job for two months. But I wasn't physically all right even after two
months and I didn't take up their offer. I am not working yet and my wife and
I got some financial help from charitable organizations like the American Red
Cross, which paid for my house rent and bills. We were very thankful for their
timely help.

To make things more difficult, two or three days after I got out of the hospital, I got a call from India. One of my brothers passed away in a train accident. I am the eldest, and I was going to leave for India immediately, but my friends advised me not to go. My family in India did not know about what happened to me in the World Trade Center. When they called, one of my friends told them that I was okay. I did not want to worry them. But if I went to India with my shaved head and 65 stitches, it would be a big shock for them. So I didn't go until January, after my hair had grown back and the stitches were removed. Still I looked bad. My mother started crying when she saw me and asked what had happened. I told her that I had fallen down walking on snow. My brothers didn't believe me, but I managed to keep that story for a week. When I finally told them the truth, my father asked me not to go back to the United States. 11

"No more U.S.A.," he said. "I want to see you alive and healthy." 12

"This was an isolated incident," I told him. "God will take care of us." 13

I have three more years on my work permit, and my wife and I expect to stay all three of those years. The U.S.A. is a great country. I am proud to be here. 14

Reading 6 Reflecting on the Reading

1 This account provides many specific details to describe what Rangaswamy experienced on September 11, 2001. Underline two or three details that you found particularly effective. Discuss the details you selected with a partner or small group.

2 In another color, underline all the details related to the passage of time. Choose two or three of these and explain to your partner or group why each one is important.

3 In your opinion, which of the words below best summarizes Rangaswamy's feelings about what happened on September 11? Find specific details in the text that support your opinion and explain your answer to your partner or group.

a terror

b courage

c gratitude

d determination

4 Working with a partner, go to a public place, such as a park or a shopping mall, and interview two or three people about their memories of September 11. Take notes – either during or after the interview – on what you learn. Report the results of your interviews to the class.

TECHNIQUES WRITERS USE

Interviewing

The techniques for effective interviewing vary somewhat depending on the specific circumstances. However, the following guidelines are helpful for most interviewing situations.

- Before the interview, make a list of questions you want to ask, but do not limit yourself to those questions.

- Encourage a relaxed atmosphere during the interview. Choose a comfortable and quiet location. You may want to offer your interviewee something to eat or drink.

- If possible, record the interview using either an audio or video recorder. If you cannot record the interview, take brief notes. Be sure to write down key words and phrases that you want to remember.

- Be an active listener and ask follow-up questions to be sure you understand or to get additional information. For example: "Could you tell me more about . . . ?" or "I'm not sure I understood what you meant. Could you explain that again?"

- Get as many specific details as possible. Asking your interviewee to tell a story often elicits details. For example: "Do you remember a specific event that happened during your early schooling?" or "Can you think of a story that would help me understand what it feels like to work in your job?"

- Do not interrupt your interviewee or talk too much yourself.

- Within 24 hours of conducting the interview, write a detailed account of what you remember. Be sure to include some direct quotations of what the person said, and remember to describe nonverbal aspects of the interview, such as the person's physical appearance, facial expressions, or body language.

Task 5.1 Analyze

1 Read the following segment of the audio transcript from Eleonor Maldonado's interview with her grandmother, who was born in Puerto Rico.

> **Question:** Grandma, can you describe your childhood in the village?
> **Answer:** Look, Granddaughter, those were dog days. We were living in a small shack built of straw and bamboo sticks. During the day the rain and the sun rays filtered throughout the many holes in the walls and ceiling, and at night we fell asleep counting the stars and praying to God for a pleasant night without rain. Also we didn't have beds. My mother slept in a hammock and my sister and I every night made a bed out of burlap sacks filled with straw. There was also no running water or toilet. The water was carried in a tin can from a nearby well, and the biological necessities were done under some bushes near the house.

Q: Who helped your mother to support the family?

A: My mother was the only breadwinner of the family, so she worked on a farm picking sweet potatoes all day and at night spent many hours weaving "Panama hats." Each Saturday morning Don Thomas, our neighbor, would take the hats to sell them at the nearby town, and with the money received he would bring us some groceries and once in a while, especially for Christmas or during the town's feasts, a piece of cloth for making dresses, a box of Pompeii face powder, or a small bottle of Evening in Paris perfume. Our diet consisted of sweet potatoes, cornmeal, and dried codfish. A half pound of coffee was blended with other toasted grains so there was enough coffee for the whole week. Meat we ate only at Christmastime, when the owner of the farm for whom my mother was working killed a pig and gave us a piece.

Q: Grandma, at what age did you get married?

A: I think I was fourteen years old when I met your grandfather. He was a very handsome Spaniard who was well known for being a good dancer. He was also very poor and at an early age started to work in the field to help his mother raise three brothers and two sisters after his father's death. He also didn't have the opportunity to go to school, so his life was a continuous struggle. A year later we got married, and while he was working in the field cutting sugarcane, I was home taking care of a few domestic animals.

Q: How many children did you have?

A: Oh, please, I don't know how to count as I didn't have the opportunity to go to school, but my oldest son said that I have eighteen alive and a couple of what people called miscarriages.

Q: Grandma, I would like to ask you something else. How do you compare the life you have today with the one you had years ago?

A: Oh my God, today I feel like a rich person. I have a house with electricity and running water. Also I have a toilet in the house. Quite a few dresses and shoes and a Social Security check. I don't have to worry about anything, but still I would like to know how to sign my name instead of making a cross symbol every time I have to sign my name.

2 Sometimes in an interview, it is only necessary to get a brief answer to a question. But most of the time, you want to encourage your interviewee to talk freely and give you as much information as possible. With a partner, look carefully at the questions the student asked. Find one question that you think is open-ended – a question that might lead to a long and detailed answer. Find another question that might lead to a short, simple answer. Now practice writing one question of each type. Then, in a mock interview with your partner, ask your questions and listen to your partner's answers. Discuss the results. Was the length of your partner's answers what you expected?

3 Because Maldonado's grandmother was such a good storyteller, there are many parts of this interview that the student might want to quote directly in her essay. Go through the transcript and underline three quotations that you think she should include. Compare your choices with those of your partner. Explain why you chose the particular quotations you did.

4 With your partner or a small group, discuss what you learned about interviewing techniques from reading this transcript and doing steps 2 and 3 above. What specific techniques do you plan to use in the interview you will conduct for your essay?

Task 5.2 *Practice*

1 Choose a classmate, friend, or family member to interview informally for about 10 minutes. Pick a person you feel comfortable with and who is enthusiastic about being interviewed. Remember that this is just a practice session and not designed to provide material for your essay.

2 Before the interview, prepare a short list of questions. The questions may be on any subject but will, of course, be influenced by the person you have chosen to interview.

3 During the interview, take notes or tape the conversation.

4 Then ask the other person to interview you.

5 After these informal interviews, freewrite on the following questions: What did you learn about interviewing? What question got the longest answer? Why? What question got the shortest answer? Why? What question led to the most interesting response? Why?

6 Discuss your results with a small group or as a class. What things will you try to do when you interview someone more formally? What will you try to avoid doing?

Formulating a Thesis Statement

A thesis statement is the main idea of an essay – a sentence that expresses the writer's position or opinion on a given topic. In personal writing, the thesis is often implied rather than stated directly, but in more formal writing it is desirable to state the main idea explicitly, usually toward the beginning of the essay. American professors consider a clear thesis statement very important in formal writing.

It is important to realize that writers often don't know exactly what their thesis statement will be when they begin to write an essay. On many occasions, writers begin to see what their most important idea is only after they have written their first draft. Then they can state this controlling idea in or near the beginning of the second draft and use it to guide their argument. The thesis statement often continues to evolve and change slightly throughout the drafting and revising of an essay. So, while having a strong thesis statement is very important in writing successful academic essays, remember that your thesis may change after you complete the first draft. Good writers continue to question and refine their thesis statements through all stages of the writing process.

In most cases, a good thesis statement meets the following two criteria:

- A thesis statement states the writer's position on the topic.

These are thesis statements:

"American family life has benefited because of women working outside the home."

"Children are harmed when their mothers work outside the home."

These are* not *thesis statements:

"In this essay, I plan to discuss the changes that have taken place in American family life as a result of women working outside the home."
   (This sentence is an explanation of the topic, not a thesis.)

"Many American women work outside the home."
   (This sentence is simply a fact, not a thesis.)

- A thesis statement is arguable.

   In other words, a thesis statement is a statement that not everyone would agree with. The writer's job in the essay is to support this arguable thesis with evidence. For example, if your thesis was the second one above, "Children are harmed when their mothers work outside the home," you would have to provide examples, statistics, and reasoning to convince the reader that your opinion is believable.

Task 5.3 *Analyze*

1 Read the sentences below, all of which make statements about the following topic: Old People in American Society.

   a The proportion of old people in American society is increasing rapidly.

   b Many American television commercials are aimed at elderly viewers.

   c Because the United States is a youth-oriented culture, old people are not respected.

   d As a larger proportion of the population becomes elderly, old people will gain more respect in American society.

2 In a small group, discuss which of the sentences above fit the definition of a thesis statement. Which sentences do not fit the definition? Explain your answers.

3 Discuss which of the sentences that you have decided are thesis statements would lead to the most interesting essay. Why?

Practice

1 With your group, choose one of the following topics and write three possible thesis statements for it:

  a The American university system

  b The difference between high school and college

  c The difference between the roles of women (or men) in your grandparents' time and today

2 Choose the thesis statement that your group feels is strongest. Have a group member write this thesis statement on the board.

3 As a class, discuss what the various thesis statements on the board have in common and how they are different. Which thesis statement would you choose if you had to write an essay based on only one of them? Why?

Clustering

A challenge writers face in more formal writing assignments is deciding how to organize their ideas effectively. One organizational strategy that students – especially students who are visual learners – often find helpful is clustering. The cluster diagram below shows how Maldonado mapped out the ideas from her interview with her grandmother (page 146).

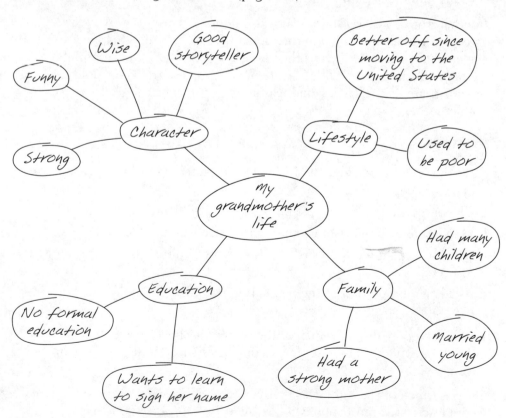

Analyze

1 Working with a partner, look at the cluster diagram and decide which of the circles in the diagram represents the most general topic, the topic that includes all the others.

2 What are the major subtopics?

3 What are three examples of supporting details?

4 Discuss how you think the student can use this diagram as she prepares to write her first draft.

Task 5.6 *Practice*

1 Working with a small group, choose one of the three topics from Task 5.4.

2 Write the topic (for example, "the American university system") in the center of a blank piece of paper and circle it.

3 Think of several subtopics and write them around the main topic. Circle each one and draw lines connecting them to the main topic.

4 Think of as many examples, facts, and specific details that relate to the different subtopics as possible. Write each one down close to the subtopic it most closely relates to, circle it, and draw a connecting line to the subtopic. Write down as many things as you can think of, even though you may not use all of them in your essay.

5 Look at these clusters and discuss which subtopics you would want to write about in an essay on your topic. Which are the most interesting to you? Which do you have the most information about?

6 As a class, look at the cluster diagrams of two or three groups. Discuss the thought process each group went through in organizing the clusters.

INTERNET SEARCH

The Internet searches you will do in Part III (Chapters 5, 6, and 7) are related to the essay assignments. The purpose of these searches is for you to gather useful information that will help you develop your essays.

In each chapter, you will be given a choice of two essay assignment options and two corresponding Internet search options. You should do the Internet search that relates to the assignment you choose. If you are not sure which essay assignment you prefer, you can begin by doing part of each Internet search. Then complete the Internet search for the assignment that seems more appealing.

In this chapter, both essay assignments are based on interviews that you will conduct. The first option is to write an essay based on a life-history interview.

Examples of essays that are responses to this type of assignment are "A Reward from Buddha" and "Unfinished Interview." The second option is to write an essay based on a topical interview, such as "My First Interview," "Interview with Andrei," and "One of Us."

Go now to page 153 for details of the two essay assignment options. Decide which one you want to do. Then proceed with the appropriate Internet search. For the assignments in this chapter, it may be more useful for you to wait until *after* you have conducted your interview to do your Internet search. Or you may decide to do the search first and then do another, more specific search after conducting your interview and writing your first draft.

Option 1 ▶ *Locating Background Information for a Life-History Interview*

1 With a partner, discuss the best keywords to locate background information that may help you to understand more about the person you plan to interview. For example, Zhong Chen, the author of "A Reward from Buddha," might do a search for the keywords *Chinese sailors World War II*. Tatyana Dyachenko, the author of "Unfinished Interview," might search for the keywords *World War II Ukraine*.

2 Type in the keywords on your preferred Web browser, such as Ask.com, Encarta.msn.com, Google.com, Looksmart.com, Lycos.com, Netscape.com, or Yahoo.com.

3 Locate two sources providing information that relates in some way to the life of the person you plan to interview. Take notes on these sources.

4 Share the results of your Internet search with a small group. Discuss what you learned about your interviewee's background and what you learned about searching the Internet from this activity.

5 Based on the information you found on the Internet and your group discussion, write two or three questions that you would like to ask in your interview.

Option 2 ▶ *Locating Background Information for a Topical Interview*

1 With a partner, discuss the best keywords to use to locate information that will deepen your understanding of the topic you plan to explore in your essay. For example, Larisa Zubataya, the author of "My First Interview," might do a search using the keywords *Jews in America*. Ahmet Erdogan, the author of "One of Us," might do a search for *homelessness* and *New York City*.

2 Type in the keywords on your preferred Web browser, such as Ask.com, Encarta.msn.com, Google.com, Looksmart.com, Lycos.com, Netscape.com, or Yahoo.com.

3 Locate two sources that provide useful information for your topic. Take notes on information that you might use in your essay.

4 Share the results of this Internet search with a small group. Discuss what you learned about your interview topic and what you learned about searching the Internet from this activity.

5 Based on the information you found on the Internet and your group discussion, write two or three questions that you would like to ask in your interview.

ESSAY ASSIGNMENT

talk [handwritten]

Angla [handwritten]
Interview my grandmother [handwritten]

Option 1 **Life-History Interview**

If you choose this option, you will interview someone about his or her life and write about an important theme in that person's life. Has the person been successful in fulfilling his or her goals? How has the person's life been shaped by economic or political forces beyond his or her control? These questions, and many more, arise when you begin to reflect on someone's personal history.

One good source for finding an interviewee is your own family. Keep in mind that older family members often have more interesting stories to tell simply because they have lived longer. In addition to your family, however, there are plenty of other possibilities for a life-history interview. For example, one of our students wrote about an interview he conducted with the parent of a friend. Another wrote about an interview with the night watchman at a dormitory. A third student interviewed a deaf teenager she tutored after school (the interview was conducted in sign language).

The purpose of this essay is to convey one or more themes that are important in the life of the person you interviewed. Think of your audience as younger members of the interviewee's family who would like to learn more about their relative's life.

Reread the writing you have already done for this chapter to see whether it gives you ideas for this assignment.

Option 2 **Topical Interview**

If you choose this option, you will focus your interview and writing on a topic of your own choice. Possible topics include major historical events, such as a war or depression; a social issue, such as the criminal justice system or the changing role of women in society; or a career or job you would like to learn more about. For example, in one class a student interviewed his uncle about the civil war in his native country of Moldova; another student interviewed a classmate to learn more about the position of women in Russia; a third student, who was researching the medical practice of cesarean section, interviewed his sister, who had had two babies delivered by this method; a fourth student interviewed a professor at her college about a career in foreign-language teaching. As you can see from these examples, you can choose to interview someone you know well or a total stranger.

For this assignment, you can interview one person, or you can interview two or three people to get different perspectives on your topic. You may want to do several short preliminary interviews with different people before you decide which person (or people) to focus on.

The purpose of this assignment is to draw a conclusion based on what you learned from your interview(s). You may decide to limit your analysis to just one person you interviewed. Or you may choose to explain how your interviewee's experience fits into some larger pattern. Think of the audience for your essay as other college students who are interested in learning more about this topic.

Reread the writing you have already done for this chapter to see whether it gives you ideas for this assignment.

Generating Ideas

For Option 1

1 To succeed in this assignment, it is important to choose a person who is willing to talk freely about his or her life history and who has interesting stories to share. Write down five people you think might be good interviewees – for example, a teacher, a friend, or your grandmother.

2 Exchange your list with a partner who is also doing Option 1. Discuss why you want to interview each of the people on your list.

3 Based on this discussion, select the one person on your list you would most like to interview and write down five questions you could ask that person.

4 Discuss these questions with your partner and, taking your partner's reactions into consideration, make any changes in your questions that seem necessary.

5 Make arrangements to conduct your interview. Before conducting the interview, review the general advice about interviewing techniques on page 146.

For Option 2

1 To succeed in this assignment, it is important to choose a topic that you sincerely wish to learn more about. Write down five possible topics – for example, a career you might want to pursue in the future, a social problem, such as homelessness, that is of concern to you, or people's attitudes toward an important issue, such as higher education or methods of childrearing.

2 Show your list to a partner who is also doing Option 2. Discuss people you could interview to get more information on each of these topics.

3 Based on this discussion, rank your three favorite topics in order, starting with your first choice. Write down five questions you would like to ask about your first topic.

4 Discuss these questions with your partner and make any changes that seem necessary.

5 Make arrangements to conduct the interview. If you cannot find a suitable interviewee for your first topic, try to find someone for your second or third choice of topic. Before conducting the interview, review the general advice about interviewing techniques on page 146.

Organizing Ideas

For Options 1 and 2

1 No more than 24 hours after you conduct the interview, spend 20 to 30 minutes freewriting about what you learned. Here are some questions to consider:

a What was the most important thing you learned from the interview?

b What was the most surprising thing?

c What were some of the nonverbal aspects of the interview – tone of voice, gestures, and so on – that caught your attention?

d Write out two or three direct quotations of the person's exact words that seemed especially important. Explain why these quotations seem significant to you.

e What one word would you choose to sum up your interview? Why did you choose this word?

2 Make a cluster diagram of ideas from your interview. Then decide which ones you could include in your essay. (Review clustering, on page 150, if necessary.)

3 In a small group of students who chose your option, discuss the results of your interviews and compare your cluster diagrams. What major theme or themes do you find in each other's interviews?

Working Toward a Thesis Statement

1 For Option 1
Taking into consideration your freewriting, your cluster diagram, and the comments of your group members, identify what you think is the most important theme in your interviewee's life. For example, in "Unfinished Interview," Tatyana Dyachenko's theme might be the hardships of war. In "A Reward from Buddha," Zhong Chen's theme might be his uncle's persistence in overcoming the obstacles he faced in his early life.

For Option 2

Taking into consideration your freewriting, your cluster diagram, and the comments of your group members, identify what you think is the most important conclusion you can draw on your topic. For example, in "One of Us," Ahmet Erdogan draws the conclusion that society, not homeless people, is to blame for the problem of homelessness. Based on "Interview with Andrei," Young Ja Lee might write, "I learned that for Andrei, working in a low-prestige job as a cleaner is 'hard labor' emotionally."

2 For Options 1 and 2

Write two or three possible thesis statements for your essay. (Review "Formulating a Thesis Statement," on page 148, if necessary.) Then decide which thesis seems to best capture the life of the person you interviewed (for Option 1), or which thesis reflects most clearly what you learned about your topic (for Option 2).

3 For Options 1 and 2

Make a list of the evidence from your interview that you could use to support your thesis statement. Write down two or three direct quotations from your interview that relate to this thesis and that you could use in your essay.

Writing Tips

- **Include specific details that reveal your interviewee's character and opinions.**
  These can include details about the setting of the interview as well as details about the interviewee's appearance, manner of speaking, and body language. For example, in Reading 4, Young Ja Lee tells readers that Andrei "leaned his chest toward the table" and that "his voice became sharp." From these details we know that he is about to say something important. Details such as these can be essential in understanding the overall meaning of the interview.

- **Vary your use of direct and indirect quotations.**
  If you include too many direct quotations, the essay will seem more like the transcript of an interview rather than your own analysis of it. In deciding which quotations to include, ask yourself what was more important: what the person said or how he or she said it. In the first case, you may be able to paraphrase the quotation, that is, to express the same idea in your own words as an indirect quotation. Use direct quotations only where the person's exact words are particularly effective or reveal his or her character. Remember that you can also use your own direct speech to add variety to your essay.

- **Introduce the quotations you select with your own words.**
  The most common way to do this is with simple phrases like "she said" or "he replied." But for variety, think of other ways. If you have trouble introducing quotations, look back at the readings in this chapter to see how other writers have done it. For example, sometimes writers refer to the

interviewee's body language, as Ahmet Erdogan does in Reading 5: "His head between his hands, he just stared ahead, and continued, 'You know, my son, many years ago we didn't have this much unemployment. Then there was no fear of being laid off. . . .'" Another possibility is to describe the interviewee's emotions during the interview, as Tatyana Dyachenko does in Reading 2: "Here, my mother saw my expression (still with a piece of cookie that stuck in my throat) and cried to me, 'How many times have I told you, don't ask me questions about it! My children do not have to know these things!'"

Writing Your First Draft

Now, keeping the writing tips in mind, write the first draft of your essay. Refer to the notes you took on your interview, your freewriting, and your cluster diagram. As you are working on this first draft, do not slow yourself down by worrying about correct grammar and spelling; it is more important just to get your ideas down on paper so you have something to work with in later drafts.

REVISING YOUR ESSAY

Once you have put your ideas down on paper by completing the first draft, you can begin the revising process.

Responding to Your Peers

1 Working with a partner or a group of three, exchange and read the first drafts of your essays.

2 Fill out a copy of the "Peer Response Form" on page 162 for each of the first drafts you read. Focus on the ideas rather than the grammar and spelling. Point out only those mistakes that interfere with understanding.

3 Using the completed peer response forms as the basis for your discussion, have a peer conference to discuss your first drafts.

Making a Plan for Revising

Many students believe that it is the teacher's job to read their essays carefully and then tell them how to "fix" their writing. As you know, we feel that students get valuable response to their writing from peers. Even more important, however, is the response you, the writer, give to yourself. After you have received feedback from your peers and perhaps from your teacher, it is extremely important for *you* to decide how you can use these comments to improve the next draft of your essay.

Beginning with this chapter, we include a "Writer's Plan for Revising" for you to fill out. The questions on these forms relate to three important concerns:

- Understanding your own writing process
- Making sure you have effectively communicated what you wanted to express about your topic
- Trying to see your essay from your reader's point of view

Professional writers know that they are their own most important readers and responders. By answering the questions on the "Writer's Plans for Revising," you will learn more about how to be a reflective reader of your own writing. As you practice the skill of responding thoughtfully to your work, you too will gradually learn how to become your own best reader.

Writing Your Second Draft

1 Fill out the "Writer's Plan for Revising" on page 165.

2 Taking into consideration the feedback you have received from your peers and your own ideas about how to improve your essay, write your second draft.

EDITING YOUR ESSAY

When you are satisfied with the content and organization of your essay, you can begin the process of editing.

Grammar in Context: Using Direct and Indirect Quotations

Understanding how to use direct and indirect quotations is important for many college writing assignments. In this chapter, you used direct and indirect quotations in an essay based on an interview. The same skills are also very important in essays based on reading and essays based on research, as you will see in Chapters 6 and 7. Every time you quote from a published source, you are using a direct quotation; every time you paraphrase, or explain in your own words what an author said, you are using an indirect quotation.

The tasks that follow will give you a chance to check your understanding of direct and indirect quotations. If you need a more detailed explanation, look up *direct quotations* and *indirect quotations* – or *direct speech* and *reported speech* – in your grammar reference book or in an online grammar resource such as Purdue University's Online Writing Lab, currently accessible at <http://owl.english.purdue.edu>.

Before you practice the tasks below, read the following guidelines (examples are adapted from Tatyana Dyachenko's essay, "Unfinished Interview"):

- A direct quotation consists of a person's exact words, either spoken or written; it is set off from the rest of the text with quotation marks.

- It is a good idea to quote a person's words exactly when the words themselves – the way the person expresses an idea – are particularly important to the point you are making in your writing.

- An indirect quotation (sometimes called *reported speech*) contains the same information found in a quotation but not the speaker's exact words; it does not use quotation marks.

Task 5.7 *Analyze*

1 Read the opening paragraph of the student essay below. It contains some direct quotations, but the quotation marks have been omitted.

2 Working with a partner, underline every example of an indirect quotation (reported speech) one time. Underline every example of a direct quotation (direct speech) two times.

3 Then punctuate the direct quotations correctly, restoring the quotation marks and adding commas and capital letters where they are needed.

Crisantina Orellana is a very old woman who was born in the quiet village of Chalatenango in the northern countryside of El Salvador. During my interview, I asked her about her age. She replied I really don't know it. The only thing I'm sure of is that I was born at some day in the past and I'm still alive. One thing is notorious in Crisantina Orellana's personality. She always looks happy and full of joy. When I asked her what was the secret that has kept her full of life, she said life is life. She told me that the only thing we have to worry about is how to live our lives. She explained that when a person has really learned how to live, he or she will understand the difference this attitude makes in how we choose to live.

4 Check your work using the Answer Key on page 260.

1 Working with a partner, you will play a game in which you have a conversation and then write a report about what you and your partner said using both direct and indirect quotations. The goal of the game is to try to persuade your partner to give you one dollar. Set a time limit of 5 minutes and keep trying until you get the dollar or the time is up. If you are the partner with the dollar, do not give the money away until your partner has convinced you that he or she really needs it or that it will be to your advantage to hand it over. Do not be cheap. Once you are persuaded by the other person's arguments, give him or her the dollar.

2 Reverse roles and play for another 5 minutes. The partner who previously gave (or did not give) the dollar should now try to persuade his or her partner to give the money.

3 Each partner should write a brief report describing what happened as you tried to persuade your partner to give you the dollar. Be sure to use a mixture of direct and indirect quotations. Tell what you said in order to get the dollar, and explain why these arguments were or were not successful.

Examples of Direction Quotations	Examples of Indirect Quotations
I asked, "Will you give me a dollar?"	I asked if she would give me a dollar. I asked her to give me a dollar. I asked my partner to give me a dollar.
I explained to my partner, "I need the dollar to buy some food. I'm very hungry."	I explained to him that I needed the dollar because I was very hungry. I explained that I needed the dollar to buy some food because I was very hungry. I explained to my partner that I needed the dollar to buy some food.

4 Exchange papers with your partner and read what he or she has written. Did your partner accurately describe your negotiation to get the dollar? Did he or she punctuate direct quotations correctly? Did he or she include some indirect quotations? If you notice any problems, discuss them with your partner and decide on the correct version.

Editing Checklist

If you are writing your essay on a computer, remember to print out your revised essay and proofread it on paper.

☐ **First proofreading: direct and indirect quotations**
Proofread carefully to see whether you used direct and indirect quotations correctly. Remember that if you quote your interviewee's words exactly, you must use beginning and ending quotation marks. Do not use quotation marks for indirect speech – that is, if you are paraphrasing what you or the interviewee said. Check (✓) the box when you have finished.

☐ **Second proofreading**
Proofread your essay a second time and correct any other errors of grammar, spelling, or punctuation that you find. Check (✓) the box when you have finished.

☐ **Third proofreading**
Print out or write a copy of your essay that includes the corrections you made in your first and second proofreading. Now proofread your essay a third time. Try to find and correct any errors that you missed. Then print out, or write in dark blue or black ink, the final draft of your essay. Check (✓) the box when you have finished.

Monday 29
June 2 Friday no class

Peer Response Form
Writing Based on Interviews

WRITER'S NAME: .... READER'S NAME: ....

DATE: ....

Focus on the ideas in the essay rather than the grammar and spelling. Discuss only those mistakes that interfere with understanding.

1 What did you like about this essay? Be as specific as possible.

2 Were there any places where the writer's meaning was not clear? If so, where were they?

3 In your opinion, what was the most important idea that emerged from the interview? In other words, what do you see as the thesis statement of this essay? If the writer's thesis statement is included in this draft, copy it below. If you do not find a thesis statement in the essay, write one or two sentences to express what you think is the most important idea from the interview.

Photocopiable   © Cambridge University Press

4 Write down one direct quotation from the interview that you thought was effective.

5 Do you feel that there are too many quotations from the interview, too few quotations, or about the right number? Explain.

6 How could the writer improve this essay when he or she revises? Make only one suggestion.

Writer's Plan for Revising
Writing Based on Interviews

YOUR NAME: .... ESSAY TITLE: ....

DATE: ....

Reread your essay, concentrating on the ideas rather than on grammar and spelling. Then write your answers to the following questions.

1 Describe your own reaction to conducting this interview. Was it easy or difficult? Why? If you had a chance to do the interview over, what would you do differently?

2 Read your essay aloud and listen to the sound of the words. If possible, audiotape your reading and then listen to the tape. What did you like most about the essay when you heard it being read aloud in your own voice?

3 What else do you want readers to understand that is not yet included in your essay? Write out these new parts and decide how you can include them in the next draft to make your essay more complete.

Families in Transition

Writing Based on Reading

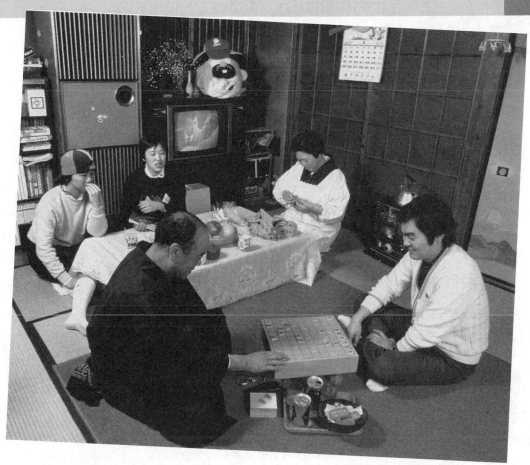

The family is, without a doubt, one of the most important elements in society. Our first lessons in life, such as how to eat, how to speak, and how to love, are normally learned within the family. However, in today's world, families are changing rapidly as a result of political and economic forces and technological developments, such as air travel, television, and the Internet. In the past few years, dramatic changes have occurred in family structures, marriage patterns, and even something as basic as the definition of what the word *family* really means. In this chapter, you will read essays by student and professional writers discussing different aspects of family life as it has changed over time. Then you will write an essay explaining your reactions to the ideas in one or more of these readings.

READINGS

Reading 1

v. s = versus

Traditional vs. Modern Family
Wan L. Lam

In this essay, a student from Hong Kong describes the dramatic transition that took place in her own family as it was transformed from a traditional to a modern family structure. Before you read, think about whether you consider your own family to be "traditional." Why or why not?

The traditional family structure no longer exists in the modern world. It's not surprising that the modern family structure has replaced it. My family, for example, has made a great leap from traditional to modern in which I can feel the existence of freedom.   1

It seems like a characteristic of traditional families that men are dominant. When I was born, my grandfather urged my mother to give me up, for I was only a girl. He suggested that my mother throw me into the sea or give me to my aunt and uncle, who didn't have any children. Under the pressure of my grandparents and relatives, my mother did give me to my aunt. But she brought me back a few hours later because of her regret in doing so.   2

In my childhood, all my family members and relatives lived in a big old building in Hong Kong. They had the same kind of job – the sculpture of ivory – and they worked together in that big building. In my family, my grandpa had the power of making all significant decisions, such as stopping my father, who was an outstanding student, from going to high school, and forcing him to work as a skilled worker in ivory sculpture.   3

There was no exception for my mother. She had to obey the men absolutely with no argument. From what my mother said, I don't think she was the daughter-in-law of my grandparents. Maidservant is a better word to describe my mother's role in the family. She had to do all the housework by herself, without any help or any machines, and had to take care of the children and the elderly parents as well.   4

By the same token, children had to obey what the older people, especially my father, said, such as going to bed by nine o'clock exactly, going home right after school, and not walking alone or with other children in the streets. We, my brother, sisters, and I, had to do whatever my father said without question.   5

The ripple of change began when we moved out of the old building. Every individual family moved to a different place. I think the reason for not living together was that my grandpa had died, and another building was very expensive. My mother began to work outside to support the family (to pay the rent on the small apartment and other expenses). We had to share the housework when my mother was out. However, my father was still stubborn and strict with us as long as we lived in Hong Kong.   6

But things really started to change when we came to the United States two years ago. My father began to be concerned about his children and tried to communicate with us. To a large extent, we now have the right to make individual choices and have a certain freedom, like coming home later at night, which we were never permitted to do before. Perhaps my parents are getting old or maybe we have grown up.

Undoubtedly, to a large extent, the modern family is better than the traditional one. At least there is a great improvement in the relationship between family members, and everybody plays an important role in the family.

The men 14/ live home to cook while the women cooked home to feed the running.

Reading 1 Reflecting on the Reading

1 In her essay, Lam includes several examples of ways in which traditional and modern families are different. Underline each example of traditional families and write a *T* in the margin next to it. Underline each example of modern families and write an *M* in the margin next to it. Then compare your answers in a small group.

2 Read the following list of categories related to family structure. In the space provided, briefly describe these categories as they relate to traditional and modern families according to Lam's essay. Then compare your answers with your group.

Category	Traditional	Modern
Where family members live	*All together*	*Only parents and children live together*
The role of men	*dominant*	*concerned about his children*
The role of women	*maids and bought the men*	*working outside to support the family*
Attitude toward the elderly	*the women had care of elderly*	*they communicate*
Relationship between parents and children	*children had to obey their*	*children can make choice*

3 In your group or as a class, discuss the points Lam makes in paragraphs 2 and 4 concerning the treatment of women. Do you know of any cases where this type of treatment still occurs? What is your opinion about this type of treatment?

4 Freewrite in your journal about the word *family*. How do you define this word? What does it mean to you? What associations does it hold for you? Then look up the word *family* in the dictionary. Write down the dictionary definition that most closely matches your own definition.

The Family in Society

Isabella Kong

In this essay, a student from Hong Kong responds to the previous essay and discusses the underlying reasons for traditional family structure. She explains why this structure is not as suitable in modern society. Before you read, think about some of the reasons that families all over the world are changing.

Nothing is perfect. The modern family and the traditional family both have their merits and demerits. What makes one more desirable than the other depends on the context of the society, the values and attitudes of the people, and the economic system. In short, we have to look beyond the culture of the society. The family patterns are the products of the culture, but they also shape the culture. 1

The traditional family, which Wan Lam described, had survival values in the primitive Chinese society for which farming was the principal economic activity. The family owned the land and depended on it for its living. If the traditional family structure had broken down, every family unit would then claim its share of land for itself. This would be disastrous as the land would be divided into such small portions that none of the family unit could survive because there would not be enough to feed them. Thus, all of the land was passed down to the eldest son. 2

Moreover, the traditional family also provides a stronger union and closer relationship among family members, which is vital if they are to defend themselves against outside threats. However, the more people living together, the more complicated their relations will be. Disputes and conflicts may often arise and thus threaten the existence of the family. As a means to counteract the disintegrating force within the family, an authoritarian leadership is needed to decide on important issues and settle disputes. This is often the job of the eldest son in the family. In turn, everyone has to obey and submit to the authorized figure; that is, they have to pay the price of giving up freedom for family union, which Wan Lam found unreasonable and disagreeable. 3

Nowadays, when individualism and equality are the most prevailing ideas in the world, people may find it very hard to adjust themselves to a traditional family. The means of production have changed so that the adaptive value of the traditional family is no longer obvious. The modern family has its advantages, as it will be more open and free, but it will also devastate the respect for the older generation that once was the dominant force in the traditional family. 4

It is clear that family structure changes in accordance with the changes in society. Yet, no matter what their differences are, all share one universal and everlasting theme of affection, companionship, and warmth, which underlies any family in any place and any time. 5

1 Formal academic writing often analyzes why things are a certain way. In this essay, Kong analyzes why the traditional family was useful in Chinese society in the past, and why it is changing in today's world. Find and underline two reasons why, according to Kong, the traditional family was so common in the past. Then find and underline, in a different color, two reasons why Kong thinks it is not as useful in modern society. Discuss these reasons with a partner or small group and decide whether you find Kong's reasoning convincing. Why or why not?

2 Select one sentence that, in your opinion, represents the more formal language of academic writing. With your partner or group, discuss your sentences and why you selected them. Then compare your answers as a class.

3 One definition of the word *culture* is "a particular society at a particular place and time." At the end of paragraph 1, Kong states, "The family patterns are the products of the culture, but they also shape the culture." Discuss what you think this sentence means. Then think of two specific examples of how changing family patterns are shaping culture in today's world. One example is that in many societies, elders don't live with the younger generation anymore. This change has shaped culture because it has made social programs that care for elders, such as Social Security and Medicare, necessary and essential.

4 In paragraph 3, Kong states that "the more people living together, the more complicated their relations will be." In your journal, freewrite about this idea. Do you agree with Kong or not? What experiences from your own life or your reading support your opinion?

Reading 3

Traditional Family and Modern Society in Africa

Papa Aly Ndaw

In Africa the family used to be of supreme importance, "one and indivisible, powerful and sacred," as this student from Senegal puts it. However, African families, like the Chinese families described earlier, are changing dramatically because of the demands of modern life. In this essay, Ndaw comments on some of the problems that can arise when families change. Before you read, think of some of the problems that modern families face.

The culture of a group can be defined as all the social, economic, and metaphysical aspects contributing to make a group specific and its members recognized as entities belonging to that group. In fact, every group, large or small, having a common past or heredity, has its own culture, even though some common cultural aspects can be found in all cultures. Another common denominator

is that almost all traditional societies are going through some cultural changes caused by the introduction of new concepts or aspects of modern life. In Africa one structure that couldn't be unaffected is the family.

In traditional Africa the family used to be one and indivisible, powerful and sacred. Every member had rights and responsibilities he could assume as long as they didn't conflict with those of the group. The family was like the body and soul of a person, the members like the different parts of the body, separate but vital in keeping the body and soul alive. 2

Today the economic and political conditions have changed, changing at the same time people's mentality and behavior. The result is a tendency to individualism, to self-concern, to division, which is not the goal of the traditional family. 3

The transition from the traditional family to the nuclear family was so quick and unpredictable that I wonder if its members were prepared for such a change in their way of living. One of the first things to change was the size of the family. It used to be a big family with Grandpa, Grandma, Mom, Dad, their brothers and sisters, and their children. Now it's a nuclear family that only includes Dad, Mom, and their own children. Many reasons are given: the house is not big enough, or it is better to have a small family so the children can have a better education, or the couple thinks their life can't be like the one their father and mother had a few years ago. And for all these reasons and many others, the family needs to change to be able to cope with the rhythm of modern life. 4

When the size of the family had decreased, the next step was to increase the rights of the nuclear family members, either by giving them more freedom or by giving them more power. The result was an establishment of new relations among the family members, who started seeing their differences and particularities. 5

The wife, whose role used to be giving a good education to the children and taking care of her husband, says she needs to be independent, and refuses to be 6 confined to just household work. Her next thought will put her out of the house, looking for a job, leaving behind her a big hole and irresponsible and unprepared children.

The children, left to themselves and without supervision, think they are free. And like the adage says, "When the cat is away, the mice will play." In fact, it was their mother's job to teach them their responsibilities, to correct them when they made mistakes, and to punish them when they violated the family's rules. Now, with Mom working outside the home, they will spend much of their time deciding for themselves, a right they didn't have before. In fact, it's a beginning of freedom!

The father, once the support of the family, feels less powerful, because his wife can now assume that function: to bring money home. To compensate for what may be called an inferiority complex, he tries to have more control over the children, who don't look at him any more as the symbol he used to be, but rather Mom's equal. At this stage, the notion of groups has lost its old power; the family has lost its traditional roots and function; every member thinks about himself first before thinking about the family.

But as we know, when society progresses, human beings gain more power over nature, bringing at the same time some changes in many aspects of life, culture included. These cultural changes, as long as they are not negative, contribute in a sense to the development of the group, because what they bring into the society are new attitudes that are needed for us to cope with the new environment in which we are living. At this time it may be too soon to understand and accept these developments, and to perceive them as achievements. The increase of women's rights, their contribution to the economic power of their countries as a working force, couldn't be accomplished if women were just household workers.

A lot of things can be said about the cultural changes in human societies, since we know that Man's life is an evolution, and evolution means improvement; and we know there is no improvement by simply repeating the old ways, but instead it comes with innovation and variety, which always lead to changes. The only thing to remember is that as long as these cultural changes bring improvement, they shouldn't be refused even though we know that every group tends to be conservative of its traditional values.

Reading 3 *Reflecting on the Reading*

1 According to Ndaw, changes in economic and political conditions have resulted in two major changes in modern family life. What are these two changes, and in which paragraphs does Ndaw discuss them? Compare your answers to these questions in a small group. Then discuss how, according to Ndaw, each change has affected the lives of different family members – grandparents, children, mothers, and fathers.

2 Circle five words in the essay that are not familiar to you. Write each of the words and the paragraph in which it appears in the chart on page 174. Then try to guess the meaning from the context – how the word is used in the essay.

Finally, look up the word in your dictionary and write down the definition that seems most appropriate. Compare your words and definitions with your group and discuss what you learned from doing this vocabulary work.

	Word	Par. No.	Guessed Meaning	Dictionary Definition
1	tendency to	3	desire	be likely to
2	nuclear	4	modern	a family with two parents
3	Cope with	5	adapt	
4	adage	7	example	a saying that
5	inferiority complex	8		a nervous feeling of not being good enough

3 In paragraphs 6 and 7, Ndaw gives his own analysis of some of the changes that occur in family life as a result of women working outside the home. Working with your group, write a brief summary of Ndaw's opinion on this issue in your own words. Then discuss whether you agree with his assessment of the situation in modern families. Why or why not?

4 In the conclusion to his essay, Ndaw writes: ". . . Man's life is an evolution, and evolution means improvement; and we know there is no improvement by simply repeating the old ways, but instead it comes with innovation and variety. . . ." In your journal, freewrite about your opinion on this statement. Do you agree with what Ndaw says? Why or why not?

Reading 4	Professional Writing

Bean Paste vs. Miniskirts: Generation Gap Grows

Nicholas D. Kristof

In this article, which was originally published in the New York Times *in 1999, the writer discusses how changes in the larger Korean society have led to changes within families. Before you read, think about how the society in which you grew up or in which you now live is changing. How do you think these changes will affect individual families?*

A blast of steam caught Park Ki Soon in the face as she peered into the caldron of beans and began stirring, feeling ever more sorry for herself. "When I was young   1

I did what my mother-in-law said," Mrs. Park, 70, said morosely as she used a wooden paddle to churn the beans. "But now my daughter-in-law doesn't listen to me. So now I'm making this bean paste, and I'm feeling miserable because I'm an old woman and she's using me. I don't know why she doesn't make bean paste herself. I think she just wants to be comfortable. She never likes hard work."

The small group of women clustered around Mrs. Park, here in the village of Hanok about 30 miles northwest of Seoul, nodded their heads in agreement. Young Koreans, they concluded, are incomprehensible and insufferable. "When I go to the cities, I look at young people, the way they dress, the way they behave, and they aren't Korean," said Choi Sam Soon, 55, who was also making bean paste. "Young people always carry credit cards, and they get money from machines! They always spend money so recklessly." "And young people abandon things that are still usable," Mrs. Choi added, shaking her head at the idea. "Some people throw out old kettles, so I pick them up and take them home and use them."

The problem, of course, is that young people are not thrilled about having their mothers or mothers-in-law rifling through other people's garbage to rescue battered old kettles. And such skirmishes are only one facet of a generation gap that many South Koreans say is greater than almost anywhere in the world.

Korea was one of the last places to open up to Western influences, for until a century ago it was an ancient kingdom that operated on Confucian traditions and deeply regimented customs. Those customs – especially respect for the elderly – permeated Korean society until the last few decades.

Since the 1960s, South Korea has been one of the fastest-changing societies in the world. The economy grew at a blistering pace, the country industrialized and urbanized, a middle class emerged, and these days respect tends to go to those with money and E-mail accounts, not to the old men and women who make great bean paste. "Generation gaps exist everywhere, but the gap is wider here, because Western culture is pouring in at an amazing speed," said Annette E. Y. Ahn, 28, a Seoul interpreter who grew up partly in the United States and Europe. "I also think it's wider here because looking back in history, we were the last country to open up to Western culture, and now the doors are open and it's pouring in."

These gaps seem to cause misunderstandings and sadness, but fewer open explosions than one might expect. Young and old alike may stew inside at the foolishness of the other, but they also describe how they go out of their way to accommodate. "It's a constant bother to live with the old folks," said Chong Kum Sook, 38, who lives in the same house as her husband's parents. "It's very hard. It's not that they complain, but I feel the burden on myself. My in-laws are early risers, so I try to get up when they do. And in the summer I can't wear skimpy clothes, because I have to dress cautiously so as not to disturb them. I should be careful not to make them unhappy."

Korean women were traditionally expected to dress very primly, and indeed a young woman was arrested for indecency just four years ago when she wore a T-shirt that exposed her navel. "When I see girls exposing themselves in short dresses, I'm shocked," said Koh Kap In, a 79-year-old matriarch who was sitting outside her house. "But I've never said a word to my granddaughters. It's the times. All the young women are in those clothes."

Most elderly Koreans say that they are often shocked privately at the laziness 8
or immorality or extravagance of young people, but that mostly they bite their
tongues. "If I complain, would they listen?" asked Kim Hae Song, 78, a stooped
woman who was outside weeding her garden. "No. That would only put them
on bad terms with me. In my heart I feel upset at what goes on, but I don't say
anything."

Mrs. Kim and her husband, Kwon Sang Mook, 81, are most offended at the 9
disappearance of traditional etiquette, which young people often breach without
even realizing it. "I see young people smoking in front of their elders," Mr. Kwon
said, shaking his head. "Young people say they are so smart, but what is the point
of knowledge if you don't know how to behave?"

The elderly often seem particularly poignant because, mixed in with the 10
outrage at the way their grandchildren or daughters-in-law behave, there is also
often pride at their education and worldliness. Sitting in her kitchen, Lee Hee Ja,
58, a housewife, served coffee and a 40-minute denunciation of young people. She
fretted that her eldest daughter-in-law will not carry on the family rituals, that her
second daughter-in-law has not minded her advice to dress modestly, that neither
can cook properly and that none of the young people are attentive enough to her
own needs. But then Mrs. Lee paused, smiled and sighed. "Maybe I'm wrong,"
she said. "Young people now are very bright. So smart! So I don't know. Maybe in
the end my daughters-in-law will be better than I was."

Reading 4 **Reflecting on the Reading**

1 Reread the first paragraph and then, with a small group, discuss why you
think a newspaper writer would decide to begin an article with an example.
How would your reaction as a reader have been different if the writer had
begun the essay with paragraph 4 instead?

2 In paragraph 2, Choi Sam Soon, a 55-year-old Korean woman, states: "When
I go to the cities, I look at young people, the way they dress, the way they
behave, and they aren't Korean." Discuss with your group what you think she
means by this statement.

3 This essay is based primarily on interviews that the writer conducted with
many Koreans of different ages. Find and underline examples of each type of
quotation below. Then compare and discuss your choices with your group.

a A quotation in which the interviewee questions the actions of the other
generation

b A quotation in which the interviewee analyzes possible reasons for the
conflict between the generations

c A quotation in which the interviewee expresses anger

d A quotation in which the interviewee expresses complex or mixed emotions

4 Now try to adopt the point of view of one of the interviewees.

   a Choose one of the Koreans who was interviewed, and write a letter from that person to a member of the younger (or older) generation. Be sure to use first-person pronouns (*I*, *me*, *my*) in this writing.

> **Example**
>
> This might be the beginning of a letter from Park Ki Soon (paragraph 1) to her daughter-in-law:
>
> Dear Daughter-in-Law,
>
> It's hard for me to talk about these things with you, and so I decided to write you a letter. I'm so tired from making bean paste all day. When I was your age, I made all the bean paste for my husband's parents, and I did a lot of other things for them too. I know you will tell me I should just buy the bean paste from the store, but it's not the same. . . .

   b Read your letters aloud in your group. Then choose one student from each group to read his or her letter to the class.

Reading 5

A Response to "Bean Paste vs. Miniskirts"

Liana Salman

In this essay, a student writer responds to the previous article, summarizing some of its main points and giving her own opinion about the changes in traditional family values. Before you read, think about the changes in family values that you have observed in your lifetime. How do you feel about those changes?

"Bean Paste vs. Miniskirts: Generation Gap Grows" is an article written by Nicholas Kristof and published in *The New York Times*. It talks about a generation gap in Hanok, South Korea, which became a conflicting situation. Korea was against westernization of their lives up until the 1960s. In the past half century, Hanok opened up to the modernization of the country, and new ideas started "pouring in." As a result, traditional, older people now have to live among concepts that they have had no time to adapt to. The article familiarizes us with views of older women of South Korea and allows us to understand their perception of this situation.

A woman named Choi Sam Soon, aged 55, talks about young people being unappreciative and imprudent with the freedom that they have. She complains that they "carry credit cards" and "always spend money so recklessly." These practitioners of Confucian traditions, who have probably never spent a dime on themselves, believe the social and spiritual way of life to be more important than the economic one. Money came to them through hardship, and it is grievous for them to see young adults take it for granted.

The women complain that their children and grandchildren are spending their earnings on modern technological devices and devious fashion. "When I see girls exposing themselves," mentions Koh Kap In, 79, "I'm shocked." It was important for women to dress properly and to respect their bodies. To the old-fashioned, nudity and sexuality is a private matter that should be shared only between a married couple. No wonder these grandmothers are upset. When you see your immature child wear skimpy clothes, the only thing you can assume is that these girls have no self-respect toward their femininity.

Korean women talk about the laziness they've seen in the newer generation. They say that these kids do not want to put effort into anything. Physical labor is for the uneducated and poor. With westernization, young people can work in offices at computers instead of in fields and kitchens. They have lost their appreciation for work that requires strength. These old-fashioned women consider the younger generation of females to be hopeless. They have lost their positions, they can't dress, they can't cook, and they can't behave.

A Hanokian couple, Kim and Kwon, feel insulted; it is like they are not existent anymore because of "the disappearance of traditional etiquette." These people complain that even though younger generations are supposed to gain intelligence with the education they are provided, they seem to be losing their good manners. "I'm an old woman and she's using me," says Mrs. Park, 70, referring to her daughter-in-law. It used to be that the older you got, the wiser and more respected you became. Now young people make fun of old people for their silly, outdated way of life. Meanwhile, the only thing these old-fashioned people have left is their strong sense of tradition and recipes for bean paste.

I have not experienced the generation gap myself because my grandparents were very open-minded people. However, I have heard stories from my mother about having to hide certain aspects of her lifestyle because they would be unacceptable to her family. My mother had to hide her addiction to nicotine because it was considered disgusting for women to smoke in her community. My grandparents don't know that she is a smoker up to this day, and she is now 42. She also had to hide her appreciation of rock n' roll and jazz music. Her family considered it to be music for hooligans and junkies, not proper young ladies. I have heard of many religious disputes between generations; older people being more dependent on faith and afterlife, and younger people on the present moment. I also remember my father telling me that he used to be punished for lying and that I ought to be treated in the old-fashioned way. He meant that life used to be harsher and harder, but it also made you a better person.

I believe that younger generations have lost and gained something by giving up old values. They have lost a sense of unity because now it is more important to be an individual. They have lost their appreciation of spiritual matters, which is the only thing that can help you sometimes when nothing else is around. They have lost their strength and devotion to hard work. Most importantly, they have lost the respect of their parents and grandparents. Now these young people will get to live their lives in comfort. Women can now depend on themselves; they can achieve higher education and choose their careers. Young adults can travel around the world and experience life to its fullest. The gain is as great as the loss. However, it is sad to see old values vanish, because I know that someday I will also be old and my way of life will also be unappreciated and forgotten.

Reading 5 *Reflecting on the Reading*

1 In academic essays, writers often focus on one main topic in each paragraph. Reread paragraphs 2, 3, 4, and 5. Working with a small group, decide what main topic Salman discusses in each of these paragraphs.

2 When professors ask students to write about something they have read, they usually expect students to summarize important ideas from the reading and then give their own opinion on these ideas. Working in your group, look through the essay and find the paragraphs in which Salman is summarizing Kristof's article. Put an S, for *summary*, next to each of those paragraphs. Find the paragraphs in which she is explaining her own opinion and put an O, for *opinion*, next to each of those. Discuss why you think Salman decided to organize her essay in this way.

3 With your group, decide in which paragraph Salman expresses her thesis statement – what she believes about the ideas in the article she has read. Choose one sentence in this paragraph that you feel expresses her thesis most clearly. Compare your choice with other groups.

4 If you were to write an essay on this same topic, what culture(s) would you discuss? What examples of generational differences could you include? Freewrite on this question, being as specific as possible. Then discuss your freewriting with a partner or small group.

Reading 6   **Professional Writing**

Gay Parents Find More Acceptance
Carlyle Murphy

As society changes, new types of family structures emerge. We can now see a growing number of gay or same-sex partners forming families and raising children, either from earlier marriages, adoption, or artificial insemination.* As you read the following excerpts from an article originally published in the Washington Post *in 1999, think about why some people might be supportive of families with same-sex parents and why others might be opposed.*

Once termed "the most planned parenthood in the world," families headed   1
by gay men or lesbians now number in the tens of thousands, according to

---

**artificial insemination*: the placement of sperm (male reproductive cells) in the female reproductive tract without sexual intercourse

Ray Drew, executive director of the San Diego-based Family Pride Coalition, which has 15,000 such families on its rolls. The overwhelming majority of about 2 million parents who are gay are raising children from earlier heterosexual marriages, according to Drew. But for gay couples who want their own children, there are more resources than ever. Scores of Internet sites offer information about adoption and sperm banks*; children's storybooks feature same-sex parents; and physicians and hospitals are more open to helping.

* * *

In addition to the increased availability of donor banks and surrogate mothers, the rise in gay-headed families has been aided by a greater willingness among adoption agencies to accept gay men and lesbians as parents. . . . "There has been a tremendous growth in the visibility of gay, lesbian, bisexual and transgender couples as adoptive parents," said Bill Pierce, president of the [Washington, D.C.]-based National Council for Adoption, an association of private adoption agencies. "It's part of the general move in the culture toward an acceptance of gays, lesbians, bisexual and transgender people."   2

Such families have also been strengthened by a growing number of judges willing to approve "second-parent" adoptions for gay couples. Long common in heterosexual marriages, these adoptions give full parental rights to the nonbiological parent, or stepparent – rights that can be crucial if the biological parent dies. . . .   3

Support groups also are flourishing. In the Washington [D.C.] area, Rainbow Families allows children of about 130 gay parents to meet other children with same-sex parents at monthly picnics, skating classes or other gatherings.   4

At the same time, however, gay activists report a growing number of bitter custody battles among couples who have split. . . . Without a "second-parent"   5

*sperm banks: medical facilities that store sperm to be used in artificial insemination adoption, the non-biological parent has little leverage. A national coalition of gay activists recently issued guidelines for avoiding custody disputes, urging parents to focus on the children's welfare. These battles, warned Kate Kendall, executive director of the San Francisco-based National Center for Lesbian Rights, "threaten the very significant but nevertheless fragile gains we have made for lesbian- and gay-headed households."

Gay parenting remains unacceptable in some circles. The Family Research Council, a conservative political organization that openly urges homosexuals to change their orientation, opposes the idea of gay men and lesbians having children. "In a homosexual household, not only is one of the sexes missing, but the children are confronted with abnormal sexuality being presented as the norm," said Robert Knight, the council's senior director of cultural studies. "Having to explain to peers that you have two mommies or two daddies is a burden no child should have to bear."

At the private Lowell School in Northwest Washington [D.C.], which actively recruits gay-headed families as part of its commitment to diversity, Director Abigail Wiebenson reports a mixed reception from parents. "Among many families there is greater acceptance, and among some families there is some leeriness," she said. The reservations arise "not because they don't like these families and their children," she added, but because "they are worried about how they can best describe to their own children families who don't look like their families."

Barry Kessler and David Hankey, a couple since 1985, spend countless hours in the nursery of their Baltimore town house with the new love of their lives. Her name is Helen, and she is 5 months old. "We just wanted to have a child so badly," said Kessler, 41, a museum curator. "There was this place in our hearts that we had this love . . . to give a child. It's just a deep feeling."

Memories of their own happy childhoods fed their longing for a child, explained Hankey, 42, a lawyer. "You're happiest when you're surrounded by people you love and who love you," he said. "And that pretty quickly translates into family."

For several years they considered adopting before they met a lesbian who agreed to be a surrogate mother. After Helen's birth, many of Hankey's corporate clients sent baby gifts, and 120 people came to her baby-naming, a traditional Jewish rite presided over by a rabbi. Kessler has taken leave from work to care for Helen, who also has two sets of doting grandparents. He and his daughter "just blend in" at a neighborhood parenting group, he said, where he and other parents "talk about whose baby is eating what food, whose baby got a rash, who's going to join the swimming pool this summer." Kessler and Hankey said heterosexuals seem to look at gay men and lesbians differently once they become parents. "You have this experience in common, and that reduces the alienation," Kessler said.

* * *

Most research on children of gay couples indicates they have no worse social or behavioral problems than children of heterosexual parents. But since most studies have, by necessity, focused on younger children, there is little research on how growing up in such families might influence a child's sexual identity. "What we know about those children is that they seem to be developing pretty much like other people's children," said University of Virginia psychology professor Charlotte J. Patterson. Opponents of gay parenting call the research "severely flawed" because, as the Family Research Council's Knight said, it covers a small number of "self-selected" subjects who favor gay parenting as a model.

Teresa Williams and Jo Deutsch, of Cheverly, who each bore one of their two 12 sons with sperm donated by friends, say they don't care what sexual orientation Jacob, 8, and Matthew, 4, have as adults. "What we express," said Deutsch . . . , "is that this is something you're going to know, and if you're gay, that's great with us, and if you're straight, that's fine with us. As long as you are comfortable with who you are."

But even if gay parents wanted to influence their children's sexual orientation, 13 said American University history professor Vanessa Schwartz, they probably couldn't. She points to her daughter, Rachel, 4, who resists suggestions that Cinderella could be happy with another Cinderella. "She says, 'No, Mom, she has to find a prince!'" said Schwartz, 35, who lives in the District* with her partner and Rachel's other mother, Rebecca Isaacs. "My own child," sighed Schwartz, "does not make the leap that Cinderella could find another Cinderella."

*the District: Washington, D.C. (District of Columbia)

<hr>

Reading 6 **Reflecting on the Reading**

1 Reread the article and underline each quotation from people who support same-sex parents. In a different color, underline each quotation from people who are opposed to such parents. Read the sections you underlined to a small group or to the class and discuss your choices. Why do you think Murphy included quotations from people on both sides of this issue?

2 Find evidence in the article that a child's sexual orientation is probably not influenced by the sexual orientation of the parents. Discuss in a small group or as a class whether you find this evidence convincing. Why or why not?

3 Working alone or with a partner, conduct some informal interviews to find out what other people think about gay parents raising children. (Review "Interviewing," on page 146, if necessary.) If you do the interviews with a partner, have one partner ask the questions and the other take notes. Talk to at least two or three people. Tape your interviews, if possible. Share the results of these interviews with a small group or as a class.

4 Write a letter to Carlyle Murphy, the author of the article, in which you express your reasons for either supporting or opposing same-sex couples raising children. Provide at least three reasons as evidence for your opinion. Read your letters to your group. Then choose one student from each group to read his or her letter to the class.

The Problem of Gay Parenting

Pui Man Wong

In this essay, a student questions the increasing acceptance in modern society of gay families. The writer is concerned about the possible negative impact on children being raised in same-sex households. As you read, consider some positive and negative aspects of same-sex parenting.

In today's society, people are gradually accepting gays and lesbians. As these people's relationships with their partners grow, they would like to start families of their own. By now, technology is more advanced, so it has become easier for gays and lesbians to produce their own children by artificial insemination. According to Ray Drew, executive director of the San Diego-based Family Pride Coalition, "the most planned parenthood in the world" is families headed by gay men and lesbians.

Gay parenting is becoming more acceptable to society nowadays. "Scores of Internet sites offer information about adoption and sperm banks; children's storybooks feature same-sex parents; and physicians and hospitals are more open to helping." "In addition to the increased availability of donor banks and surrogate mothers, the rise in gay-headed families has been aided by a greater willingness among adoption agencies to accept gay men and lesbians as parents. . . ." More and more gays, lesbians, bisexuals, and transgender couples are being accepted as adoptive parents. "Children . . . meet other children with same-sex parents at monthly picnics, skating classes, or other gatherings."

However, in my opinion, gay parenting might have negative effects on the child. "In a homosexual household, not only is one of the sexes missing, but the children are confronted with abnormal sexuality being presented as the norm." Children might be confused about their own sexuality. "Having to explain to peers that you have two mommies or two daddies is a burden no child should have to bear." In the end, the child will be the one getting hurt. Even a four-year-old girl knows that "[Cinderella] has to find a prince."

Society needs to address the issue of gay parenting and the problems that will inevitably arise. We need to examine how much impact these controversial lifestyles will have on future generations. In my opinion, gay parenting has nothing to benefit the child. It will leave the child confused about his or her sexuality and wondering why he or she is the one chosen to have two mommies or two daddies. They might even think that life is unfair to them.

Reading 7 *Reflecting on the Reading*

1 Underline the places in Wong's essay in which she points out the advantages for gay families of society's increasing acceptance of them. In a different color, underline the places that point out the disadvantages of the increasing

acceptance of gay families. Discuss with a small group or as a class why you think Wong arranged the advantages and disadvantages in this order.

2 Put an A next to any sentences of the essay with which you agree. Put a D next to any sentences with which you disagree. Then discuss your choices with a partner or small group. Explain and support your opinions.

3 Wong does not identify the source of the many quotations she uses. Not giving the source for quoted material is considered a serious mistake in academic writing. In fact, all of these quotations are from "Gay Parents Find More Acceptance," on page 179. Working with your partner or group, select three direct quotations in Wong's essay. Then find the original quotations in Murphy's essay. Give the name of the person who originally made each statement and identify the person. For example, Robert Knight is the Senior Director of Cultural Studies for the Family Research Council. Finally, for each quotation, discuss any possible connections between the person's job affiliation and his or her opinion on gay parenting.

4 Write a letter to Wong expressing your opinion about her essay. Point out specific parts of the essay with which you agree or disagree. Read your letters to a small group. Then choose one student from each group to read his or her letter to the class.

A Positive View of Gay Parenting

Alana Vayntraub

In this essay, a student expresses a positive view of same-sex parenting. She argues that children raised in gay families do not seem to suffer any negative effects from being raised by same-sex parents. As you read, think about whether most people you know would agree or disagree with the writer's opinion.

Society has many different outlooks on a controversial situation. The majority of the public is small-minded, or shall I say narrow-minded about these issues. So when gay parenting becomes an issue, many outlooks are presented that conflict with each other. You have the people who support it and the people who oppose it. I support it.

In the article entitled "Gay Parents Find More Acceptance," Carlyle Murphy reported intense research on this conflict and different people's opinions. The subject was analyzed thoroughly. I will begin to summarize the supporting ideas.

Ray Drew, executive director of the San Diego-based Family Pride Coalition, says, "Families headed by gay men or lesbians now number in the tens of thousands." He is one of the people in support of this lifestyle. Drew explains how gay couples can find out information about adoption and methods of artificial fertilization. According to Murphy, "the rise in gay headed households has been

1

2

3

aided by a greater willingness among adoption agencies to accept gay men and lesbians as parents."[That helps the gays and lesbians to become a family and live their lives as other couples do. If society fully accepts these families, then being gay or lesbian won't be abnormal in the years to come.

In Washington, D.C., a support group is forming called the Rainbow Families,   4
which meets monthly. The group consists of about one hundred and thirty gay parents and their children. They meet other children with same-sex parents. They have picnics and skating classes. It is extremely comforting to these families to get together and relate to one another.

As I continued to read the article, I started to feel deeply for the couples. Barry   5
Kessler says, "We just wanted to have a child so badly . . . There was this place in our hearts that we had this love . . . to give a child. It's just a deep feeling."

That was extremely emotional, and reading something like that allows me to   6
support same-sex parents and their beliefs. The way these parents express their emotion toward children demonstrated with no doubt that these parents are loving people, just looking out for the benefit of their kids.

According to psychology professor Charlotte Patterson, the long-term research   7
suggests that children of same-sex couples "seem to be developing pretty much like other people's children." In the years to come, maybe due to all the positive attributes of gay and lesbian parenting, this type of parenting will be accepted and not looked at differently from that of heterosexual families. Possibly the gay and lesbian family could provide greater love for their children than some so-called "normal families."

Reading 8   *Reflecting on the Reading*

1 In her introduction, Vayntraub states that she is in favor of gay parents. In paragraph 2, she explains that she will summarize Murphy's evidence in support of gay parents to back up her own view. Working with a partner or small group, underline each piece of evidence in support of gay parents that Vayntraub summarizes. Discuss whether you find Vayntraub's use of supporting opinions effective. Why or why not?

2 Put an A next to any sections of the essay with which you agree. Put a *D* next to any sections with which you disagree. Then discuss your choices with your partner or group. Be prepared to explain and support your opinions.

3 Put a check (✓) in the margin next to sections of the essay that deal with emotions. Discuss whether you think these sections make the writer's argument more convincing. Why or why not?

4 At the end of her essay, Vayntraub writes: "Possibly the gay and lesbian family could provide greater love for their children than some so-called 'normal families.'" In your journal, freewrite about your reactions to this statement, providing evidence for your opinion from television news reports, your reading, or your own understanding of what is important in children's lives.

TECHNIQUES WRITERS USE

In this chapter, you will write an essay in which you respond to ideas presented in something you have read. This is the most typical kind of essay assigned for college courses. The key task in this type of writing is to express your opinion about what you have read. In order to do this effectively, you need to explain relevant ideas from the reading, using the techniques of summarizing, paraphrasing, and quoting. It is important to remember, however, that you are the author of the essay, so you need to select ideas from the reading that will support the point or points you wish to make.

Summarizing Information from Written Sources

Summarizing – explaining someone else's ideas in your own words – is done for several purposes. For example, students often summarize when they are taking notes on what they have read. But they also need to summarize when they refer to this information in their own writing.

A good summary should meet the following criteria:
- The first part of a summary should include
   - identification of the written source, including the title and author
   - a statement of the main idea of the material being summarized.
- A summary should be much shorter than the original source.
- It should cover the most important points in the original but leave out small supporting details and examples.
- It should not change or add to the ideas contained in the source.
- It should explain only the ideas contained in the source; it should not include the summary writer's ideas.
- It should be written in the summary writer's own words, although it may include brief quotations from the source. Quotation marks must be used around any words copied directly from the source.
- It should be written clearly and in a logical order.

Task 6.1   *Analyze*

1 Reread "Bean Paste vs. Miniskirts" (on page 174). Then reread the first paragraph of "A Response to 'Bean Paste vs. Miniskirts'" (on the next page), in which Liana Salman summarizes the main ideas of the article.

> "Bean Paste vs. Miniskirts: Generation Gap Grows" is an article written by Nicholas Kristof and published in *The New York Times.* It talks about a generation gap in Hanok, South Korea, which became a conflicting situation. Korea was against westernization of their lives up until the 1960s. In the past half century, Hanok opened up to the modernization of the country, and new ideas started "pouring in." As a result, traditional, older people now have to live amongst concepts that they have had no time to adapt to. The article familiarizes us with views of older women of South Korea and allows us to understand their perception of this situation.

2 Working with a partner, do the following:

a Underline the place where Salman identifies the title and author of the article she is writing about. What punctuation is used to set off the article title?

b In a different color, underline the place where Salman identifies the newspaper in which the article appeared. What kind of type does she use to indicate the newspaper title?

c Find the paragraph in the original article by Kristof that contains most of the ideas mentioned in Salman's summary. Why do you think she decided to begin her summary with ideas from this particular paragraph?

d Underline twice the place where Salman quotes from the article itself. Why do you think she did this?

3 Compare your answers as a class.

Task 6.2 *Practice*

1 As a class, choose one of the following essays for all students to summarize:

"The Family in Society" by Isabella Kong (page 170)

"Gay Parents Find More Acceptance" by Carlyle Murphy (page 179)

2 Working individually, reread the essay several times and underline information that you think is important. Make notes in the margin of things you want to include in your summary.

3 Write down the most important questions the essay answers.

Examples

Why was traditional family structure beneficial in a society based on agriculture?

Why are there so many more gay parents today than in the past?

4 Now write a summary of the essay. Be sure to follow the general guidelines for summarizing on page 186.

5 Working in a small group, read each other's summaries. Then discuss and evaluate them by answering the questions below that are based on the summary guidelines on page 186. If the summary is written correctly, the answer to each question below will be yes.

   a Does the summary give the essay title and author correctly?

   b Does the summary state the main idea of the essay?

   c Is the summary much shorter than the essay?

   d Does the summary give only the main ideas of the essay, without including too many examples or small details?

   e Does the summary include only the ideas in the source? (In other words, it should not include the ideas of the summary writer.)

   f Is the summary written mostly in the summary writer's own words?

   g If a direct quotation is included in the summary, is it copied correctly and placed in quotation marks?

6 Decide which of the summaries is the strongest and discuss why.

7 Revise your summary based on the feedback you received from your group.

Paraphrasing Information from Written Sources

Paraphrasing – restating another writer's ideas in your own words – is used frequently in academic writing when a writer needs to explain someone else's ideas. Paraphrasing is an important academic skill, but it is a skill that students often find difficult. Usually, professional writers say things effectively, and it is hard for students to say them equally well using their own words. In Western academic writing, however, it is essential not to copy the exact wording of another text unless you put the words in quotation marks and state their source.

Using another author's words as if they were your own is called *plagiarism* and can lead to serious penalties, such as getting an F on the paper or failing the course. In some cases, plagiarism even leads to suspension from a university. With the widespread use of the Internet, plagiarism has become even more common than it was in the past. But it is also much easier for teachers to detect. Therefore, it is important for every college student to practice the essential writing technique of paraphrasing.

The following guidelines will help you to paraphrase effectively. (Examples are taken from "Bean Paste vs. Miniskirts" on page 174.)

- The most obvious way to paraphrase is to change the wording.

> **Original Sentence** *(from paragraph 6)*
> "These gaps seem to cause misunderstandings and sadness, but fewer open explosions than one might expect."
>
> **Acceptable Paraphrase**
> In Korea differences between the generations result in confusion and unhappiness, but they rarely cause open conflict.

- Another useful technique is to change the order of ideas.

> **Original Sentence** *(from paragraph 4)*
> "Those customs – especially respect for the elderly – permeated Korean society until the last few decades."
>
> **Acceptable Paraphrase**
> Until fairly recently, respecting one's elders was an important value in Korean culture.

- Certain key words cannot be successfully explained in other words and therefore must be included in a paraphrase.

> **Original Sentence** *with key words underlined (from paragraph 3)*
> "And such skirmishes are only one facet of a generation gap that many South Koreans say is greater than almost anywhere in the world."
>
> **Acceptable Paraphrase** *with key words underlined*
> Many South Koreans explain that the generation gap in their country is very big and therefore results in many conflicts between the young and the old.

- Occasionally, you may want to quote brief phrases from the original in your paraphrase.

> **Original Sentence** *(from paragraph 6)*
> "Young and old alike may stew inside at the foolishness of the other, but they also describe how they go out of their way to accommodate."
>
> **Acceptable Paraphrase**
> Although members of one generation sometimes "stew inside" because of the behavior of the other generation, they explain that they "go out of their way" to get along.

- Remember that copying more than a few key words without using quotation marks is considered to be plagiarism and is not acceptable.

> **Original Sentence** *(from paragraph 6)*
> "Young and old alike may stew inside at the foolishness of the other, but they also describe how they go out of their way to accommodate."
>
> **Unacceptable Paraphrase** *with copied words underlined*
> Young and old Koreans may stew inside at the foolishness of the other, but they explain that they go out of their way to accommodate.

Task 6.3 *Analyze*

1 Working with a partner or small group, read these attempted paraphrases of sentences from "Gay Parents Find More Acceptance" (page 179). Compare each of the attempted paraphrases to the original sentence and discuss why it is or is not an acceptable paraphrase.

a **Original Sentence** (from paragraph 1)
"The overwhelming majority of about 2 million parents who are gay are raising children from earlier heterosexual marriages, according to Drew."

Attempted Paraphrase
The overwhelming majority of gay parents are raising children from earlier heterosexual marriages.

b **Original Sentences** (from paragraph 6)
"Gay parenting remains unacceptable in some circles. The Family Research Council, a conservative political organization that openly urges homosexuals to change their orientation, opposes the idea of gay men and lesbians having children."

Attempted Paraphrase
Some people are still opposed to gay parenting. For example, the conservative Family Research Council, which encourages gay people to become straight, is against homosexuals becoming parents.

c **Original Sentence** (from paragraph 11)
"Most research on children of gay couples indicates they have no worse social or behavioral problems than children of heterosexual parents."

Attempted Paraphrase
Much of the existing research on children who are raised in gay families suggests that "they have no worse social or behavioral problems" than children raised by straight parents.

2 If you decided that an attempted paraphrase was not acceptable, rewrite it so that it *is* acceptable. Check your work using the Answer Key on page 260.

Practice

1 Write a paraphrase of each of the following sentences from "Traditional Family and Modern Society in Africa" (page 171):

   a "In fact, every group, large or small, having a common past or heredity, has its own culture, even though some common cultural aspects can be found in all cultures." (paragraph 1)

   b "Today the economic and political conditions have changed, changing at the same time people's mentality and behavior." (paragraph 3)

   c "One of the first things to change was the size of the family." (paragraph 4)

2 Compare your paraphrases with a small group. Then discuss the following:

   a Which of the paraphrases do you consider to be acceptable? In other words, which ones explain the ideas from the original sentences without copying the exact wording?

   b Did you find any examples of plagiarism? Explain.

   c As in summarizing, it is not acceptable in a paraphrase to change or add to the ideas of the original sentences. Did any of the paraphrases do this?

Outlining

Outlining, like clustering (discussed on page 150) is a tool to help you in organizing ideas. But unlike clustering, outlining organizes ideas in a linear way. Students who approach problems analytically often prefer this approach. Here is the outline format for a traditional academic essay.

   I.   Introduction and thesis statement

   II. First major supporting idea
       A. Relevant evidence
           1. Example or explanation
           2. Another example or explanation
       B. Relevant evidence
           1. Example or explanation
           2. Another example or explanation

   III. Second major supporting idea
       A. Relevant evidence
           1. Example or explanation
           2. Another example or explanation
       B. Relevant evidence
           1. Example or explanation
           2. Another example or explanation

   IV. Additional supporting ideas [optional]

   V. Conclusion

An outline can be written either before or after a draft. Some writers like to get their ideas down in outline form before they begin to write. Then they follow their outline as they write. Others choose to write a draft first and then do an outline afterward to see how their ideas are related. In this case, writers can analyze the outline of a draft and then decide how to improve their organization in the next draft.

Task 6.5 *Analyze*

1 Reread "The Family in Society" by Isabella Kong (page 170).

2 Working with a partner or small group, write an outline for this essay. Be sure to express each of the points in your outline in a complete sentence.

3 Compare your outline with the one in the Answer Key on page 260. Discuss how the outlines are similar and different. After seeing the Answer Key, is there anything you would change in your outline? Why?

Task 6.6 *Practice*

1 Working individually, imagine that you have been asked to write an essay explaining why you prefer to live either in a traditional or a modern family.

2 First, write two or three possible thesis statements for an essay on this topic. (Review "Formulating a Thesis Statement," on page 148, if necessary.)

3 Choose the one thesis statement that you would most like to work with, and develop an outline for a possible essay on this topic. Remember to express your ideas in complete sentences.

4 Exchange outlines with a partner and discuss them. Which outline was more detailed? Which one listed more convincing evidence?

INTERNET SEARCH

Do the Internet search that relates to the essay assignment option you choose. If you choose Option 1, you will write about changing family structures. The essay "A Response to 'Bean Paste vs. Miniskirts'" (page 174), is an example of a response to this assignment. If you choose Option 2, you will write about gay parents. The essays "The Problem of Gay Parenting" (page 183) and "A Positive View of Gay Parenting" (page 184) are examples of responses to this assignment.

Go now to page 194 for details of the two essay assignment options. Decide which one you want to do. Then proceed with the appropriate Internet search. (If you are not sure which essay assignment you prefer, you can begin by doing part of each Internet search to get a better idea of the difference between the two assignments.)

Option 1 *Changing Family Structures*

1 Do an Internet search using the keywords *family structure in* [name of country or name of group]. For example, you could use *family structure in the United States, family structure in Pakistan, family structure Italian Americans,* or *family structure Japanese Americans.*

2 Look for articles that are based on recent information and select two or three of the most interesting ones to read carefully.

3 Take notes on the articles you selected. Be sure to identify your sources by including the following information at the end of your notes for each article:
  • The name of the article
  • The name of the newspaper, magazine, or journal from which it was taken
  • The address of the Web site (URL)
  • The date you accessed the Web site

4 Write a summary of the most important things you learned from reading these sources. (Remember that copying from the Internet is plagiarism and can lead to serious penalties.)

5 Share your summary with a small group of students who chose the same topic. Then discuss what you learned about searching the Internet from this activity.

Option 2 *Gay Parents*

1 Do an Internet search using the keywords *positions on gay parents.*

2 Read several articles and select two articles to read carefully: one that is in favor of gay parenting and one that is against it.

3 Take notes on the articles you selected. Be sure to identify your sources by including the following information at the end of your notes for each article:
  • The name of the article
  • The name of the newspaper, magazine, or journal from which it was taken
  • The address of the Web site (URL)
  • The date you accessed the Web site

4 Write a summary of the different reasons each of the two sources give to justify their positions. (Remember that copying from the Internet is plagiarism and can lead to serious penalties.)

5 Share your summary with a small group of students who have chosen the same topic. Then discuss what you learned about searching the Internet from this activity.

ESSAY ASSIGNMENT

Option 1 *Changing Family Structures*

In paragraph 4 of "The Family in Society," Isabella Kong states:

> Nowadays, when individualism and equality are the most prevailing ideas in the world, people may find it very hard to adjust themselves to a traditional family. The means of production have changed so that the adaptive value of the traditional family is no longer obvious. The modern family has its advantages, as it will be more open and free, but it will also devastate the respect for the older generation that once was the dominant force in the traditional family. (page 170)

Write an essay in which you discuss the statement above, following these guidelines:

- The purpose of your essay is to express your opinion about the ways in which families are changing. Imagine your readers to be other college students who are interested in learning the views of their peers on this topic.
- Use examples from two or more of the following essays:
    "Traditional vs. Modern Family" (page 168)
    "The Family in Society" (page 170)
    "Traditional Family and Modern Society in Africa" (page 171)
    "Bean Paste vs. Miniskirts" (page 174)
- Use examples from your Internet search.
- Use examples from your own reading, if possible.
- Summarize and paraphrase ideas from the readings to which you refer.
- Include at least one direct quotation.
- If you wish, you may use examples from your own experience or the experiences of other people you know.

Reread the writing you have already done for this chapter to see whether it gives you ideas for this assignment.

Option 2 *Gay Parents*

Write an essay in which you discuss the issue of gay parents, following these guidelines:

- The purpose of your essay is to express your opinion on the issue of gay parenting. Imagine your readers to be other college students who have not yet decided how they feel about this issue.
- As your main source, use "Gay Parents Find More Acceptance" (page 179) by Carlyle Murphy. In your essay, explain some of the signs indicating, according to Murphy, that gay parenting is becoming more acceptable in the United States. Explain some of the problems that gay parents and their children still face, according to Murphy.

- Use examples from your Internet search.
- Use examples from your own reading, if possible.
- Summarize and paraphrase ideas from the readings to which you refer.
- Include at least one direct quotation.
- If you wish, you may use examples from your own experience or the experiences of other people you know.

Reread the writing you have already done for this chapter to see whether it gives you ideas for this assignment.

Generating Ideas

For Option 1

1 Write a paraphrase of paragraph 4 of Isabella Kong's essay (quoted at the top of page 194). Review "Paraphrasing Information from Written Sources," on page 188, if necessary.

2 Write down three examples of changes in family structure taken from the readings you plan to discuss in your own essay.

3 Discuss your paraphrases and examples in a small group.

  a According to Kong, why have families moved to a modern family structure? How has this change affected older family members?

  b Compare the examples of changing family structure that you plan to use in your essay. In what ways do the different examples relate to Kong's statement, "The modern family has its advantages, as it will be more open and free, but it will also devastate the respect for the older generation that once was the dominant force in the traditional family"?

For Option 2

1 Reread "Gay Parents Find More Acceptance" and, in the margin next to each paragraph, write down the topic being discussed.

2 Discuss the topics you found with a partner or small group. In which paragraphs is Murphy giving examples that relate to gay parenting becoming more acceptable to society? In which paragraphs is he focusing on problems that gay parents still encounter? Which example or examples are the most important for you in forming an opinion on this issue?

3 Review your answers and notes from the "Reflecting on the Reading" activities (page 182) that follow Murphy's article.

Organizing Ideas

For Options 1 and 2

Organize the ideas you generated by making an outline (see page 191) or a cluster diagram (see page 150). For Option 1, put the topic "how families are changing" at the top of your outline or in the center of your cluster diagram; for Option 2, use the topic "gay parenting."

Working Toward a Thesis Statement

For Option 1

1 Write your answers to each of the following questions in one to three sentences:

  a What general statement can you make based on the advantages and disadvantages you have noted?

  b What is your own opinion about the ways in which families are changing in the modern world? Do you see these changes as positive, negative, or positive *and* negative?

2 Considering your answers to the questions in step 1, write several possible thesis statements for your essay. Review "Formulating a Thesis Statement," on page 148, if necessary.

3 Analyze your thesis statements. Which thesis comes closest to expressing your own opinion? For which thesis do you have the strongest supporting evidence? Which thesis would result in the most interesting essay?

4 Choose what you feel is your strongest thesis statement. This tentative thesis will guide you as you write your first draft. It is important to remember, however, that your original thesis may change or become more complex as you draft and revise your essay.

For Option 2

1 Considering all the evidence Carlyle Murphy included in his article and all of the comments he quotes or paraphrases, what general position do you think Murphy is presenting about gay parenting? Write down what you think this position is in one or two sentences.

2 Do you agree with Murphy's position as you have expressed it in step 1? Why or why not? List the evidence you have to support your own opinion.

3 Now write out your own position – your thesis statement – about gay parenting in one sentence. This will be your tentative thesis statement, which will guide you as you write your first draft. It is important to remember, however, that your original thesis may change or become more complex as you draft and revise your essay.

Writing Tips

- **Give your essay a title.**

  Thinking of a title can help you focus on your main idea. The title should inform the readers of what your topic is and also make them want to learn more about what you have to say. Look back at the titles of the readings in this book to get ideas about what makes a title effective. Before you begin to write your first draft, think of two or three titles that would be appropriate. Then choose the one that seems best. After you finish your draft, you can decide whether your title accurately reflects what you wrote. At that point, if you feel that your title does not communicate your ideas effectively, you can always decide on a different title.

- **Write an effective conclusion.**

  The conclusion is an important element of your essay, so you should spend time thinking about it carefully. The conclusion serves to sum up an essay and let the reader know it is coming to an end. In addition, the conclusion can emphasize your thesis, suggest a way to solve a problem, or explain what you have learned. Review the conclusions of some of the readings in this book to get ideas about what makes a conclusion effective. After you finish your draft, decide whether your conclusion is effective and accurately reflects your ideas. If you are not sure, write a different conclusion (or two) and see which one you like best.

- **Organize your essay clearly.**

  Make an outline of your essay before you start to write. Seeing an outline of your ideas and supporting evidence will help you write a clear and logical essay. (Review "Outlining" on pages 191–192, if necessary.) After you finish your draft, you should check to see whether you followed your outline. If you did not follow your outline, you can then make a second outline that reflects the order of ideas and evidence as you actually wrote them in your first draft. When you compare the two outlines, decide which one is the most logical and effective and the one you want to follow as you revise.

Writing Your First Draft

Now, keeping the writing tips in mind, write the first draft of your essay. Use your thesis statement and refer to the writing you did for "Generating Ideas" (page 195) and "Organizing Ideas" (page 196). As you are working on this first draft, do not slow yourself down by worrying about correct grammar and spelling; it is more important just to get your ideas down on paper so you have something to work with in later drafts.

REVISING YOUR ESSAY

Once you have put your ideas down on paper by completing the first draft, you can begin the revising process.

Benefiting from Teacher Comments

Throughout this book, we emphasize getting peer response to your writing before you revise. We hope you will continue this practice in future writing situations. But, of course, students can also learn a great deal from their teachers' comments. Some teachers want to comment on each draft that you write. Other teachers prefer to comment on the last draft before the final essay. Still other teachers will comment only on the final draft, although they may want to see your previous drafts. Whichever procedure your teacher prefers, the following suggestions will help you to get the most from your teacher's comments:

- Soon after getting your essay back, reread it, paying careful attention to what your teacher wrote.
- Take notes about the following:
  What comments did your teacher make that you agree with?
  Are there any areas where you don't agree?
  Are there any comments that you don't understand?
- Sometimes it helps to discuss the teacher's comments with a classmate you trust. Does your friend see anything in the comments that you missed? Can your friend help you to understand the teacher's comments?
- If there are comments that you do not agree with or do not understand, or if you would just like to talk to your teacher about your paper, try to arrange a conference either before or after class.

Responding to Your Peers

1 Working with a partner or a group of three, exchange and read the first drafts of your essays.

2 Fill out a copy of the "Peer Response Form" on page 202 for each of the first drafts you read. Focus on the ideas rather than the grammar and spelling. Point out only those mistakes that interfere with understanding.

3 Using the completed peer response forms as the basis for your discussion, have a peer conference to discuss your first drafts.

Writing Your Second Draft

1 Fill out the "Writer's Plan for Revising," on page 205.

2 Taking into consideration the feedback you have received from your peers and perhaps from your teacher and your own ideas about how to improve your essay, write your second draft.

EDITING YOUR ESSAY

When you are satisfied with the content and organization of your essay, you can begin the process of editing.

Grammar in Context: Using Modal Auxiliaries

Modal auxiliaries are necessary to add important shades of meaning to verbs. Sometimes called helping verbs, they indicate different degrees of ability, possibility, permission, advisability, or necessity.

Here are some of the most common modals:

can	*have (has, had) to*	*might*	*shall*	*will*
could	*may*	*must*	*should*	*would*

The tasks that follow will give you a chance to check your understanding of the correct usage of modal auxiliaries. If you need a more detailed explanation, look up modal auxiliaries or modal verbs in your grammar reference book or in an online grammar resource such as Purdue University's Online Writing Lab, currently accessible at <http://owl.english.purdue.edu>.

Because it is difficult to explain the exact meanings of modals, it is best to observe how they are used in speech and writing and then to experiment with using them yourself. Notice that the modals never change their form (for example, by adding -*s* or -*ed*), as other verbs do.

Task 6.7 *Analyze*

1 Read the following passage, taken from paragraph 6 of "Bean Paste vs. Miniskirts" by Nicholas D. Kristof (page 174), and draw one line under all the modals and two lines under the verbs they modify.

> These gaps seem to cause misunderstandings and sadness, but fewer open explosions than one might expect. Young and old alike may stew inside at the foolishness of the other, but they also describe how they go out of their way to accommodate. "It's a constant bother to live with the old folks," said Chong Kum Sook, 38, who lives in the

same house as her husband's parents. "It's very hard. It's not that they complain, but I feel the burden on myself. My in-laws are early risers, so I try to get up when they do. And in the summer I can't wear skimpy clothes, because I have to dress cautiously so as not to disturb them. I should be careful not to make them unhappy."

2 Working with a partner, discuss each of the modals you identified. Which of the following meanings does each one suggest: ability, possibility, permission, advisability, or necessity?

Example

"Disputes and conflicts <u>may</u> often <u>arise</u> and thus threaten the existence of the family."

In this sentence, taken from Isabella Kong's essay, "The Family in Society," *may* refers to possibility: It is possible that disputes and conflicts will arise.

3 Compare your explanations with those given in the Answer Key on page 261.

Task 6.8 *Practice*

1 Working with a partner, fill in the blanks with the correct modals to solve the mystery of the missing students. Choose your answers from the following: *might, must, should, would.*

An American professor was rushing to the classroom to give his first   1
lecture at a Brazilian university. When he arrived, he was surprised
to find Room 101 was empty. He didn't know what had happened.
However, being a professor, his mind went to work, and he came up
with some interesting theories.

The professor's watch .... have stopped. Or the   2
students .... have forgotten that a class was scheduled
for that day. Or possibly, they all .... have decided to
drop the class.

There were other possibilities as well. The university   3
.... have closed early that day for a strike or protest.
But surely if there had been a strike, the professor ....
have heard about it from someone. Maybe there was a cultural
explanation. Perhaps in Brazil, it .... be acceptable for
students to come late to class or not to come to class at all.

As it turned out, the answer was quite simple. As a professor,   4
he .... have known better, but he obviously had not

> checked the schedule of classes carefully enough. Although he had copied down the day and time correctly, he .... have made a mistake about the room. He had gone to room 101 when, in fact, he .... have gone to Room 110, which is where all his students were waiting.

2 Check your work using the Answer Key on page 261.

Editing Checklist

If you are writing your essay on a computer, remember to print out your revised essay and proofread it on paper.

☐ **First proofreading: modal auxiliaries**
Proofread your essay carefully to check your use of modal auxiliaries. Remember that the modals do not change their form because of subject-verb agreement. Check (✓) the box when you have finished.

☐ **Second proofreading**
Proofread your essay a second time and correct any other errors of grammar, spelling, or punctuation that you find. Check (✓) the box when you have finished.

☐ **Third proofreading**
Print out or write a copy of your essay that includes the corrections you made in your first and second proofreading. Now proofread your essay a third time. Try to find and correct any errors that you missed. Then print out, or write in dark blue or black ink, the final draft of your essay. Check (✓) the box when you have finished.

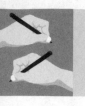

Peer Response Form
Writing Based on Reading

WRITER'S NAME: .... READER'S NAME: ....

DATE: ....

Focus on the ideas rather than the grammar and spelling. Discuss only those mistakes that interfere with understanding.

1 What was one thing you learned about the topic from reading this essay?

2 Did the writer include a thesis statement explaining the main idea of the essay? If so, copy it in the space below. In which paragraph did this thesis statement appear?

3 Find one example of a quotation from an outside source that was included in the essay and copy it in the space below. Was the source for the quotation identified clearly and correctly? If not, what was missing?

Photocopiable   © Cambridge University Press

4 Did the quotation effectively support a point the writer was making? Why or why not?

5 Find one example of a paraphrase from an outside source that was included in the essay and copy it in the space below. Was the source for the information identified clearly and correctly? If not, what was missing?

6 Did the paraphrase effectively support a point the writer was making? Why or why not?

7 Has the writer included enough background information so that readers who are not familiar with the essay topic will easily understand the points he or she is making? If not, what additional information should the writer add in the next draft?

Writer's Plan for Revising

Writing Based on Reading

YOUR NAME: .... ESSAY TITLE: ....

DATE: ....

Reread your essay, concentrating on the ideas rather than on grammar and spelling. Then write your answers to the following questions.

1 What part of this essay are you most pleased with? Why? Explain in as much detail as possible.

2 What parts of this essay were the most difficult to write? Are you satisfied with them? If not, how could you improve these parts in the next draft?

3 Without looking at your essay, write out what you now believe about your essay topic (your thesis statement) at this stage of the revision process. If this opinion is different from the one you expressed in your present draft, how will you revise your essay to reflect the changes in your thesis statement?

Identity is the answer to the question "Who am I?" For some people, race or skin color may be the most important element of identity. For others, it may be language, nationality, religion, culture, or profession. The question of identity is often complicated when someone belongs to several groups, such as children whose parents are of different races or immigrants who feel loyal to the country of their birth as well as to their new country. Issues of identity also arise when people from different races or ethnic groups fall in love and have to consider the effects of marrying someone from another race or culture. In this chapter, you will read and discuss essays about identity; most of them include research data from interviews, public opinion polls, and statistical analysis. Then you will conduct some research of your own and write an essay in which you report the results of this research.

READINGS

An American Success Story
by Samuel Nakasian

A big part of American identity is related to the "American dream," in which a poor immigrant comes to America with no money and works his or her way to the top. Samuel Nakasian, a successful lawyer who immigrated to the United States from Armenia, gave this speech to a group of new American citizens more than 20 years ago. As you read the speech, think about Nakasian's description of America. Is it realistic? How does it compare to the experience of people you know?

Some forty years ago, in a U.S. District Court in New York – a court in the   1
neighborhood of the Statue of Liberty and Ellis Island, where I entered America – I
applied for American citizenship and received it, just as you did today in the same
time-honored ceremony. I was given my naturalization certificate, as you were
given yours today. May I share with you what this certificate has meant to me?

This is my American birthright. I have cherished it above all other possessions   2
for forty years. It means something very special, for no other country in the world
offers as much as this certificate guarantees.

If you came here to escape discrimination because you are a member of a   3
minority in your religious beliefs, ethnic origins, or political preference, *here* you
are guaranteed your religious rights and personal freedom. This court and other
courts are here to serve you by protecting your rights and to hear your petitions
with impartial justice. If you came here to make a better life for yourself and your
family, to have the opportunity of formal education to the highest level of your
capacity, ours is one of the few countries where you can climb the economic,
intellectual, and cultural ladder to the top.

I must now, unavoidably, become personal – to emphasize this point. I was   4
brought here very young, very poor, by one surviving parent of a massacre, and
shortly after arriving in the United States I was orphaned. After a few years in
an orphanage, my first job was as a farm hand. I had a dream to be a lawyer;
thereafter, I made steady progress: educationally, professionally, and economically.
Taking advantage of America's opportunities, I was able to support a family of
four children, each of whom now has a college education at my expense and has
employment of his or her choice. And how nice it is that my wife and I are not
financially dependent on our children as we approach the later years.

Do you know what I hate to hear? "You are a self-made man." I am not a   5
self-made man. I am the product of this great country and its generous people.
America made me!

The opportunity to work is here. The schools are here and available, whether or   6
not you can afford the tuition for college or graduate school. If you have dreams and
make the effort, *you* can make it or – more accurately – America can make *you*.

The major difference in America is the 200-year-old system. I know the   7
difference firsthand, because since World War II, I have traveled to almost every
country in the world as a representative of our government and as an overseas
negotiator for American companies. Whatever the country of origin, people who
come to America are remade by our free society system. They become dedicated
Americans regardless of their ethnic origins. . . .

Before World War II, immigrants were regarded one or two notches below   8
the social level of old American families. The greatest social prestige came from
having an ancestor on the Mayflower or in the War of Independence. . . . Today,
all is changed. You are respected for your diligence and honor. It doesn't matter
that your skin is darker, eyes more slanted, or speech heavily accented. You are
respected for what you can contribute to your family, community, and country.

Read the awards of the Nobel Prize; read the list of distinguished scientists;   9
read the election forms; read *Forbes* magazine listing the richest Americans today.
You will find immigrants in all those records of achievement. . . .

In recent years immigrants fly in, so perhaps many of you have not had the   10
opportunity to see the Statue of Liberty. Would you, the first chance you get, visit
there and read what is inscribed? The statue is the symbol of America's outreach
to the world's people. America is great because it is composed of almost every
race and religion in the world. It is a community which has been enriched by
what immigrants brought here and planted here to flourish in a free society – a
society based on government as the *servant* of the people and not government as
the *master* of the people. What you do with your lives is your decision, not the
government's. . . .

Finally, let me say this. A popular song goes, "If I can make it here [in New   11
York], I can make it anywhere." I believe that. I also believe that if you can't make
it in *America*, you were not likely to make it anywhere else.

You will make it here, no doubt, because you came here to work. You will find,   12
as I did, that America's rewards are generous.

Reading 1   Reflecting on the Reading

1 List all the advantages of life in the United States that Nakasian mentions.
Next to each advantage, write a possible disadvantage that Nakasian does not
mention. For example, Nakasian says that in the United States people are
guaranteed personal freedom. He supports this by explaining that the legal
system protects people's rights. But he does not mention that you must have
enough money to hire a lawyer or that pursuing a legal case can take years.
Discuss your list of advantages and disadvantages with a small group.

2 With your group, discuss in what ways Nakasian's audience probably
influenced what he said. How might his speech have been different if he had
been addressing a group of high school students, for example, or a group of
welfare recipients who were born in the United States?

3 Nakasian's view of America is idealistic; that is, he talks only about the positive things and ignores the darker side. Discuss which of the following statements might explain Nakasian's positive outlook:

a He is not aware of such things as discrimination, language problems, or poverty because he never experienced them himself.

b He knows that problems exist in the United States, but he wants to offer encouragement to new citizens.

c He is proud of his adopted country and wants people to see the positive things as opposed to the negative things often reported in the press.

d He truly believes that the United States allows anyone to succeed who really wants to.

4 Imagine that a friend who lives outside the United States has read "An American Success Story." Your friend has been so impressed by what Nakasian says about opportunities in the United States that he or she is planning to immigrate to America as soon as possible. Write a letter to this friend giving your own opinion about the ideas in Nakasian's speech. What advice would you give your friend about whether to immigrate to the United States? Read your letter to your group. Then choose one student from each group to read his or her letter to the class.

Reading 2

Response to "An American Success Story"

Jowita Drazkowski

Jowita Drazkowski was born in Poland and came to the United States in the 1990s. In responding to Nakasian's speech, she points out some problems immigrants often encounter that he did not mention. Before you read, think about some of the problems you, your family, a friend, or someone you heard about faced after coming to the United States.

Some people think that America is a country full of opportunities – a society where everyone can achieve what he or she wants if that person tries hard enough. They think that people who live here are themselves products of this country and that being an American means there are built-in guarantees of success. They feel able to overcome any obstacles on the way to fulfill their dreams. The author of the essay "An American Success Story," Samuel Nakasian, belongs to the group of people who think like that. He has a very idealistic view of living in America, with which I do not agree.

Nakasian states that every immigrant who comes to America has an equal opportunity for achieving his goal. He doesn't see the difference in whether or not an immigrant came to this country as a child or as an adult. He seems not to have an idea that knowing the language is not only helpful to achieve one's goal, but also it is a key to personal success. He also says, "It doesn't matter that your skin is darker, eyes more slanted, or speech heavily accented." I wonder what makes him think that. Racial discrimination, for example, is one of the most controversial and very current issues in the media these days. There are countless incidents touched upon in newspaper articles or on TV that involve hatred between people of different ethnic, cultural, or national backgrounds living in America. Nakasian was only a few years old when he arrived in America. Most likely he can speak English with no apparent foreign accent. Therefore, he might never have experienced how people who speak with accents are treated here. I, in contrast, do speak with a foreign accent, and occasionally I find myself in circumstances where I'm sure I would be treated better if I were a native speaker in America. It's not to say that people have no rights. For instance, a person could openly be opposed to immigration. Everybody has a right to have independent views and to express them. However, we shouldn't close our eyes and pretend that problems don't exist. Therefore, I do not agree with Nakasian on these points.

Another way in which my opinion differs from Nakasian's is that he declares 3
that education is available for everyone if they want to study. I think it is not true. The people who have a lot of money can afford to go to any school they want. The people who are very poor can study with government help. Yet what about people who are in the middle? What about people whose income is too high to obtain financial aid and at the same time too low to pay for their education? These are very important questions which Nakasian doesn't take under consideration, but I do.

Fortunately, I agree with Nakasian in the case of personal freedom and 4
guarantees about religious rights. In this country, no one feels like a stranger if their beliefs differ from somebody else's. In every area of the United States, we can find examples of religious freedom. Synagogues, mosques, Catholic and Protestant churches, or even Buddhist temples can be found here. People celebrate their own holidays without worrying that someone can abuse them for doing it. Everyone can feel comfortable while speaking out their opinion.

Nakasian mentions that "If you have dreams and make the effort, *you* can 5
make it or – more accurately – America can make *you*." I agree with him, but only partly. I believe that working hard helps people to reach their goals. Yet I think that every one of them needs something more than only work. They need to have some luck. The word *luck* doesn't mean to win millions of dollars in the lottery. The word *luck* means not to have too many obstacles or obstacles one cannot overcome on the way one has chosen to reach his or her goals.

I am an immigrant from Poland. I came to the U.S. five years ago. I have 6
chosen this country to stay in, perhaps forever. It's a country that has been built on the basis of immigration. When I came here, I had a feeling that I would not be rejected by the society, and I would feel more comfortable here than anywhere else in the world. I think that America is the right place for me to live and a great place to fulfill my dreams. I have been working hard, and I will continue to work hard to achieve my goals, and with some luck, which until now has not left me, I will make it here.

1 Like all good writers, Drazkowski identifies the written source to which she is responding and clearly explains specific ideas from that source that she wishes to comment on in her own essay. Working with a partner, find the following:

a The place where Drazkowski first identifies the written source

b An example of an effectively used quotation from the source

c An example of a clearly written paraphrase of an idea from the source

2 In paragraph 2, Drazkowski states that "we shouldn't close our eyes and pretend that problems don't exist [in America]." Underline each of the problems that she points out in paragraph 2. Discuss these problems with your partner or a small group. Based on your own knowledge or experience, do you believe these problems are as serious as the writer thinks they are?

3 In paragraph 4, Drazkowski says: "In this country, no one feels like a stranger if their beliefs differ from somebody else's. . . . Everyone can feel comfortable while speaking out their opinion." Working with your partner or group, think of an example from your own experience or a news story that contradicts (does not support) this statement. Now write a statement that qualifies (modifies or limits) Drazkowski's original statement so that it can be supported. Here are some qualifying words you might use: *usually, often, in many cases, more than, many, some.* Then compare your examples and statements with those of other pairs or groups.

4 In paragraph 5, Drazkowski says that being successful in America depends partly on luck, which she defines as "not to have too many obstacles or obstacles one cannot overcome on the way one has chosen to reach his or her goals." In your journal, freewrite about your definition of luck. Is luck something that just happens to you, or can you make your own luck? Why, in your opinion, do some people always seem lucky while others seem to attract bad luck?

Reading 3   **Professional Writing**

America 2050: Immigration and the Hourglass

Alejandro Portes

In this article from Crosscurrents, *the Institute for Global Studies Newsletter, Alejandro Portes, a Cuban-born sociologist currently teaching at Princeton University, discusses the influence of immigration on the future of American society. Will increased immigration have the tendency to fragment or weaken American society, as some people fear? On the other hand, will immigration strengthen America by providing new sources of unskilled and skilled labor, additional business, and more upwardly mobile professionals? As you read, think about whether immigration hurts or helps American society.*

Adapting to the United States is not what it used to be. The general trend at the turn of the century* was to find a blue-collar job and stay within the ethnic community for the first generation. Then the second generation gradually moved up to the supervisory jobs, and the third generation joined the middle classes. Today, the society is far more differentiated than it was at the turn of the century. You have increasingly an hourglass economy, with a lot of minimally paying low-level jobs and a lot of well-paying professional jobs. At the same time, there are greater expectations of consumption and achievement. The new immigrants are in a very real race against time to jump from the entry-level jobs, pass through that narrow center of the hourglass, and reach the professional mainstream. But, increasingly, many second-generation children do not make it because of the shape of that economy. They are frustrated because they are Americans and have in a sense already assimilated the aspirations and the patterns of consumption of the society. Thus, for both parents and children, it's a one-generation race to make it – which makes it a very demanding adaptation experience.

Fortunately, the resources of the ethnic community help in different ways. They help in allowing first-generation immigrants to become entrepreneurs,* and, through that route, place their children in a better position to climb up through the narrow center. That is the case of many Chinese, Lebanese, and Korean shop owners whose children we now see in colleges and universities.

Second, the ethnic communities offer a certain reinforcement of immigrant parental values, not least of which is the significance of hard work and achievement. In one study of the children of immigrants, we found a perfect positive relationship between homework hours and academic performance, and a perfect negative relationship between hours of TV watching and academic performance.

*turn of the century: the years around 1900

*entrepreneurs: business owners

Third, the immigrant community can offer a safety valve for those who do not make it here by providing access to the home networks. For instance, some immigrants find a way to send their kids home to be educated when they see them in danger here. In many ways, we are witnessing more functional adaptations that combine instrumental* learning of U.S. culture with strong bonds within the immigrant community. 4

These adaptations reflect the increasing complexity of U.S. society. Instead of a clearly dominant mainstream culture preaching certain virtues associated with a puritan ethic,* we now have a number of differential lifestyles and orientations, and a number of perils along the way as well. Clearly, mass culture as diffused by the media is a double-edged sword. It is a means to get a lot of information about the rest of the world and to be entertained. But it is also often a means to foster expectations that may not be within the immediate reach of particular groups. 5

That gap creates processes of relative deprivation, which, in turn, evolve in different directions. The native-born Americans with long experience in the country have developed different lifestyles as a way to selectively adapt to these messages and to navigate a complex society. The immigrants arrive for the most part with the belief that the streets of America are paved with gold, that they are going to make it here. What they find is a very different reality. Their fate is often problematic in terms of the resources they can bring to bear on these issues. . . . 6

* * *

Stereotypes feed on labels that impose a certain form of symbolic violence in the conceptualization of ethnic groups. For example, the labels Hispanic American or Asian American are often void of content from the point of view of the groups of designation. The experience of Mexican Americans in the West, a profound experience of generations of exploitation, is closer to that of black Americans in the East than to the experience of immigrants from the rest of Latin America, who happen to be coming often from privileged backgrounds. So the idea of incorporating a Rodriguez in the Hispanic group because he happens to be Rodriguez is symbolic violence exercised against the individual and also against the history of the group. Similarly, to lump all Africans, Jamaicans, Haitians, and so on as "black" will lead to confusions. I have argued repeatedly that the identities that count are for the most part national, because that's where individuals are rooted in a particular history. 7

Of course, national identities cut both ways. Thus, chauvinistic* and xenophobic* observers are often afraid of the new immigrants. They think that this country is falling apart, and they generate a lot of writing about the fragmentation of America. There was a book by a former governor of Colorado called by that label, *The Fragmentation of America*. 8

Those fears are unfounded. Most immigrant communities are very keen on making it in America and having their children make it in America. Their 9

*instrumental: necessary, essential

*puritan ethic: a value system that emphasizes rewards for hard work

*chauvinistic: being overly proud of one's country or nationality

*xenophobic: being afraid of anything "foreign"

loyalties and ties are not set up in an adversarial sense toward the mainstream of the society. Rather, they aim to adapt better economically and socially, and in an instrumental sense, to that mainstream.

The more xenophobic commentators fail to see this process of adaptation and the role it gives to the transition between generations. The first generation may remain culturally closed and so are its ethnic communities. But because of the achievements of that first generation, members of the second generation are very often able to jump into a good college education. These second-generation kids are Americans. In our data, we find that by age fourteen, children of immigrants speak English fluently, almost without exception, and about 85 percent prefer to speak English over their parental language – even if living in the middle of an ethnic community and going to bilingual schools, as it happens in Miami. In a sense, what is at risk in the second generation is not Americanness or the English language. What is at risk is *the preservation of the parental language,* which is a resource for these kids. It would be better to speak two languages rather than one. So some of them will go to college and will painfully relearn the language of their parents, the very one they lost when they were children. In short, fragmentation does not happen as predicted.

Further, it is important to realize that the immigrant flow does not occur as an "invasion" from the Third World. Immigration is certainly pushed, but it is also pulled by the interests of politically influential groups within the U.S., such as growers and other employers, who have managed to keep the immigration door open *de facto,** if not *de jure.** In a sense, the nation needs to get better control of its borders and implement more orderly programs of entry, but, by and large, immigration has been positive for America. The variety, the energy, the cultural diversity of the country that we see today in American cities are consequences of immigration.

The most concrete recommendation that comes from research on the new immigration is to pay attention, first, to context. If you receive people, make the contextual setting one in which they can at least swim. In many cases, people are being irresponsibly admitted when they are almost certain to drown, at least economically. The second lesson is: allow likes to be with likes. Do not be too concerned if in the first generation enclaves and communities are created here. These practices are not anti-American, and they do not lead to back-door fragmentation. Rather, that is often the first step toward successful adaptation, economically and socially.

The new migrations will certainly modify the categories through which Americans see themselves and are seen by others. At the turn of the century, white natives of northwestern European extraction used to look at southern and eastern Europeans as individuals of different races that would somehow change the character of the nation, pollute America, and turn it into a second-rate country. The categories at that time singled out southern and eastern Europeans, and there were projections that by the end of the century, over half of the population

10

11

12

13

de facto: in reality

de jure: according to law

would be made up of these people. Well, today nobody remembers, because they have all become "white." So the very process of adaptation to America has made the category "white" inclusive enough to accommodate both southern and eastern Europeans. In southern Florida and southern California today, it doesn't matter if your grandparents were Italian, Polish, or English. I think that by the year 2050, a number of descendants of current immigrant groups that are today categorized as mestizo,* Hispanic, or Asian will be white as well, sociologically, and that adaptation will change the categories. . . .

*mestizo: of mixed race

Reading 3   Reflecting on the Reading

1 In his title and throughout this essay, Portes uses the metaphor of an hourglass to describe the American economy. Reread paragraph 1. Then, with a partner or a small group, discuss what Portes means when he says that the center of the hourglass is narrow. Where on the hourglass are the jobs in "the professional mainstream"? Where are "the minimally paying low-level jobs"?

2 Discuss the meaning of this quotation from paragraph 5: "mass culture as diffused by the media [radio, television, movies, newspapers, etc.] is a double-edged sword." What does the author mean by a *double-edged sword*? What are some of the benefits of the media for immigrants? What might be some problems in the way the media presents American society to immigrants?

3 Look up the word *deprivation* in the dictionary and explain the definition to your partner or group in your own words. Then look at the beginning of paragraph 6, where Portes claims, "That gap creates processes of relative deprivation. . . ." Which of the following best summarizes what the writer means?

  a The media creates realistic ideas about what immigrants can expect in America.

  b The media makes it seem that everyone in America is rich.

  c The media creates false impressions about what immigrants can expect in America.

  d The media has no influence on what immigrants think about American society.

4 At the end of paragraph 7, Portes explains: "I have argued repeatedly that the identities that count are for the most part national, because that's where individuals are rooted in a particular history." In your journal, freewrite about how you define your own identity. How much of your identity consists of personal aspects (personality, family relationships, interests)? How much of your identity is related to group characteristics (nationality, language, race, religion, etc.)? Which aspects do you consider more important – group aspects or personal aspects?

Identity

Shanan Marie Lynch

In this personal essay, Shanan Lynch, a student at New Jersey City University, describes the difficulty she had reconciling the different aspects of her own identity. Before you read, think about what the word identity *means to you.*

Defining who I am has never been an easy task for me. My ethnic background declares that there is more to me than what you see. It is a brilliant rainbow that defines me, adding a hint of mystery. I am a Christian woman of Panamanian, Irish, and black descent. 1

Over the years, I have struggled to fit into these three ethnic groups in search of my identity. I know what it's like to be lost in a world that doesn't recognize who you are. I fought to make myself visible to a world that looked through me instead of inside me. The greater part of my life was spent trying to discover who I was. I believe that most people want to be loved, to reveal themselves entirely to another person and be embraced by their acceptance. I set forth in search of that acceptance. 2

My grandfather was the most prominent male figure in my life. He was an Irishman – kind, gentle, and loving. He had the most beautiful blue eyes. I needed only to look into them when I was afraid and I felt safe. I was the first of his grandchildren. He named me Shanan after the Shannon River in Ireland. (My mother chose to spell it differently.) He showered me with attention and spoiled me rotten. Grandfather's love was the epitome of acceptance. Color was never an issue. It never occurred to me that he was different from me. I had always viewed him as a lighter version of myself. It was no surprise that my first attempt to discover myself took place within the "Caucasian" ethnic group. 3

At an age as early as seven, I began excluding myself from the other components of my ethnic background. I distanced myself from other Hispanics and blacks who were not part of my immediate family. I believed that for true acceptance, I had to come *alone*. As a teenager, I began dating white males exclusively. (Most of them had blue eyes.) I found that acceptance among white males was considerably easier than among white females. It seemed that males tolerated me while females discarded me. I changed the way I spoke, dressed, and styled my hair. I avoided wearing braids and bright colored clothing in an effort to blend into their culture. I straightened my hair, wore bangs and ponytails, and dressed primarily in jeans and T-shirts. 4

After all of my efforts, I obtained only two female friends. One was Irish and the other was Italian. They invited me into their circle of peers. It wasn't long before I felt the animosity stirring in the midst of the group. I became increasingly uncomfortable in their presence, but, determined to belong, I continued to remain in their company despite the tension. Finally, I found an opportunity to exhibit authentic verification of my membership in the Irish community. I decided that I would participate in the St. Patrick's Day Parade. 5

I had always celebrated St. Patrick's Day with my grandfather. It was as normal 6
to me as celebrating Christmas. I thought if they could see how natural I looked,
they would be forced to accept me. I stood in the middle of the school courtyard
covered with green from head to toe as blank stares of disbelief pierced my very
soul. Rejection blistered my bleeding heart. I realized that I would never be
accepted.

Various episodes of rebuff followed. Someone once said to me that I was 7
too pretty to be black. I never understood what that meant. Was I a member
of something society deemed ugly? Did that account for the hatred that was
frequently thrust my way? By whom was I being judged? And by what law was I
convicted? It all seemed so strange. I couldn't understand what people saw when
they looked at me. They were so different from Grandfather. He always maintained
that I was the most beautiful girl he had ever seen. Why couldn't others see me
through his eyes? Perhaps love was the veil that prevented Grandfather's eyes
from seeing the *evil* in me that others saw.

The older I got, the more aware I became of the hatred that existed among 8
races. When my two white friends were invited to a pool party at a neighbor's
house, I was sure I'd be able to go. After all, I was well acquainted with everyone
in the neighborhood. My friends got there just before I did. I watched them enter
the house as I approached from down the street. When I arrived at the door, I was
told that the pool was being cleaned and I couldn't come in. As the door closed, I
heard the sounds of laughter in the background. I walked home in agony.

I attempted to heal my wound by assuring myself the pool was being cleaned 9
and that the laughter was only coming from the usual band of egotists whom no
one wanted to be around. I often made excuses for their behavior toward me. It
was easier than facing the possibility that something might be wrong with me.
Even when I was left standing in the garage of my Italian boyfriend's house while
my two girlfriends accompanied him inside, I convinced myself that there was a
perfectly logical explanation for it. I would have believed that was true if his little
brother hadn't whispered in my ear that their mother didn't like blacks. I was
crushed. I quickly came to the conclusion that although there were some whites
who treated me fairly, they were the exception rather than the rule. I no longer saw
them as a source of comfort but as a source of pain. I decided to move on, but the
wounds they inflicted scared me. I had nightmares that Grandfather would one
day join his cultural colleagues in their hatred against me.

I never spoke to Grandfather about the prejudice I endured. I was haunted 10
by the fear that any mention of such repulsion against me might cause him to
see me as others did. Grandfather passed away some time ago. There are times
while riding the bus or on the subway that I see kindly old men who remind me
of him. Looking at them, I wonder if they could be capable of the kind of love
that Grandfather had. Occasionally, when I smile at them, they smile back. For a
moment it's like seeing Grandfather again.

My next attempt to define myself took place within the Hispanic ethnic 11
group. Following the same pattern of exclusion, I surrounded myself with Spanish
speakers. I was confident that I would be accepted in this group. After all, I was
a certified member. Unfortunately, things did not work out the way I had hoped.

I was quickly made aware of the friction that exists within Hispanic subcultures. There are so many different dialects and diversities that the language is often disputed between groups. The "correct" pronunciation of certain words or phrases could quite literally start a fight. In general, I spoke well enough to get by, but there were some discrepancies along the way. Disputes about my choice of wording caused me to become less confident in my ability to communicate effectively outside my home. Surrounded by a group of peers that consisted mainly of Puerto Rican Americans, I had no one to corroborate my position, and I became uncomfortable speaking in public.

Hair was also an issue with my new group of acquaintances. I was the only 12 one in the group whose hair was different from everyone else's. Within the group, several of the girls wore their hair down. They often requested that I do the same. The length of my hair wasn't as much of a problem as the thickness of it. If my hair were to get tangled during the course of play, I would be forced to sit teary eyed for at least an hour while my mother combed through it. They always seemed puzzled by my refusal to let my hair down. Unlike the Caucasian group, they didn't seem to understand that a person could be both black and Hispanic – which in my case was the reason for my differences. I became depressed. I began to hate who I was. "Why can't I fit in?" I asked my aunt (whose hair was exactly like that of my Hispanic cohorts), "Why am I so different?" She said that differences are what make people beautiful. How dull the world would be if everyone were the same. I smiled as she kissed me and walked away, but deep inside I still wanted to be more like her. It wasn't long before my distinctions caused me to separate from the Spanish-speaking group as well.

I rarely acknowledged the fact that I was Hispanic. I tried to submerge myself 13 within the "black" culture. Even there I could not find acceptance. There were those who detected an accent when I spoke and were disturbed by it. There were those who deemed me conceited just because I had light skin. Overall, I realized that I would never fit into any *one* ethnic group. There were just too many variations within me.

Finally, I came to the realization that I was multicultural and that no one thing 14 was more a part of me than another. I understood that I could not divide my identity into pieces. Each piece is a part of who I am. Coming to this conclusion, however, offered no consolation for the isolation I felt. I still craved love and acceptance. I wanted to belong. I needed to find a place where I fit in.

Some time passed before I realized that my quest for group acceptance was in 15 vain. I had loved the Lord for as long as I could remember, and He loved me. He had always accepted everything that was uniquely me. I belonged to Him. I was a Christian and thus a part of that group. I discovered that there were variations among Christians as well, and it was in the Church that I felt most accepted.

I conclude that identity is not what you are a part of, but rather what is a part 16 of you. Each group I attempted to fit into was a reflection of each part of me. I have learned to love who I am. I was blessed to have been born a part of so many different cultures. It's possible that if I had been born to just one, I might have been infected with the hatred that existed around me.

1 Before reading this essay, you were asked to think about what the word *identity* means to you. Now write out your definition of this word. Underline three or four details in the essay showing different parts of the writer's identity that fit your definition. Discuss your definition and the details you chose with a small group.

2 This essay is organized chronologically according to periods in the writer's life when she attempted to fit into different groups. Using the time-chunk categories below, list some important events in the development of the writer's identity. (Review "Time Chunks," on page 46, if necessary.)

a Preschool years

b Elementary school years

c Teenage years

d Adult life

3 Reread the introduction and the conclusion of the essay. Then, in your own words, write one sentence that explains the main idea of the essay. Discuss your sentence with your group. Choose one or two students from the group to read their sentences to the class.

4 Underline two or three examples of unfair treatment that Lynch describes. Then think about a time in your life in which you were treated unfairly, and freewrite in your journal about your experience. Provide details, such as your age at the time of the incident, where it took place, and who was involved. How was your experience similar to or different from Lynch's?

Reading 5   **Professional Writing**

The Color of Love

Maria P. P. Root

When two people of different races marry, questions of identity often arise. In this essay, a professional psychologist writes about some of the joys and problems associated with intermarriage – marriage between people of different racial or ethnic backgrounds. Before you read, think about any advantages or disadvantages that might exist for couples who decide to intermarry.

With at least three million people in the United States in interracial marriages, racially mixed marriage is no longer a rarity. And with one degree of separation – all the family members of these couples – it touches many millions more. Allowing a second degree of separation – friends, coworkers, acquaintances – intermarriage likely affects most people in this country. Younger people, on average, are far more open to intermarriage than those who grew up in an era of segregation.* This   1

*segregation: a social system that provides separate facilities for minority groups in such areas as housing, transportation, and education

trend is a major gain for tolerance and pluralism in America, and families that successfully navigate the challenge of interracial marriage often become more open generally. But large pockets of discrimination continue to exist.

In the twentieth century, segregationists expressed concern that civil rights* 2 would ultimately lead to greater acceptance of intermarriage. And in a sense, they were right. With more interracial contact has come less fear and more acceptance of the racial "other," and the ultimate form of acceptance is personal love and the marriage bond.

A 1997 Gallup poll found the highest approval rating of interracial marriage 3 ever by both black (77 percent) and white (61 percent) Americans. The National Opinion Research Center (NORC) also has found increased acceptance. By 1994, when people were asked, "Would you favor a law against racial intermarriage?" 84.9 percent of 1,626 white Americans answered in the negative. Even more black Americans – 96.8 percent of the 258 polled – also answered no.

Nevertheless, interracial marriage can create deep conflict within families. 4 Opposition reflects not just bigotry. It can reflect fears about loss of valued traditions and concerns that children and grandchildren will suffer society's lingering prejudice. A NORC poll in 1990 asked Jews, blacks, Asians, and Hispanics how they would feel about a close relative marrying someone from outside their racial or ethnic group. Blacks were most strongly opposed, with 57.5 percent of

*civil rights: the rights of citizens to political and social freedom and equality

1,362 respondents against it; next came Asian Americans at 42.4 percent; then Hispanic Americans at 40.4 percent. Jews were the least opposed, at 16.3 percent, but also had the largest response neither favoring nor opposing intermarriage of a closer relative (63.1 percent). Just over 46 percent of Asian Americans and Hispanic Americans were neutral on the question. These data show that despite the increasing acceptance of intermarriage in this country, people are not necessarily pleased when it becomes personal. Families remain highly protective of their most significant "product": future generations.

In their book *Multiracial Couples: Black and White Voices*, Paul C. Rosenblatt,   5 Terry A. Karis, and Richard D. Powell suggest that disowning interracially married family members may be a way of disowning racially different in-laws. Through denouncement, families attempt to avoid possible contamination by an undesirable status or stigma. The NORC data and my own interviews indicate that people of all races sometimes fear contamination, though for different reasons. Whites may fear loss of privileged status for their children and grandchildren, while people of color may fear loss of cultural identity.

If the couple has children, as most couples do, the children have a blood tie   6 to both clans, which strengthens – and complicates – the links immeasurably. Parents who resisted the intermarriage of a child may soften their opposition when grandchildren come. Or their resentment may harden because of the embarrassment of a blood relation who is a mixed-race child. Late marriages (those that occur past child-bearing age) may receive less opposition for this reason.

My attempts to answer the question "What differentiates those families   7 who can welcome someone racially different from those families who cannot?" led me to think about families as open or closed systems of relationships. Open families most resemble an individualistic society in which interdependence is maintained and intermarriage is acceptable. Families that I term "pseudo*-open" may encourage interracial or interethnic friendships and be fine with interracial dating, but they oppose interracial marriage. Other families are "pseudo-closed"; they are sometimes able to grow over time to greater acceptance of an interracial marriage – but this often takes years, and sometimes the birth or death of a family member. Closed systems typically correspond with monarchical family models, show less tolerance of individual deviation, and see race as a critical piece of the image or product and property of the family.

The hallmark of closed families is the rigidity of rules maintaining distance   8 between "us" and "them." These families, while seemingly democratic in times of peace and harmony, tend to become monarchical in the disowning process, directing other family members' behavior toward the banished member. Communication moves in a single direction from the decision makers to the lower-ranking members – that is, from parents to children. The flow of communication may not change even when children are grown and well into their adult years. Cultural, ethnic, or religious traditions are often key parts of identity and help determine the boundaries that mark in-group and out-group status.

pseudo: fake or false

One immigrant group that has recently had great difficulty breaking closed   9
ranks are adult children of South Asian families. Many were born or raised from an
early age in the United States and are very Americanized. Intermarriage naturally
emerges as a possibility for this generation, but their parents often insist that they
marry someone culturally similar who has similar class standing. Some parents
have hired private investigators to find out whether their children are having
secret relationships; and some try to arrange marriages or place newspaper ads for
suitable spouses for their children. They are often openly rude to girlfriends and
boyfriends who are not of the "correct" racial, cultural, and class background.

Much of this rigidity stems from unchallenged prejudices or unrealistic   10
expectations. In a culturally and racially diverse nation with tremendous
geographic mobility, educational opportunities away from home, and integrated
workplaces, it is unrealistic not to consider the possibility that a son, daughter,
grandson, granddaughter, niece, or nephew will fall in love with a member of an
"out" group.

Until it comes to crossing the color line, closed families are not necessarily   11
dysfunctional families – which are unstable and chaotic, lack the capacity to
nurture, and can be abusive. But they do tend to have certain rigidities, fears, and
prejudices that are not easily changed by facts or experience. Their ability to act
lovingly in the face of these feelings is limited or nonexistent. Interracial dating
is explicitly forbidden. Closed families do not always engage in overt forms of
racial discrimination, but they usually do their best to pass on a way of thinking
that perpetuates the borders between the races, a way of thinking that forecloses
critical thinking about race.

Often the prospect of an interracial marriage takes on mythical proportions   12
and the partnership is seen as an act of blatant disloyalty, even as an act of war.
Filial piety is assumed; sons and daughters are indebted to their parents and must
repay them for their sacrifices. Marrying the right partner is a filial obligation. The
children of these families are caught in a horrible bind: sacrifice their own needs
and desires or alienate their parents, perhaps permanently.

Closed families have narrow criteria for whom they will accept as one of the   13
clan. They will open their ranks only to persons who guarantee betterment of the
family position. Regardless of how a family becomes closed, the opportunities for
growth and change are limited. In an extreme example of a closed family, Randall,
an African American in his mid-forties, spoke about his ex-mother-in-law's
inability to see him as a person.

> My daughter and my son are black and white. To make it brief,
> my wife called her mother in California one Christmas day and put
> our daughter on to talk to grandmother. She didn't say a word to our
> daughter and my wife gets back on the phone and her mother says,
> "What the hell is the matter with you? I don't want a nigger in my
> family!" And this is her grandchild!

Such behavior is not limited to parents and grandparents. Sometimes adult   14
children disown their parents, as in the case of Linda, who married a white man
years after being widowed by her Filipino husband. "My [Filipina] daughter really

disowned me for several years," she said. "It is only this Christmas that we got a card. But in the card she didn't mention anything about having feelings against us or for us. She just sent the card to me."

In his 1944 study of race relations, *An American Dilemma: The Negro Problem and Modern Democracy*, Swedish sociologist Gunnar Myrdal echoed W. E. B. DuBois's observation half a century earlier that the color line would be the problem of the twentieth century in the United States. Today, at the dawn of the twenty-first century, Jim Crow laws* and other legal barriers are gone but not forgotten and we still struggle with race.   15

I doubt that intermarriage is the solution to all of America's race problems; nor is it necessary for all or even most Americans to intermarry. But it does provide one avenue for the challenging of stereotypes, particularly when it involves an extended kinship network of different-race and mixed-race kin. It is an opportunity to move into a different dialogue about race, a dialogue in which the voices of multiracial adult children and women and people of color can also be heard. And beyond its benefits to racial tolerance, interracial marriage demands democracy, openness, and tolerance within families.   16

*Jim Crow laws: laws passed in the United States in the late 1800s through the mid-1900s establishing separate schools, transportation, and other public facilities for blacks and whites

Reading 5 Reflecting on the Reading

1 With a small group, discuss which of the statements below reflects Root's opinion regarding intermarriage today. Be prepared to point to specific lines in the essay to support your choices.

   a She thinks that there is a growing acceptance of intermarriage in the United States.

   b She thinks that there are still many people who oppose intermarriage.

   c She thinks couples that intermarry mainly face problems from outside their own families.

   d She thinks that intermarriage is the only way to overcome racial prejudice.

2 Root uses several forms of evidence to convince readers that the points she is making are valid ones. For example, in paragraph 5, she cites an opinion stated in a book to support her own ideas. Working with your group, find examples of at least three other types of supporting evidence the author uses. Then compare your examples with those of another group. As a class, discuss whether you think the supporting evidence the author has chosen is convincing. Why or why not?

3 Working individually, write a definition in your own words of the term *open family* and write a definition in your own words of the term *closed family*. Share your definitions with your group. Then compare your definitions to those given by the author in paragraphs 7 and 8. Discuss what Root means by the terms *pseudo-open* and *pseudo-closed* families.

4 In relation to intermarriage, which of the four terms below best describes your own family? In your journal, freewrite about why you chose this particular term.

a open   **b** pseudo-open   **c** closed   **d** pseudo-closed

Reading 6

Color or Real Love?
Yanqin Lan

In this essay, which is a response to "The Color of Love," Yanqin Lan, a student from Surinam, reports the results of her research on interracial marriage. Before you read, think about your own views about marriage. What is more important in choosing a partner – love and sexual attraction or cultural and racial background?

We are now living in the twenty-first century, a century where almost everything is changing. Still we have to struggle with the problem of racism. Racism is still an issue today but not as strong anymore as in the past. This has resulted in the changing of people's minds about choosing a partner from other than their own race or color. This type of marriage – a marriage between people of two different races, mixed marriage – is called an interracial marriage. Interracial marriage has increased and become more acceptable over the years in many countries including America, especially among the young generation. Maria P. P. Root explains this in the article "The Color of Love": "With at least three million people in the United States in interracial marriages, racially mixed marriage is no longer a rarity" (220). Every woman is looking for Mr. Right and vice versa, but who is the right one? What is more important when choosing a partner with whom you want to share the rest of your life? One with the same race and culture or just someone you love because of his personality, no matter what race he is?

I think when someone is looking for a marriage partner, we don't need to look at his skin color or what culture and religion he has. The more important thing in choosing a marriage partner is true love, good communication, and understanding; as long as the couple loves each other and can live harmoniously together for the rest of their lives, the other problems are secondary. Of course, still there are disadvantages and advantages in an interracial marriage.

One of the problems could be communication, especially when the couple speaks different languages. Misunderstanding of the meaning of a word or sentence may cause big trouble when they are arguing about something. However, in some cases it may be better because they don't understand each other, so they cannot fight or have arguments. I have a friend who is Chinese. When she came here, she didn't speak English. Then she met an Italian-American man. After a couple months of dating, they married. At that time they walked with dictionaries in their hands because she couldn't speak English and he couldn't speak Chinese. Before this marriage he was married to a Caucasian. When I had just arrived here, I spent a couple weeks with them. One day I asked him why he married my friend, since they have difficulty understanding each other. He answered, "Even though you understand each other and can communicate well, you can still end in a divorce." Now they have two beautiful sons. She has learned some English, and so they communicate in broken English. But I can see that they are a happy and warm family.

Sometimes the couple has to overcome other problems, especially when the parents on both sides cannot accept their interracial relationship. This is the problem that most couples have to struggle with. Although interracial marriage has become more common in most countries, still there are some races that don't accept it. Some groups still have conservative thinking and are afraid of losing their cultural identity or losing their color. Root explains in "The Color of Love" that one immigrant group, South Asian families, often oppose interracial marriages. Most of their children were born and raised in the United States. Interracial dating or marriage is very common for this generation, but their parents demand that they marry someone with the same culture, color, and class. Some of these parents even try to arrange marriages for their children. They are openly not accepting of someone who is not from the right racial, cultural, and class background (Root). But some whites and people of color also don't accept mixed marriage. They are also afraid of losing their culture. As Root states, "Whites may fear loss of privileged status for their children and grandchildren, while people of color may fear loss of cultural identity" (222). In the Internet source "Is Love Colorblind?" Steve Sailer also supports this statement: "What's fascinating, however, is that in recent years a startling number of nonwhites – especially Asian men and black women – have become bitterly opposed to intermarriage." This statement shows that there are still some groups who are against interracial marriages, even though interracial marriage has increased recently.

There are also a lot of advantages in an interracial marriage. If the couple comes from different cultural backgrounds, they can learn the other culture from each other. Language, food, and customs are some examples. Interracial marriage may bring more advantages for the children, because these children can learn the cultures of both parents and can speak more than one language in some cases. In this way we learn how to communicate with other races, and maybe this can help to solve the racism problem, because you cannot know someone well unless you get a closer relationship with this person.

We cannot judge whether a marriage between people of the same race or an interracial marriage has a better chance of succeeding because problems can occur, whether it is an interracial marriage or not. Although the marriage partners are from the same race, culture, and class background and speak the same language, their marriage can also end in a divorce when a problem comes up. The couple has to prevent these problems and try to understand each other and solve the problems instead of divorcing. I think this is the same whether a couple is from the same race or different races. If an interracial marriage couple chooses one of their races and brings the children up accordingly, I don't think that their children will have more problems than the children of a couple with the same race. We have a great example from the memoir *The Color of Water*, written by James

McBride. McBride writes about his childhood and his success in this book. He and his eleven brothers and sisters are children from interracial marriages between a Jewish Orthodox woman and two black men. (After the mother's first husband died, she married again.) Although McBride's mother was white, she cut off all ties with her relatives and renounced her Jewish religion. She raised all of her children in the black community, and they attended Christian churches. All these twelve children had a hard childhood and had to struggle because of their skin color. James was the one in the family who especially had problems with his race, but today all twelve children are well educated and have successful professions in society. McBride has even benefited from having parents of two different races. He wrote the book *The Color of Water*, explaining his two racial backgrounds, and became a successful author.

Like many other people who accept interracial marriage, I also can accept   7
it, but my parents, especially my father, are against it. I think he is like other immigrants, afraid of losing his cultural identity. My mother is more afraid of communication problems, as she cannot speak other languages than Chinese. I have never talked about this subject with my father because I am afraid to argue with him about this. However, I know what his statement is about interracial marriage. I used to talk to my mother about it, as I can bring up any subject with her. I remember one day when we were having dinner, I started to ask my mother what her opinion was about interracial marriage. I asked her whether it was fine if I choose someone who is not Chinese to be my marriage partner. She didn't reject this idea immediately, but she said many things, which meant no in the end. She said, "As long as you love each other, but I'd rather you take a Chinese who can speak Chinese because when you two have problems, as a mother I can help you." Then the next day, she announced to all of her children, "Your father said if one of you marries another race than Chinese, that is equal to having one child less." I laughed at that time, although she said it seriously. I think this may not be a big problem for my older brother and sister, as they already have a partner of the same race, but for me and my younger brother it may cause some problems if we both fall in love with someone of a different race. We both were born in China, but we grew up in Surinam. Like many other immigrants who grew up here in the United States and can accept interracial marriage naturally, so do I. My parents don't think in this way.

Although my prospective husband's personality and his love for me and mine   8
for him are more important than our color, still I hope I don't have to struggle with this problem in the future, as I don't want to disrespect my parents or cause trouble or any arguments with them because my parents are very important to me. But I really hope that one day my parents can understand this and also can accept interracial marriage as many parents do.

Works Cited

McBride, James. The Color of Water. New York: Riverhead Books, 1996.
Root, Maria P. P. "The Color of Love." The American Prospect April 8, 2002: 54–55.
Sailer, Steve. "Is Love Colorblind?" Retrieved May 9, 2003, from <http://www.isteve.com/IsLoveColorblind.html>.

1 Reread the first paragraph of Lan's essay. With a partner or small group, discuss the different techniques she uses to capture the reader's interest in her first paragraph. Do you think this introduction is effective? Why or why not?

2 Find and underline the disadvantages and potential problems of interracial marriage that Lan points out. Then find and underline, in a different color, the advantages and positive aspects of interracial marriages presented in her essay. Compare what you found with your partner or group.

3 Lan uses both direct quotations and paraphrases from the sources she consulted. Find one direct quotation and one paraphrase that you think are used effectively. With your partner or group, discuss why you chose these particular examples.

4 In your journal, freewrite about your parents' views on intermarriage. How do you think they would react if you were going to marry someone of another race or ethnicity? If you are a parent yourself, how would you feel if your child decided to intermarry? If you are married to someone from a different race or ethnic group, describe your family's reaction to your marriage.

Reading 7

Interracial Marriages

Igor Faynzilbert

Igor Faynzilbert, a student from Russia, considers the question of interracial marriages using examples from his own experience as well as from his research. Before you read, think of an example from your experience (or from a movie or TV show) that relates to the topic of interracial marriage.

Interracial marriage is a very popular topic for discussion in our time. The most important question is: is it accepted by society or not? A lot of people, especially those who belong to the younger generation, think that interracial marriage is acceptable. However, the elders very often don't agree with marriages between different races.

My opinion is that interracial marriages are not so terrible, and I truly believe that they are even stronger than marriages between partners of the same race because they are based on love, not on money or other material things. I think that the most important thing in marriage is love and understanding. Race, culture, or religion can be connected with food preferences, traditions, celebration of holidays, etc. Before marrying, people of different races should discuss everything from cuisine and clothes to religion and traditions because all these differences can put love and acceptance for the other to the test, and their marriage can collapse very easily and soon. I believe that those who said that "Marriages are made in heaven" were absolutely right, and I doubt that they thought about any racial or cultural differences.

What is more, I suppose that children whose parents are from different races will know a lot about both races and have appreciation and respect for other races, cultures, and religions. The children of mixed marriages can have the best features of both parents.   3

I know a girl whose father is a "person of color" and whose mother is white. She has a lot of respect for other races, and she is a zealous fighter against racism. In college we were asked to read *The Color of Water* by James McBride (1996). In that book, McBride described the story of his interracial family, where his mother was a white woman and his dad was a black man. He showed all aspects of such marriages. He knew what it meant to be connected with two different cultures and that the most important things were understanding and respect for others.   4

On the other hand, many people claim that interracial marriages have more disadvantages than advantages. They say that the most important and painful problem is that such marriages ". . . can create deep conflict within families" (Root, 2002, p. 221), and in many cases partners in an interracial marriage would not be accepted by relatives and other people. The language problems can be very important because misunderstanding can lead to viewing a son- or daughter-in-law as an outsider. An important role for both spouses is to explain to the families the differences between races and make them believe that interracial marriage isn't so terrible.   5

The problem is that many people are very old-fashioned and think that marriages must be between people of one color of skin. More than that, some of them may have some racist feelings, and letting a person of another race into the family is a source of shame for them. In "The Color of Love," Maria P. P. Root (2002) described the case of a white woman who had a black son-in-law and a black granddaughter. On Christmas, when that grandchild wanted to talk to her grandmother on the phone, the woman wouldn't even say "Hi" because the child was black.   6

Another serious problem of interracial marriages, which is perhaps the worst one, is that children can suffer from being biracial. They can be badly treated or humiliated in schools and beaten on the streets. They can be trapped in themselves and have a feeling that they are the worst part, or even not a part of society. Moreover, they can have doubts about what religion they should follow if their parents have different religions. The questions "Which religion should a child be brought up in?" and "Which language should be adopted?" are very important. The children may find themselves "the odd ones out" in school and out of school if society is not ready to accept them. Another story that I heard about this situation concerns a girl whose parents were black and white. She was always humiliated by her classmates and teachers in school. She couldn't live with that nightmare; that's why she decided to commit suicide.   7

During the Olympic Games in Moscow in 1980, a lot of black athletes came to Russia. Many of them stayed there and entered universities. They began to form families and have children. Those children were treated badly by everybody; they were referred to as "The Insulted and Humiliated" in schools, and people   8 sometimes called them "Olympic children." Another example was included in *The Color of Water* (McBride, 1996). The author described a situation where he was ashamed that his mother was white. He wanted her to be black as he was, so people in their all-black neighborhood wouldn't look at them oddly or with disgust.

The last drawback, but not the least, is that the opinion of other people, who 9 are not even relatives, plays a very big role. Society itself pushes interracial couples to divorce. On the Internet I found an article about an interracial couple who lived in the suburbs in one of the southern states. They were insulted and debased by neighbors, who didn't want to accept them. The pressure was so heavy that the couple had to divorce (*Interracial Marriages*, n.d.).

In conclusion, I'd like to say that I have nothing against interracial marriages. 10 I really believe that they are stronger than marriages between people of one race, despite the problems and disadvantages. Although all these barriers are very difficult, love can transcend everything. What is more, our society has become less skeptical than it was 50 years ago. Now interracial marriages and mixed-race children are becoming more and more acceptable.

As for my family, I have never asked them about this question, but I'm sure 11 that they would accept any woman whom I love, despite racial, cultural, or other problems. My parents always did everything to make me happy, and they never had anything against other races. What is more, they taught me how to respect and understand other nations, races, and religions.

I'm a Jew. During the history of existence, my people suffered from many 12 national and religious persecutions. The biggest of them was the Holocaust at the time of the Second World War. More than 6 million Jewish people were brutally killed in Nazi camps such as Majdanek and Treblinka. That's why children in Jewish families are brought up with respect for other nations, religions, and races. What is more, a 1990 National Opinion Research Center poll found that "Jews were the least opposed [to interracial marriages], at 16.3%. . . ." (Root, 2002, p. 222).

However, interracial marriages have always been a big problem of society, and 13 they would hardly improve the problem of racism. Today interracial marriages are not unusual phenomena; nevertheless, people still think about such marriages with prejudice. Many years will pass until our society accepts all races, nationalities, and religions and all people will live in peace.

References

Interracial marriages. (n.d.). Retrieved May 23, 2003, from <http://www.bbngg.com/articles/interracial.html>

McBride, J. (1996). *The color of water*. New York: Riverhead Books.

Root, M.P.P. (2002, April 8). The color of love. *The American Prospect*, 54–55.

1 Working with a partner or small group, find and underline the thesis statement of this essay. Then find and underline, in a different color, the counterarguments (points that contradict the thesis) that Faynzilbert includes. Discuss why you think he included these points. Do you feel that the use of these counterarguments strengthens or weakens the effectiveness of the essay as a whole?

2 Find one place in this essay where Faynzilbert includes an example from his own experience. How is this example related to the thesis statement? Compare the example you selected with those of your partner or group. Discuss whether these examples make the writer's argument more convincing or less convincing.

3 Find one place where Faynzilbert uses statistics to support a point he is making. Discuss whether you think this use of statistics is effective. Are there any other statistics that you would have liked him to include?

4 Before reading this essay, you were asked to think of an example from your own experience (or from a movie or TV show) that relates to the topic of interracial marriage. In your journal, freewrite about this example. Be as detailed and specific as possible. How does your example relate to Faynzilbert's opinion as explained in his essay?

TECHNIQUES WRITERS USE

Many of the skills you practiced in Chapters 5 and 6 will serve you well in this chapter as you write an essay based on research. The same techniques of summarizing, paraphrasing, and quoting are needed for research writing. In addition, you will learn how to locate reliable sources, find support for your ideas with evidence from your research, cite your sources properly in the body of your essay, and prepare a bibliography (a list of the books, articles, and Internet sources you consulted).

Supporting Ideas with Evidence

Just as lawyers working in a courtroom have to support their case with evidence, writers also need to give convincing evidence for the ideas in their essays. Especially in research writing, it is not enough just to state that something is true. You must convince your reader that your ideas are sound by providing various types of evidence: for example, quotations or paraphrases from reliable written sources (journal or magazine articles, newspapers, books, or the Internet); information taken from interviews; statistics; and logically presented reasoning. The tasks that follow will help you to understand how writers support their ideas with evidence.

Analyze

1 In "The Color of Love" (page 220), underline or highlight one example of each of the types of evidence listed below. Use a different color for each of the four types:

   a A quotation from an interview that the author conducted

   b A paraphrase of something originally stated in a book

   c The use of statistics from a respected public opinion poll

   d A detailed example of the attitudes toward interracial marriage of a particular immigrant group

2 Working with a partner or a small group, compare your examples. Which ones seem most convincing to you? Which ones seem least convincing? Why?

Task 7.2 *Practice*

1 Imagine that you are going to write a research essay on the topic of interracial marriage. Think about the kinds of evidence you might need to support various points in your essay, such as examples from your own experience, articles, interviews, and statistics. Work with a partner or small group to answer the questions below. You can use more than one type of evidence for each point.

   a What type of evidence could you use to support the idea that interracial marriage is becoming more common in the United States?

   b What type of evidence could you use to support the idea that many people still oppose interracial marriage even though it is becoming more common?

   c What type of evidence could you use to support the idea that in some families, the parents do not support interracial marriage and would treat their child harshly if he or she married a person from another cultural or ethnic group?

   d What type of evidence could you use to support the idea that interracial marriage used to be illegal in the United States?

2 Now discuss with your partner or group how you could locate the different types of evidence you identified.

Paraphrasing and Quoting to Add Support

In research writing, one of the most common ways of adding support is by paraphrasing or quoting from other written sources. Remember that when you include quoted material in your writing, you need to introduce the quotations with your own words so that they fit smoothly into your essay. You also need to be sure that you have clearly indicated the source of the material. Ideally, you should indicate to the reader why you have chosen a particular quotation. For example, if you have quoted something that you agree with, you need to explain how this quotation supports your point of view. If you have quoted something you disagree with, you need to explain that although some people hold the opposing view, you see the matter differently; then explain why your view is a more valid one. The phrases below show some simple ways of introducing quotations.

> As [author's name] states, ". . ."
> According to [author], ". . ."
> [Author] explains, ". . ."
> In the words of [author]: ". . ."
> I agree with [author] that ". . ."
> [Author] states, ". . ." However, in my opinion . . .

Task 7.3 Analyze

1 Working with a partner, find and underline each example in "Color or Real Love?" (page 225) of a *quotation* from a written source or interview. For each example, circle the words that Lan used to introduce the quotation.

2 Now find examples of Lan's use of *paraphrasing* of an idea from a written source or interview. Bracket [ ] the paraphrased portion. For each example, discuss which of Lan's points the paraphrase supports.

Task 7.4 Practice

1 Imagine that you are writing an essay in which you state that intermarriage is becoming more acceptable in American society. You are using "The Color of Love" (page 220) as your source material. Working with a small group, choose relevant information from "The Color of Love" that you would like to paraphrase to support your point.

2 Working individually, write your paraphrase.

> **Example**
> This is a paraphrase based on information from paragraph 1 of "The Color of Love":
>> In the United States, people's attitudes toward intermarriage are becoming more positive. In "The Color of Love," Maria P. P. Root says that many Americans know someone who is in an interracial marriage and that Americans, especially younger people, are becoming more accepting of so-called "mixed" marriages.

3 Discuss your paraphrase with your group. Based on your group's feedback, make any changes in your paraphrase that you think are necessary.

4 Imagine that you want to use the quotation below from paragraph 16 of "The Color of Love" in your essay. With your group, write an introduction to this quotation that you could use.

> "[Interracial marriage] does provide one avenue for the challenging of stereotypes, particularly when it involves an extended kinship network of different-race and mixed-race kin."

5 Working individually, practice supporting the idea that intermarriage in American society is becoming more acceptable by directly quoting some of Root's exact words.

a Choose the words you want to quote and copy them on a piece of paper.

b Write an introduction to the quote and punctuate your introduction and the quote correctly.

c Share your work with your group. Based on your group members' feedback, make any changes that you think are necessary.

6 Compare your answers to the questions in step 5 with those of another group. Then choose several examples to write on the board and share with the class.

Giving Credit to Sources

In writing for American colleges and universities, it is very important to state where you got your information. This enables interested readers to consult the sources to get more information and also gives credit to the person who first stated the idea. (The only time that you are not expected to mention the source of information is when you are stating a commonly known fact, such as "The United States is one of the most diverse societies in the world.")

The importance of acknowledging the sources of ideas may derive from the emphasis on the individual in Western culture. People's ideas are thought to "belong" to them, like property. And if you use these ideas without acknowledging their source, it is considered similar to stealing; the name given to this type of "theft" is plagiarism, and the penalties can be severe, ranging from failing an assignment to being expelled from college. (See "Paraphrasing Information from Written Sources," on page 188.) Most plagiarism is not intentional but occurs because students do not know how to credit their sources properly.

It is important to find out which method of crediting sources your teacher prefers and use that method. Two of the most commonly used methods are those of the American Psychological Association (APA) and the Modern Language Association (MLA). The APA style is usually preferred in the social sciences, which include such subjects as psychology and anthropology; the MLA style is used more often in the humanities, which include such subjects as literature and languages. With both methods, you are required to cite the source of the ideas briefly within parentheses in the text of the essay and then provide complete information in a bibliography at the end.

In this book, we introduce you to the basic APA and MLA styles. Both of these styles are explained in more detail in writer's handbooks available in college bookstores. If you are asked to write research essays frequently, you should consider purchasing one of these handbooks.

The examples that follow show the form used for citing sources within the text of your essay and for creating a bibliography at the end of your essay. You do not need to memorize this information. Refer to these examples as a guide when you are writing your research essay. Pay careful attention to the differences in punctuation and capitalization between the two styles.

When citing sources within a text in both APA and MLA style, it is important to include the author's last name. If you are using the APA style, you also include the date of publication, but you do not give a page number unless you have included a direct quotation from the source. If you are using the MLA style, you do not include the date of publication, but you do include the page number for all references.

Examples of APA Style In-text Citations

Author not mentioned in text
Expressive language is personal and related to everyday conversation (Britton, 1982).

Author mentioned in text
According to Britton (1982), expressive language is personal and related to everyday conversation.

Author mentioned in text, direct quotation included
According to Britton (1982), expressive language is "close to the self" and "relies on an interest in the speaker as well as the topic" (p. 96).

Author not mentioned in text, direct quotation included
Expressive language is "close to the self" and "relies on an interest in the speaker as well as the topic" (Britton, 1982, p. 96).

Internet source with author
One study suggests that positive emotions such as joy or contentment help to promote survival (Frederickson, 2000).

Internet source without author
The pressure on one interracial couple was so heavy that the couple had to divorce (*Interracial Marriages*, n.d.).

Examples of MLA Style In-text Citations

Author not mentioned in text

Expressive language is personal and related to everyday conversation (Britton 96).

Author mentioned in text

According to Britton, expressive language is personal and related to everyday conversation (96).

Author mentioned in text, direct quotation included

According to Britton, expressive language is "close to the self" and "relies on an interest in the speaker as well as the topic" (96).

Author not mentioned in text, direct quotation included

Expressive language is "close to the self" and "relies on an interest in the speaker as well as the topic" (Britton 96).

Internet source with author

One study suggests that positive emotions such as joy or contentment help to promote survival (Frederickson).

Internet source without author

The pressure on one interracial couple was so heavy that the couple had to divorce ("Interracial Marriages," retrieved May 23, 2003).

Here are examples of entries in APA style bibliographies. APA bibliographies are titled References. Center the title on the page.

References

Book with one author

Banton, M. (1983). *Racial and ethnic competition.* Cambridge, England: Cambridge University Press.

Book with two or more authors

Glazer, N., & Moynihan, D. P. (1970). *Beyond the melting pot: The Negroes, Puerto Ricans, Jews, Italians, and Irish of New York City.* Cambridge, MA: MIT Press.

Article in a magazine

Gibbs, N. (1995, July 3). Working harder, getting nowhere. *Time, 146,* 16–20.

Article in a scholarly journal

Hirschman, C. (1983). America's melting pot reconsidered. *Annual Review of Sociology,* 397–423.

Article in a newspaper

Kamm, H. (1995, January 26). Poland reawakens to its history as communism's mirror shatters. *The New York Times,* pp. A1, A10.

Internet source with author
>Frederickson, B. L. (2000, March 7). Cultivating positive emotions to optimize health and well-being. *Prevention & Treatment, 3,* Article 0001a. <http://journals.apa.org/prevention/volume3/pre0030001a.html>.

Internet source without author [Note that a retrieval date is necessary because the article is not from a dated publication.]
>"Ho Chi Minh." Retrieved May 15, 2003, from <http://www.lonelyplanet.com/destinations/south_east_asia/ho_chi_minh>.

Here are examples of entries in MLA style bibliographies. MLA bibliographies are titled Works Cited. Center the title on the page.

Works Cited

Book with one author
>Banton, Michael. Racial and Ethnic Competition. Cambridge: Cambridge UP, 1983.

Book with two or more authors
>Glazer, Nathan, and Daniel P. Moynihan. Beyond the Melting Pot: The Negroes, Puerto Ricans, Jews, Italians, and Irish of New York City. Cambridge: MIT Press, 1970.

Article in a magazine
>Gibbs, Nancy. "Working Harder, Getting Nowhere." Time 3 July 1995: 16–20.

Article in a scholarly journal
>Hirschman, Charles. "America's Melting Pot Reconsidered." Annual Review of Sociology, 9 (1983): 397–423.

Article in a newspaper
>Kamm, Henry. "Poland Reawakens to Its History as Communism's Mirror Shatters." New York Times 26 Jan. 1995, late ed.: A1, A10.

Internet source with author (Note that "13 Mar. 2003" indicates the date the researcher retrieved the article from the site.)
>Frederickson, Barbara L. "Cultivating Positive Emotions to Optimize Health and Well-Being." Prevention & Treatment. 13 Mar. 2003 <http://journals.apa.org/prevention/volume_3/pre0030001a.html>.

Internet source without author (Note that "15 May 2003" indicates the date the researcher retrieved the article from the site.)
>"Ho Chi Minh." Lonely Planet. LonelyPlanet.com. 15 May 2003 <http://www.lonelyplanet.com/destinations/south_east_asia/ho_chi_minh>.

1 Working with a partner, compare the bibliographies of the two student research essays in this chapter, "Color or Real Love?" (page 225) and "Interracial Marriages" (page 228). Which of these essays used the APA style of citation? Which one used the MLA style?

2 With your partner, make a chart like the one below. List all the differences in style (for example, punctuation and capitalization) that you find between the APA and MLA methods. Then compare your information as a class.

APA	MLA
In-text reference	
• Comma between name of author and year of publication	• No comma between name of author and year of publication
Bibliography	
References	Works Cited
• Initials of author's first and middle names given	• Full first name of author given; middle initial given

3 Find out which of the two styles your teacher wants you to use for your research essay.

1 Working with a partner, write a bibliography for the sources listed below. Use the style that your teacher wants you to use for your research essay (APA or MLA). As you work, use the sample bibliography items given on pages 236–237 as a guide. Notice that each line after the first line should be indented. Be sure to arrange the entries in alphabetical order by the author's last name.

 a Ethnic Identity: The Transformation of White America. This is a book by Richard D. Alba published in New Haven, CT, in 1990 by Yale University Press.

 b The Debate in the United States over Immigration. This is an Internet source. The author is Daphne Spain. The article was retrieved from the following site on October 19, 2003: <http://usinfo.state.gov/journals/itsv/0699/ijse/spain.htm>

c The Color of Love. This is an article by Maria P. P. Root published in the April 8, 2002, issue of The American Prospect, a magazine. It appeared on pages 54–55.

2 After you have styled each of the entries and arranged them in alphabetical order, check your work using the Answer Key on page 262.

INTERNET SEARCH

Do the Internet search that relates to your choice of the essay assignment options. If you choose Option 1, you will write about immigrants and identity. If you choose Option 2, you will write about interracial marriage.

Go now to pages 240–241 for details of the two essay assignment options. Decide which one you want to do. Then proceed with the appropriate Internet search. (If you are not sure which essay assignment you prefer, you can begin by doing part of each Internet search to get a better idea of the difference between the two assignments.)

Option 1 ▶ *Immigrants and Identity*

1 Make a list of keywords that might lead to information you could use in a research essay about the identity of immigrants. For example, the keyword *assimilation*, meaning the process by which immigrants are absorbed into the dominant culture, might lead to some useful information. Do an Internet search for the keywords you have listed.

> **Examples of keywords**
> immigrants assimilation
> immigrants assimilation into American society
> immigrants citizenship
> immigrants home ownership

2 Another source of reliable and up-to-date information on this topic is the U.S. Census Bureau, currently accessible at <http://www.census.gov>. Go to this Web site and see whether you can find information on your topic.

Option 2 ▶ *Interracial Marriage*

1 Do a search using these keywords:

> interracial marriage opinions

2 Think of other keywords that might give you information about interracial marriage and do a search using these keywords.

For Options 1 & 2:

3 Choose two or three sources that you think are appropriate for your topic. Select sources that are reliable, fairly recent, and provide information you might be able to use in your essay.

4 Print out any articles that you might be able to use in your essay. Avoid printing excessively long documents.

5 On each article, write the information needed to identify it as a source in the documentation style your teacher wants you to use (APA or MLA). Be sure to write down the date on which you retrieved the article.

6 Using your own words, write a one-page summary of what you learned about your topic from your Internet search.

7 Attach the Internet sources you printed out and your summary to your essay when you give it to your teacher.

ESSAY ASSIGNMENT

Whichever option you choose (1 or 2), your essay should include the following:

• At least three research sources that support your opinion, one of which should be from the Internet
• Ideas or facts based on one of the readings in this chapter
• Paraphrases of ideas from your research sources
• At least two direct quotations, each from a different research source
• Some statistical information to support your opinion
• APA- or MLA-style identification of your sources within your essay
• APA- or MLA-style bibliography of your sources at the end of your essay

Option 1 ▶ **Immigrants and Identity**

There is an ongoing debate among United States citizens about how immigration influences people's identity. Many believe that America is a "melting pot," in which people originally from other countries blend together to become Americans. Others use the metaphor of the "tossed salad," saying that new and old Americans mix together but retain much of their original identity like the different ingredients in a salad that retain their individual characteristics. Still others feel that immigrants do not assimilate into American society but remain "outsiders" who are loyal to their countries of origin and who primarily speak their first languages. People who hold this view often feel that immigrants threaten the integrity of American society.

Write an essay in which you explore the topic of immigrants and identity. How do the majority of immigrants define their identity? In your opinion, do immigrants assimilate into society, or do they remain separate from the rest of society and unchanged by the immigration experience? The purpose of this essay is to use evidence from research to support your conclusion about the identity of immigrants. Imagine your readers to be people born in the United States who would like to understand more about the different factors that influence the identity of immigrants.

Reread the writing you have already done for this chapter to see whether it gives you ideas for this assignment.

Option 2 ▶ *Interracial Marriage*

As you know from the readings in this chapter, interracial marriage is becoming much more common in the United States. However, there are still many people who oppose the idea of marriage between people of different racial or ethnic backgrounds. Write an essay in which you express your opinion about interracial marriage using information from several research sources to make your opinion convincing. Use "The Color of Love" (page 220) as your source from this chapter. The purpose of this essay is to use evidence from research to support your opinion on interracial marriage. Imagine your readers to be young, unmarried people who have not yet made up their minds how they personally feel about interracial marriage.

Reread the writing you have already done for this chapter to see whether it gives you ideas for this assignment.

Generating Ideas

For Option 1

1 Reread the summary you wrote based on your Internet search. Are you satisfied with the articles on the identity of immigrants that you found? If not, keep looking for better ones. Keep in mind that articles taking a position you disagree with can also be very useful sources to refer to in your essay – to show the counterarguments to your own position. Remember to print out any sources you think you might use, and be sure you have the information necessary to identify them properly according to the style your teacher wants you to use (APA or MLA).

2 Reread the writings in this chapter listed below that relate to the topic of immigrants and identity. Make notes about ideas and passages in these writings that you might want to refer to or quote.

"An American Success Story" by Samuel Nakasian (page 208)

"Response to 'An American Success Story'" by Jowita Drazkowski (page 210)

"America 2050: Immigration and the Hourglass" by Alejandro Portes (page 212)

3 Go to the library and look for additional published material on your topic. If you are not sure how to do this, ask your librarian for guidance.

4 Meet with a small group of students who have chosen Option 1, and describe the sources you have selected to refer to in your essay.

5 Discuss the following questions with your group:

a Why did you select these sources?

b What ideas do you have now about the assimilation of immigrants to the new country?

c Based on the sources you consulted, how does the process of assimilation usually take place?

d How does the assimilation process affect the identity of immigrants?

e Do immigrants threaten native-born inhabitants of the new country?

6 Write notes about any new information or ideas that you got from your group discussion.

For Option 2

1 Since one of the sources you will be using is "The Color of Love" by Maria P. P. Root (page 220), you will need to summarize relevant ideas from her text in your essay. Reread "The Color of Love," and then write a summary of it. Remember that a summary should not include all of the evidence and supporting details, but it should cover all of the author's major points. (Review "Summarizing Information from Written Sources," on page 186, if necessary.)

2 Reread the summary you wrote based on your Internet search. Are you satisfied with the articles on interracial marriage that you found? If not, keep looking for better ones. Keep in mind that articles taking a position you disagree with can also be very useful sources to refer to in your essay – to show the counterarguments to your own position. Remember to print out any sources you think you might use, and be sure you have the information necessary to identify them properly according to the style your teacher wants you to use (APA or MLA).

3 Go to the library and look for additional published material on your topic. If you are not sure how to do this, ask your librarian for guidance.

4 Meet with a small group of students who have chosen Option 2. Exchange your summaries of "The Color of Love" and read them carefully. (If possible, make photocopies of each summary for each group member.) Using the criteria for summary writing on page 186, decide which summaries are successful. Why?

5 Explain which sources other than "The Color of Love" you have selected to refer to in your essay.

6 Based on your reading of "The Color of Love," your other research sources, and your personal experience, discuss the following questions:

    a Why did you select these sources?

    b What is your own opinion about interracial marriage?

    c What support do you find for your opinion in the research sources?

    d What are some of the possible effects of intermarriage on the marriage partners, their children, other family members, and society?

7 Write notes about any new information or ideas that you got from your group discussion.

Organizing Ideas

For Options 1 and 2

1 Gather together all of the research sources you plan to use in your essay as well as all your notes and summaries.

2 On a separate piece of paper, make a list of the most important idea(s) you found in each of your sources. Use the appropriate model below for your list.

For Option 1

Most important idea	Research source & page number
1.	
2.	
3.	
etc.	

For Option 2

Reasons to support interracial marriage	Research source & page number
1.	
2.	
3.	
etc.	

Problems faced by interracial couples	Research source & page number
1.	
2.	
3.	
etc.	

3 Make an outline on which to base your first draft.

Working Toward a Thesis Statement

For Options 1 and 2

1 Now that you have done some research, write several paragraphs to explain your own position on this topic. Here are some questions that you can use to focus your writing.

For Option 1

- Does immigration to another country always result in changes to a person's identity? What examples or evidence do you have to support your opinion on this question?

- In your opinion, is assimilation a desirable goal for most immigrants? Why or why not?

- What are some outward signs that an immigrant has become assimilated into American society?

- How does an immigrant's educational level and social class influence the processes of assimilation and identity adjustment?

- How are the identity issues of first-generation immigrants (those who actually made the decision to move to a new country) different from those of the next generation (those born in the new country)?

For Option 2

- What is more important in choosing a marriage partner: group factors, such as race, culture, language, and religion; or personal factors, such as personality type, sexual attraction, and love?

- Which type of marriage has a better chance of not ending in divorce – a marriage between people of the same race or an interracial marriage?

- Which type of marriage is better for the children?

- Think about your own family situation. How would your family respond if you were to marry a person of another race? How might this affect you and your marriage partner and eventually your children? If your children were to marry interracially, how would you react? If you are married to someone of another race, what problems have you faced?

2 A day or two after you have written about your position, reread what you wrote. Then review your summaries, research, and notes to make sure you have enough evidence to support your position.

3 Now decide on the thesis statement for your research essay and write it down. Remember that you may need to revise this initial thesis as you continue to draft and revise your essay.

Writing Tips

- **Express your opinion clearly.**
  You are the author of this essay, and your opinion should be clearly expressed. Use information from your research to support your opinion, but do not let your sources become the focus of your essay.

- **Include brief quotations from at least two outside sources.**
  Choose effective quotations and introduce them with your own words, explaining how they fit in with what you are saying. Be sure to identify the source of each quotation in parentheses.

- **Include some statistics to support your opinion.**
  In research writing, the use of statistics (numerical information) as support for the author's point of view is a common way of adding credibility to an essay.

- **Identify your sources properly.**
  Be sure you know which style (APA or MLA) your teacher wants you to use. Include an in-text citation every time you refer to information you got from an outside source. Include a bibliography at the end of your essay. (See pages 236–237 for APA and MLA guidelines.)

Writing Your First Draft

Now, keeping the writing tips in mind, write the first draft of your essay. Use your thesis statement and refer to your research and the writing you did for "Generating Ideas" (page 195) and "Organizing Ideas" (page 196). As you are working on this first draft, do not slow yourself down by worrying about correct grammar and spelling; it is more important just to get your ideas down on paper so you have something to work with in later drafts.

REVISING YOUR ESSAY

Once you have put your ideas down on paper by completing the first draft, you can begin the revising process.

When Does Revising End? A Word on Meeting Deadlines

We hope that the techniques presented in this book have given you some practical help in revising your writing. One student who had used some of these methods expressed it this way: "I think what helped me the most was that the draft was read by a classmate and by my teacher, and they both gave me confidence and made me see what I did right and what I was doing wrong. . . . When I revised, I tried to put myself in the reader's place; I wanted to help the reader picture what I was thinking about when I was writing."

As you become more skilled as a writer, you will probably find yourself doing more, not less, revising. But there comes a time when this process has to end – when you have to stop improving your essay and simply turn it in. Donald Murray, a successful writer and teacher of writing, concludes his essay on revising by explaining this fact of life: "A piece of writing is never finished. It is delivered to a deadline, torn out of the typewriter on demand, sent off with a sense of accomplishment and shame and pride and frustration. If only there were a couple more days, time for just another run at it, perhaps then . . ."

Responding to Your Peers

1 Working with a partner or a group of three, exchange and read the first drafts of your essays.

2 Fill out a copy of the "Peer Response Form" on page 250 for each of the first drafts you read. Focus on the ideas rather than the grammar and spelling. Point out only those mistakes that interfere with understanding.

3 Using the completed peer response forms as the basis for your discussion, have a peer conference to discuss your first drafts.

Writing Your Second Draft

1 Fill out the "Writer's Plan for Revising" on page 253.

2 Taking into consideration the feedback you have received from your peers and perhaps from your teacher and your own ideas about how to improve your essay, write your second draft.

EDITING YOUR ESSAY

When you are satisfied with the content and organization of your essay, you can begin the process of editing.

Grammar in Context: Using the Active and Passive Voice of Verbs

Checking your essay to be sure you have used the active and passive voice of verbs correctly is important in essays based on research because it is in this type of essay that you will most often find it useful to include the passive voice. The active voice is much more common than the passive voice in most writing, even in research writing. But there are certain situations in which the passive voice is preferred, particularly if the writer does not wish to emphasize who or what performed the action. The tasks that follow will give you a chance to check your understanding of the active and passive voice. If you need a more detailed explanation, look up *active and passive voice* in your grammar reference book or in an online grammar resource such as Purdue University's Online Writing Lab, currently accessible at <http://owl.english.purdue.edu>.

There is an old story about the definition of news: If the headline reads "Dog bites man," that's not news. But if it says "Man bites dog," *that's* news. The point is that who performs the action of the verb can make a big difference. And this is also the key to understanding the difference between active and passive voice. Both of the headlines quoted above are in the active voice. Notice how they change when they are rewritten in the passive voice:

Active		Passive
Dog <u>bites</u> man.	=	The man <u>is bitten</u> by the dog.
Man <u>bites</u> dog.	=	The dog <u>is bitten</u> by the man.

Notice the different emphases of the following sentences:

Active		Passive
The judge <u>sentenced</u> the murderer to 25 years in prison.	=	The murderer <u>was sentenced</u> to 25 years in prison.

The first sentence puts more emphasis on its subject, "the judge," which is not necessary because most people know that only judges can sentence criminals to prison. A newspaper article on this case would probably use the passive voice to put the emphasis on "the murderer."

Note that when verbs are in the passive voice, the first verb is a form of *to be*, followed by the past participle form of another verb. Occasionally, the verb *to get* is used in passive constructions, as in the sentence "My parents <u>got married</u> in 1966."

Task 7.7 *Analyze*

1 Working with a partner, underline each example of the passive voice in the following excerpt from paragraph 12 of "The Color of Love" (page 220).

> Often the prospect of an interracial marriage takes on mythical proportions and the partnership is seen as an act of blatant disloyalty, even as an act of war. Filial piety is assumed; sons and daughters are indebted to their parents and must repay them for their sacrifices. Marrying the right partner is a filial obligation. The children of these families are caught in a horrible bind: sacrifice their own needs and desires or alienate their parents, perhaps permanently.

2 Check your work using the Answer Key on page 262.

3 For each of the passive voice constructions that appears in this passage, discuss why you think the author decided to use the passive rather than the active voice.

Practice

1 The verbs in the following questions are in the active voice. Working with a partner, answer each question using the passive voice.

> **Example**
> **Q:** Should we grant legal status to all of the illegal immigrants currently living in the United States?
> **A:** Yes, they should be granted legal status.

  a Should the United States provide education and health care for the children of illegal immigrants?

  b Does the United States offer equal opportunities to all people living in this country?

  c In your opinion, does the language a person speaks influence his or her identity?

  d Should parents allow children to choose their own marriage partners?

  e Can partners in an interracial marriage overcome the problems they face?

  f How will the children of interracial couples define their identity?

2 Compare your answers with the samples given in the Answer Key on page 262.

Editing Checklist

If you are writing your essay on a computer, remember to print out your revised essay and proofread it on paper.

☐ **First proofreading: active and passive voice of verbs**
Proofread carefully to check your use of the active and passive voice of verbs. Remember that even in more formal writing based on research, you should be careful not to overuse the passive voice. In most cases, the active voice is more direct and interesting for readers. Check (✓) the box when you have finished.

☐ **Second proofreading**
Proofread your essay a second time and correct any other errors of grammar, spelling, or punctuation that you find. Check (✓) the box when you have finished.

☐ **Third proofreading**
Print out or write a copy of your essay that includes the corrections you made in your first and second proofreading. Now proofread your essay a third time. Try to find and correct any errors that you missed. Then print out, or write in dark blue or black ink, the final draft of your essay. Check (✓) the box when you have finished.

A NOTE AS YOU COMPLETE THE COURSE

In Part III of this book, you have used writing as a way of exploring ideas – your own ideas and those of others. We hope that in the process of writing and revising more formal essays, you have developed new interests and new strengths.

As you complete the course, take the time to reflect on your progress as a writer by filling out "Assessing Your Progress: A Closing Survey" on page 254.

PARTING WORDS FROM THE AUTHORS

We wrote this book because we were excited by our students' writing, and we felt that if more people could read stories and essays by student writers, they might be inspired to explore their own ideas for writing. We have found that it is not necessary to be a professional author to write well. We hope that you agree.

We would appreciate hearing about your reactions to the book. How has your writing changed? What activities helped you the most? Were there any activities that were not helpful? If you were especially pleased with any of the writing you did, we would like to read it.

Send any correspondence or essays to:
    Rebecca Mlynarczyk, <rmlynarczyk@kbcc.cuny.edu>
    Steven Haber, <shaber@njcu.edu>

Now you have come to the end of this book, but we hope it will mark the beginning, not the end, of your writing career.

Peer Response Form
Writing Based on Research

WRITER'S NAME: .... READER'S NAME: ....

DATE: ....

Focus on the ideas in the essay rather than the grammar and spelling. Discuss only those mistakes that interfere with understanding.

1 What is the topic of this essay?

2 What is the writer's opinion about his or her topic?

3 Where in the essay is the writer's opinion stated?

4 Give one example of a place where the writer used a paraphrase or quotation from an outside source effectively.

Photocopiable   © Cambridge University Press

5 Give one example where the use of outside research was not handled so well – a place where you got confused or needed more explanation.

6 Look at the bibliography at the end of the essay. Has the writer given credit to all of the outside sources cited in the essay? Check the citations and the bibliography carefully and note any places where there are problems.

7 How could the writer improve this essay when he or she revises? Make only one suggestion.

Writer's Plan for Revising

Writing Based on Research

YOUR NAME: .... ESSAY TITLE: ....

DATE: ....

Reread your essay, concentrating on the ideas rather than on grammar and spelling. Then write your answers to the following questions.

1 What did you like about writing an essay that required you to do outside research? What did you find difficult about doing this assignment? Be as specific as possible in your answers.

2 How was your original opinion about this topic influenced by doing research using outside sources? Explain in as much detail as possible.

3 In this draft, have you included the opinions of any people who disagree with your own view on the topic? If so, explain how you used these opposing viewpoints to strengthen your own argument. If not, do you plan to include any opposing viewpoints in your next draft? Why or why not?

Assessing Your Progress
A Closing Survey

YOUR NAME: .... DATE: ....

Reread your responses to "A Beginning Survey" and "A Midterm Survey." Then answer the following questions.

1 What new strengths have you discovered in your writing during this course?

2 Which of the essays you have written for this course are you especially pleased with? Explain.

3 What aspects of writing are still difficult for you? Explain.

4 Has your attitude toward writing changed as a result of this course? Explain.

Photocopiable   © Cambridge University Press

5 Look at your answer to question 3 in "A Beginning Survey." In what ways has your approach to the writing process changed? What new techniques have you discovered to help you improve your writing?

6 Look at your answer to question 5 in "A Beginning Survey." Which of the things listed were, in fact, most helpful to you? Were these the things you thought would help? Explain.

7 Look at your answer to question 4 in "A Beginning Survey." Did your writing improve in the ways that you hoped it would? Are you satisfied with your progress in this course? Why or why not?

ANSWER KEY

Chapter 2

Task 2.7: Practice (page 57)

In the Cyber Game Room

A few years ago, I had a best friend. His name is Eric Chan. He **comes** from Hong   1
Kong. He has light skin, big eyes. Maybe it's because he thinks a lot. His head looks
really big, especially the upper part around his brain. And he has very straight hair,
which stands up 3 inches on top of his head.

Back in the high school days, we **spent** a lot of time together. Usually this was   2
after school at the "cyber game room." It **was** a room that **had** a lot of computers.
So people **paid** money to play computer games or do stuff on the computer and
the Internet. When we were in front of the computer, we became partners. He **was**
a great teacher. He **showed** me how to play the game and **gave** me examples like
strategies about how to play. He **gave** me his ideas, **explained** how to catch what's in
the enemy's mind, and **told** me how to make the enemy play my own game. He **led**
me into battles. We **fought**, we **bled**, and we **won**. We never lost since we **became**
experts. We were as good as all those professional gamers out there in the world.

When we **stayed** in the "cyber game room," he always **had** a cigarette in his hand   3
or mouth. He **smoked** a pack of cigarettes every day. He **said**, "Having a cigarette, I
am 100% sure what I am doing," and "A cigarette is like a battery; it can recharge
the energy for my body." So after a few times with him in the cyber game room, I
started to learn how to smoke.

After two years of our friendship, things **began** to cool down a little. We both **met**   4
the same girl. . . .

Note: There is more than one way to correct the verb tenses in these paragraphs.
It is clear from things the writer says in the first and the last paragraphs that
although Eric Chan is still alive, the friendship between Eric and King is over;
it is in the past. Therefore, we made the decision to keep most of the verbs in
the first paragraph in the present tense. These statements about Eric Chan are
still true. We decided to use the past tense for most of the verbs in the second
paragraph because they are describing things that happened "back in the high
school days," which are now past. Most of the verbs in paragraphs 3 and 4 are
in the past because these events are clearly in the past. Notice, however, that
the verbs in the direct quotations from Eric in paragraph 3 should be left in the
present because these are the exact statements he made at the time.

Chapter 3

Task 3.6: Analyze (page 85)

Note: The delete sign (ɣ) indicates that the small letter should be replaced with a capital.

A Woman I Admire

I met her at a park near Chinatown. She was an old, healthy Chinese lady. I thought she had a wealthy family and a happy life. Since we both spoke the same dialect, we didn't have any trouble understanding each other. After we had met a couple of times, I learned that she got married when she was only fifteen. Her husband left his family in China for Singapore and then for the United States five months later. They did not meet each other again until she came here twenty-eight years later, when she was forty-three years old. Unfortunately, they did not have any children. She is living alone in this country now.

Task 3.7: Practice (page 85)

Note: The delete sign (ɣ) indicates that the punctuation mark should be removed or changed, or that the size of the letter should be changed.

The Third Day Behind the Wheel

When I was twenty-one, I got my first driver's license. Living in the suburbs of New Orleans, I was forced to drive a car in order to get from one place to another. At the place I lived, called Violet, nobody dared to cross the street on foot.   1

Before I took the road test, I had driven for two hours at a shopping mall parking lot. On the day after I got my license, I was already forcing my eight-year-old Ventura to fly seventy miles per hour on a two-way highway.   2

The next day I decided to check the Ventura's speed ability. I took her on a divided highway with two lanes going each direction. In the middle was neutral ground full of potholes. On both sides along the highway were ditches filled with snakes, mud, and water. In the distance, the skeletons of dead trees greeted the haunted travelers.   3

It was the beginning of dusk. When I passed the Judge Perreze Bridge and accelerated to ninety-six miles per hour. When the car wasn't going any faster, I had a glimmering thought of slowing down. Suddenly, the Ventura started bouncing from side to side and went off the road to the left. First I noticed the headlights of oncoming cars, so I was preparing myself mentally for a head-on collision. A second later, however, I had the panorama of eternal wetness and started subconsciously to press the brakes with all my might. The idea of dying in a swamp somehow didn't fit me. The Ventura was still turning. She made another cycle and a half and stopped, to my surprise. It took me a few deep breaths to recover my full awareness, but soon I was back on the highway again.   4

Chapter 4

Task 4.6: Analyze (page 116)

In my childhood memories, I have many favorite places, but I will write about the   1
one that I prefer. It is the tree of my secrets. I began my journey in the Dominican
Republic with my tree, and it was there at the end of my journey.

A long time ago, when I was a young child, my parents decided to travel to the   2
United States to get better opportunities and enhance the quality of our family's
life. My parents left me in the Dominican Republic, and I lived in different family
members' houses. When I first came to live with Uncle Pipe Sosa and my godmother,
Ramona, in 1981, the tree was young like I was. At the age of four, I started to enjoy
the company of my tree. I played around it with my two younger sisters, neighbors,
and friends. Then my godmother and my uncle decided to sell the house and move
to a big empty place.

Task 4.7: Practice (page 117)

I Was a "Little Devil"

In the summer of 1980, I had to attend a chemistry class because my father   1
thought I was doing poorly in it. I admired karate very much at the time, but my
father always gave me good reasons not to take lesson. Therefore, instead of going
to chemistry class, I skipped school and took karate at a little school nearby, without
my father's permission.

After I had taken a few lesson, I became one of the most annoying kid in the   2
neighborhood. I always made plan for us (our kid gang) to fight with the other kids
on the surrounding block. This was one of the game that we enjoyed most. But as
you may guess, every wild start must have an end. In my case, this was how I ended
my karate lesson.

One day when I got out of my karate lesson, two of my friend and I were all   3
excited because the next day would be the big contest to go a step higher in karate.
Suddenly I bumped into somebody. When I looked up, it was a guy who was around
my age, but by appearance stronger than me. However, I didn't notice that, but stood
up and started a fight with him. Even though he said "Sorry" many time and asked
me to forgive him, I didn't. We took off our shoe and started. The kid surrounding us
were cheering, and their yelling made me even more excited. I was winning for the
first several minutes, but my strength left me as the fight went on. Finally, the guy
punched me so hard that he completely knocked me down. I sat on the ground with
bruise on my body and a bloody nose. He came over, looked at me, and asked: "Are
you okay? I didn't want to fight, but you insisted. I'm sorry." After that he left. I was
sitting on the ground feeling like a total fool.

On my way home, I didn't cry out loud, but tear⁵ kept rolling down my face. After ₄
crying, I began to laugh about my stupidity and decided to give up physical fighting
for the rest of my life. That was the end of my karate lesson⁵.

Chapter 5

Task 5.7: Analyze (page 159)

Crisantina Orellana is a very old woman who was born in the quiet village of
Chalatenango in the northern countryside of El Salvador. During my interview,
I asked her about her age. She replied, "I really don't know it. The only thing I'm
sure of is that I was born at some day in the past and I'm still alive." One thing is
notorious in Crisantina Orellana's personality. She always looks happy and full of joy.
When I asked her what was the secret that has kept her full of life, she said, "Life
is life." She told me that the only thing we have to worry about is how to live our
lives. She explained that when a person has really learned how to live, he or she will
understand the difference this attitude makes in how we choose to live.

Chapter 6

Task 6.3: Analyze (page 190)

a **Unacceptable paraphrase.** Too much of the language of the attempted
   paraphrase is copied directly from the original.

b **Acceptable paraphrase.** The language, except for a few key words such as
   "Family Research Council," has been changed.

c **Acceptable paraphrase.** Most of the original language has been changed. A
   key point from the original has been quoted, but quotation marks have been
   used to signal the quote.

Task 6.5: Analyze (page 192)

Outline of "The Family in Society" by Isabella Kong

I. Family structures reflect the culture in which they occur, but they also
    help to shape that culture. (Thesis Statement)
II. Traditional family structures work well in agricultural societies.
    A. If the family had broken into smaller units, the land would have been
       divided into small lots, and families would not have been able to raise
       enough food to survive.
    B. To prevent the division of the land in traditional families, the oldest
       son typically inherited all of the family's land.
III. Another feature of traditional families is that they lead to closer
     relationships among family members and greater family unity.
    A. This type of unity helps the family defend itself against aggressors.
    B. This type of family also produces more conflicts among family
       members.
       1. To keep these conflicts under control, a leader has to be
          designated – usually the oldest son.
       2. Giving over a lot of authority to one family leader often results in
          a loss of freedom.

IV. In modern families, people value individualism and equality, and they resent the authoritarianism of traditional families.
   A. A major reason for this change in family structure is the change in how families make their livings.
   B. Modern family structure gives more freedom to individual members.
   C. Modern family structure leads to a weakening of respect for the elders.
V. Although family structure changes as societies change, all family structures emphasize the values of "affection, companionship, and warmth." (Conclusion)

Task 6.7: Analyze (page 199)

These gaps seem to cause misunderstandings and sadness, but fewer open explosions than one <u>might expect</u> [**possibility: fewer explosions than one thought were possible**]. Young and old alike <u>may stew</u> [**possibility: it is possible that young and old people will stew (meaning: be upset)**] inside at the foolishness of the other, but they also describe how they go out of their way to accommodate. "It's a constant bother to live with the old folks," said Chong Kum Sook, 38, who lives in the same house as her husband's parents. "It's very hard. It's not that they complain, but I feel the burden on myself. My in-laws are early risers, so I try to get up when they do. And in the summer I <u>can't wear</u> [**ability or permission: she isn't able or doesn't have permission to wear**] skimpy clothes, because I <u>have to dress</u> [**necessity: it is necessary for me to dress**] cautiously so as not to disturb them. I <u>should be</u> careful [**advisability: it is advisable (meaning: it is a good idea) for me to be careful**] not to make them unhappy."

Task 6.8: Practice (page 200)

Note: The answers given are examples of one way to complete this task, but other correct answers are possible. If your answer is different from the one given, discuss your reason for choosing a particular modal with your partner or teacher and decide if your answer would also be correct.

An American professor was rushing to the classroom where he was scheduled to give his first lecture at a Brazilian university. When he arrived, he was surprised to find Room 101 was empty. He didn't know what had happened. However, being a professor, his mind went to work, and he came up with some interesting theories. 1

The professor's watch _might_ have stopped. Or the students _might_ have forgotten that a class was scheduled for that day. Or possibly, they all _might_ have decided to drop the class. 2

There were other possibilities as well. The university _might_ have closed early that day for a strike or protest. But surely if there had been a strike, the professor _would_ have heard about it from someone. Maybe there was a cultural explanation. Perhaps in Brazil, it _might_ be acceptable for students to come late to class, or not to come to class at all. 3

As it turned out, the answer was quite simple. As a professor, he _should_ have known better, but he obviously had not checked the schedule of classes carefully enough. Although he had copied down the day and time correctly, he _must_ have made a mistake about the room. He had gone to room 101 when, in fact, he _should_ have gone to Room 110, which is where all his students were waiting. 4

Chapter 7

Task 7.6: Practice (page 238)

APA Style:

References

Alba, R. D. (1990). *Ethnic identity: The transformation of white America*. New Haven, CT: Yale University Press.

Root, M. P. P. (2002, April 8). The color of love. *The American Prospect*, 54–55.

Spain, D. (2003, October 19). The debate in the United States over immigration. http://usinfo.state.gov/journals/itsv/0699/ijse/spain.htm

MLA Style:

Works Cited

Alba, Richard D. Ethnic Identity: The Transformation of White America. New Haven, CT: Yale UP, 1990.

Root, Maria P. P. "The Color of Love." The American Prospect 8 April 2002: 54–55.

Spain, Daphne. "The Debate in the United States over Immigration." 19 Oct. 2003 <http://usinfo.state.gov/journals/itsv/0699/ijse/spain.htm>.

Task 7.7: Analyze (page 247)

Often the prospect of an interracial marriage takes on mythical proportions and the partnership is seen as an act of blatant disloyalty, even as an act of war. Filial piety is assumed; sons and daughters are indebted to their parents and must repay them for their sacrifices. Marrying the right partner is a filial obligation. The children of these families are caught in a horrible bind: sacrifice their own needs and desires or alienate their parents, perhaps permanently.

Task 7.8: Practice (page 248)

Note: The answers given are merely samples. Your own answers will probably be different. But check to be sure that all of your answers are in the passive voice.

a Should the United States provide education and health care for the children of illegal immigrants?
Sample Answer: Yes, education and health care should be provided for all children in the United States.

b Does the United States offer equal opportunities to all people living in this country?
Sample Answer: No, all people living in this country are not provided with the same opportunities.

c In your opinion, does the language a person speaks influence his or her identity?
Sample Answer: Yes, a person's identity is greatly influenced by language.

d Should parents allow children to choose their own marriage partners?
Sample Answer: No, children should not be allowed to choose their own marriage partners.

e Can partners in an interracial marriage overcome the problems they face?
Sample Answer: Yes, in most cases, the problems of interracial marriages <u>can be overcome</u>.

f How will the children of interracial couples define their identity?
Sample Answer: The identity of children born to interracial couples <u>will be defined</u> by these children in their own ways.

INDEX

CREDITS

Text Credits

Nicholas D. Kristof, "Hanok Journal: Bean Paste Vs. Miniskirts," from *The New York Times*, May 5, 1999. Copyright ©1999 by The New York Times Co. Reprinted with permission.

Carlyle Murphy, "Gay Parents Find More Acceptance," from *The Washington Post*, June 14, 1999. Copyright ©1999, *The Washington Post*. Reprinted with permission.

Dean E. Murphy, *September 11: An Oral History*, copyright ©2002 by Dean E. Murphy. Used by permission of Doubleday, a division of Random House, Inc.

Alejandro Portes, "America 2050: Immigration and the Hourglass," from *Crosscurrents in Culture, Power and History*, Volume II, Number 1 and 2: Winter–Spring 1994–1995. Reprinted with permission of the author and the Institute for Global Studies in Culture, Power and History.

Maria P. P. Root, "The Color of Love." Reprinted with permission from *The American Prospect*, Volume 13, Number 7: April 8, 2002. The American Prospect, 11 Beacon Street, Suite 1120, Boston, MA 02108. All rights reserved.

Photo Credits

3 ©Marc Romanelli/Getty Images
4 ©Gary Conner/Photo Edit
29 ©Michael Newman/Photo Edit
34 ©Michael Newman/Photo Edit
49 ©Creatas
55 ©Premium Stock/Corbis
59 ©Charles & Josette Lenars/Corbis
68 *(left)* ©Mark Scott/Getty Images; *(right)* ©Janine Weidel/Alamy
74 ©Rob Crandall/Alamy
76 ©Tomas Johanson/Alamy
93 ©George D. Lepp/Corbis
101 ©Index Stock
105 ©Réunion des Musées Nationaux/Art Resource,NY
127 ©Michael Newman/Photo Edit
139 ©Gideon Mendel/Corbis
143 ©Roy Gumpel/Getty Images
167 ©Paul Chesley/Getty Images
172 ©Liba Taylor/Corbis
180 ©Queerstock
207 ©Spencer Platt/Getty Images
213 ©Justin Sullivan/Getty Images/NewsCom
221 ©Getty Images